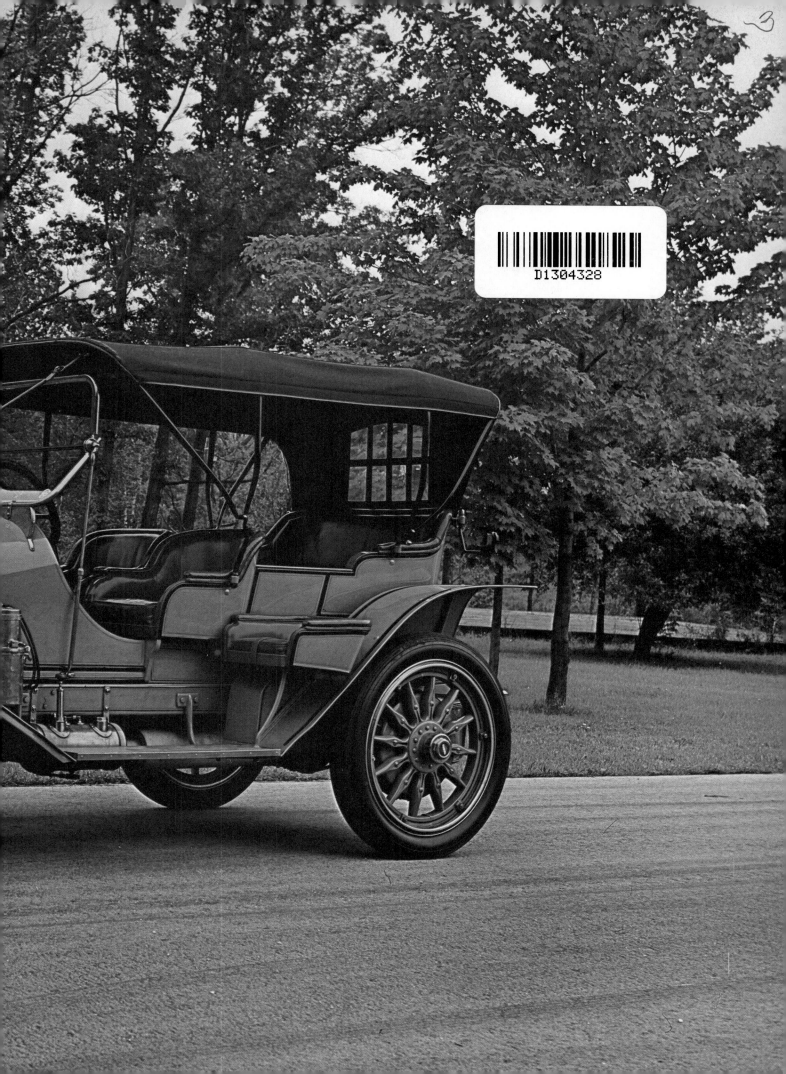

Classic Cars

Classic
Cars

George Bishop

Optimum

Copyright © The Hamlyn Publishing Group Limited 1979

This edition published by Optimum Books 1979

ISBN 600 321134

Printed in Italy by Group Poligrafici Calderara, Bologna

Contents

Chapter 1 What is a Classic Car?

A car which is worth keeping, or listing (like an ancient building) must have some special merit to deserve its place, whether in posterity or in the motor museum. Although it must be outstanding, however, it can be so in more than one way; it need not relate to performance in the sense of being fast or having sporting attributes. It might be small and slow but still rate preservation because of some special feature. For example, the Volkswagen Golf Diesel should be listed because it was the first small popular family car to be diesel-powered and offer reasonable standards of performance, silence and economy.

The purist might throw up his hands at the thought of such a device being admitted to the ranks of Great Cars. He would be entitled to his prejudices, but the little VW has a genuine claim as a classic because it was the first of its kind, just as Cadillac had the first self-starter, Chrysler the first hydraulic brakes and so on. They might be horrid cars in other ways, but the Diesel Golf should have its own pedestal, as should the first car that ever ran, the first electric car, the first steam car, the first to do 100 kilometres or miles per hour and, indeed, any other vehicle which introduced an important new feature affecting the future of transport. You do not have to *like* a car (or a person) for it to rank as Great.

So the cars in any list must be outstanding, but under any one of ten or more headings: Practicability, Performance, Durability, Economy, Luxury, Quality, Roadholding, Handling, Innovation, Cleverness of Design, or the use of new Materials. Some of these may overlap but they will do as a basis for discussion; no doubt there are

The first small family car to be produced with a diesel engine, VW's remarkable Golf may be a pointer to the car of the future with adequate performance and 58 miles per gallon of fuel.

other headings which have been overlooked.

Choosing The Greats is not an exact science, with cars any more than it is with racing drivers. Most people will say 'Nuvolari, Fangio, Moss, Clark, Stewart' and then argue about the rest. It is the same with cars. To add a little spice, some people would list ten manufactures who never made a bad car, or ten who never made a good one, but one could never achieve agreement over this, nor would one expect to. Taking them alphabetically, those who never made a bad car were: Alfa Romeo, Bentley, Bugatti, Duesenberg, Ferrari, Jaguar, Lancia, Mercedes, Rolls-Royce, and Talbot. People will cite the 4.0 litre Bentley of 1930/31 as a disaster, but it was a smooth, pleasant machine and only compared unfavourably with the 4.5 litre, the

Speed Six and the 8 litre because it was over-heavy and under-powered, but there were good reasons for this.

On the other hand, the following never made a good car: Alvis, Austin, Invicta, Lagonda, MG, Morris, Rover, Singer, Vauxhall, and Wolseley. Now there are many people about to hurl this book across the room because they happen to be *afficionados* of one or more of these makes. And just as we picked out the 4.0 litre Bentley as being not so good as some others, so we must make an exception of the 30/98 Vauxhall, which had many merits in spite of its flexible chassis and its complete lack of brakes. Fewer people are likely to defend the late, unlamented, Wolseley marque, except perhaps the police, who had good service from their cars when there was nothing better at the price.

Alvis cars, on the other hand, just got worse and worse, until the company turned to making armoured cars and tanks – a role for which the weight of their cars always suited them. The early

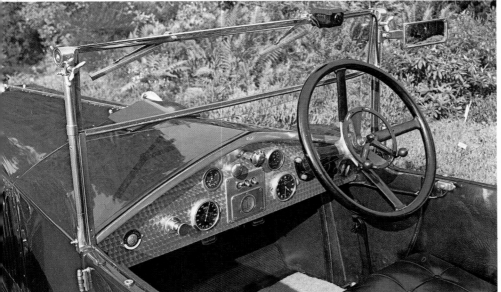

Vauxhall's immortal 30/98 set high standards in 1924, although the company's subsequent efforts have not met with universal approval.

The instrument panel was a joy to behold – functional, without frills and all engine-turned.

12/50 model was much loved, and the 4.3 litre tourer was fast for its time, but it had no steering lock, an enormous appetite for fuel and engine bearings, and a most peculiar method of valve spring operation in which eight (or was it nine?) separate little coil springs jostled each other for position around each and every valve in a frenzied tango.

And surely nobody will defend those Invictas, which either spun on their own axis or turned upside down on the driver; or the 2.0 litre Lagondas which consumed gearbox bushes with the regularity of cows chewing the cud; or the ghastly Singer Le Mans, which danced about the road like a superannuated ballet dancer?

A ducks-back Alvis 12/50, looking much more modern than its 1928 origins would suggest. It was one of the few cars from Alvis to find any favour among collectors.

7

Then there were Morris and MG models – and Wolseleys – which turned their dynamos on end and used them as camshaft drives, with the result that they filled with engine oil and were quite unable to perform the tiresome task of producing electricity. Then there was the Wolseley Hornet, whose chassis sagged in the middle to make a highly original, banana-shaped car.

These pieces of folklore do not help us select a classic, except that there is no reason why a banana-shaped car should not qualify, so long as it had some other quality which made its owners love it; certainly the various MG models must have had *something*, as well as built-in anachronism, to make so many people suffer their lack of suspension and luggage space.

Le Mans was where Bentley became famous. This 4.5 litre was racing there in 1929, complete with a four-seat body (demanded by the regulations).

1905 Vauxhall with a three-cylinder, two-stroke engine of 9 hp and chain drive.

The famous Sarthe circuit at Le Mans played an important part in the development of the automobile. This is a Type 13 Bugatti at the 1911 race.

Nobody is going to exclude the works of Walter Owen Bentley, not even the devotees of M. Ettore Bugatti, whose jewel-like confections have often been compared to Swiss watches alongside the burbling Bentleys. Certainly the external appearance of a Bugatti engine, with hardly a wire or a pipe in sight, like an oblong memorial of polished metal erected to the honour of an artist, qualifies his cars as immortals, irrespective of the fact that they also won hundreds of races.

One way not to treat a collector's piece: this jewel of a 1926, Type 35 Bugatti appears to have modern, fat tyres on the back. Men have been shot for less.

Signor Ettore Bugatti's little sayings have become somewhat hackneyed, but convey his arrogance and impatience with worldly people who bothered too much about trivialities. They are worth repeating, even at the risk of boring those already familiar with the sayings of this artist in metal. One owner had

the temerity to complain that his Bugatti would not start easily in the mornings, whereupon the Patron said, with a curl of the lip, 'A gentleman should have a heated motor-house'.

Another, too worried about his own skin, said that the brakes did not work too well, whereupon Ettore shouted: 'My cars are made to go, not to stop!'

Moving down the list of Good Cars, Duesenbergs were made in such small numbers and cost so much money that very few people have ever driven one, and no legends have been handed down about their weaknesses. Ferrari? Well, can Enzo Ferrari do any wrong? His 330GT has not earned a high regard among lovers of the make, but the only thing 'wrong' with it is that it is not as good as some of the other Ferraris, although it is still streets ahead of most other cars. Jaguar have always offered fabulous value for money, and – if early XKs were a bit short on brakes – their cars went so much faster than most other things that nobody had time to find out how to stop 1.5 tons of metal from 120 mph. Fortunately, modifications improved matters before the supply of drivers ran out.

Lancia have always loved complexity for its own sake and have gone in for peculiar engine configurations, to say nothing of using a trans-axle (on the Aurelia) before it was made respectable by Alfa Romeo and Ferrari. There does seem to be some communion between Italian engineers and their machinery which has given that country the three, major, high-performance producers and a plethora of ingenious, exciting or just plain workable designs, ranging from the Fiat Mouse to the Lamborghini Fighting Bull. Certainly, most Lancia models must rank among the immortals, and if there is one which should be excluded, it does not spring readily to mind. The Aprilia was a legend in its day,

There is no such beast as a bad Ferrari.
This selection from a French
enthusiast's collection includes a
330 LM (with blue stripe), a 375
Spyder, a GTO (behind owner Pierre
Bardinon and racing driver Jacky
Ickx), a 330 P4 and a 250 TR.

brought new standards, and so it has gone on.

Alphabetically, next in line are Mercedes, who have been building good cars for a long time. Some of the earlier ones can be criticised by today's standards, but in their day they were tremendous. The sporting, open two-seater 190SL, for example, was perhaps not a real sports car, but it was handsome and handy on the boulevard. Their 38/250 SSKL looked like an attacking tiger and had a savage masculinity which endeared it to the hairy-chested. Maybe they were heavy and thirsty and unrefined, but they offered something unique in their time. Modern Mercedes are leaders in the field of everyday transport, with superb engineering, suspension, comfort, performance and every other attribute endearing them to the keen driver and the connoisseur of magnificent

From a company who never made a bad car, the Lancia Aurelia B52 closed coupé, which had a vee six engine and featured a genuine transaxle.

machinery.

So to Rolls-Royce, who were accused of being backward because they did not rush to use the disc brake and all-independent suspension from the moment they were invented, while they have still not adopted the steel-braced radial tyre, but RR like ten years or so to try things out and make sure there is no hidden snag; an awful lot of people certainly like the result. That old crack about their cars being a triumph of workmanship over design is a bit dated now. The old original, the Silver Ghost, did not need an advocate, nor do the modern Shadows. Some of the intervening models, like the Phantoms and the Silver Dawn (which was a Mark VI Bentley) had some weaknesses in their character, but may now be all the more likeable for that. Hydraulic tappets can be converted, and there are ways round the over-heating problems of ageing Phantom IIIs.

Another to put on a list of Good Cars is Talbot, although there are

Opposite, top
Size alone can be enough to convey immortality. This is the pocket-sized Fiat Topolino.

Opposite, lower
At the other extreme, this 1965 Cadillac Sixty Special should have room for a whole flock of Topolinos in its boot.

lots of people ready to throw things at the work of George Roesch, the inimitable Swiss who had something in common with Bugatti in the cleanliness of his engines and the absence of external wires, pipes and other protuberances. Roesch's failings are well-known, but his sporting cars – particularly the 105 – were superb and will be suitably lauded in the appropriate chapter. His cars did not always start too well, with 3.5 gallons of SAE 30 oil to be churned round without benefit of a reduction gear by only 24 volts, but the answer – like Ettore's heated garage – was to live on top of a hill, which surely was not too much to ask in return for something so innately valuable.

Top
It may have lacked the performance of a real sports car, but the Mercedes 190 SL was solid and reliable and led to better things, in the shape of the much faster 250 SL.

Centre
Exuding masculine magnificence and brutal beauty, the Mercedes 36/220 of 1927 may have been clumsy, but its looks have never been surpassed.

We must now move to the baddies, headed by that unheavenly trio of MG, Wolseley and Singer, about whom some comment has already been made.

Alphabetically, Austin should have out-ranked them but, apart from the spindly Seven, surely nobody would want to put an Austin in a museum, and even the Seven would only be there for its curiosity value and as a milestone in the story of putting the man-in-the-street on wheels. It had little other merit and one had to be pretty small to fit into an early Chummy, a model which was supposed to have been designed on a billiard table.

Alvis always appeared as pretenders to the throne of Bentley: not quite royalty, but too expensively dressed for a commoner. The company also tended to use slightly inferior body-builders, while the superior ones worked for Rolls and Bentley, so that Alvis bodies tended to become rattly and tatty as the stiff springs and flexible chassis attacked the woodwork. The transverse, independent leaf spring at the front was not liked as much as the in-line cartsprings of the pre-1932 types, but the cars had their merits.

Lagonda is a musical name and some of their engines could be musical too. The big bangers from Meadows ('a good engine for marine purposes') did not like to run over 4,500 rpm, but then neither did anything else at that time. Lagonda made very nice-looking cars, although the 16/80 was a look-alike of the 2.0 litre and was never

A very rare machine indeed, this two-cylinder Rolls-Royce of 1905 is now back in the possession of its manufacturers. When it was in production, it went by the romantic name of the Ten Horse Power.

14

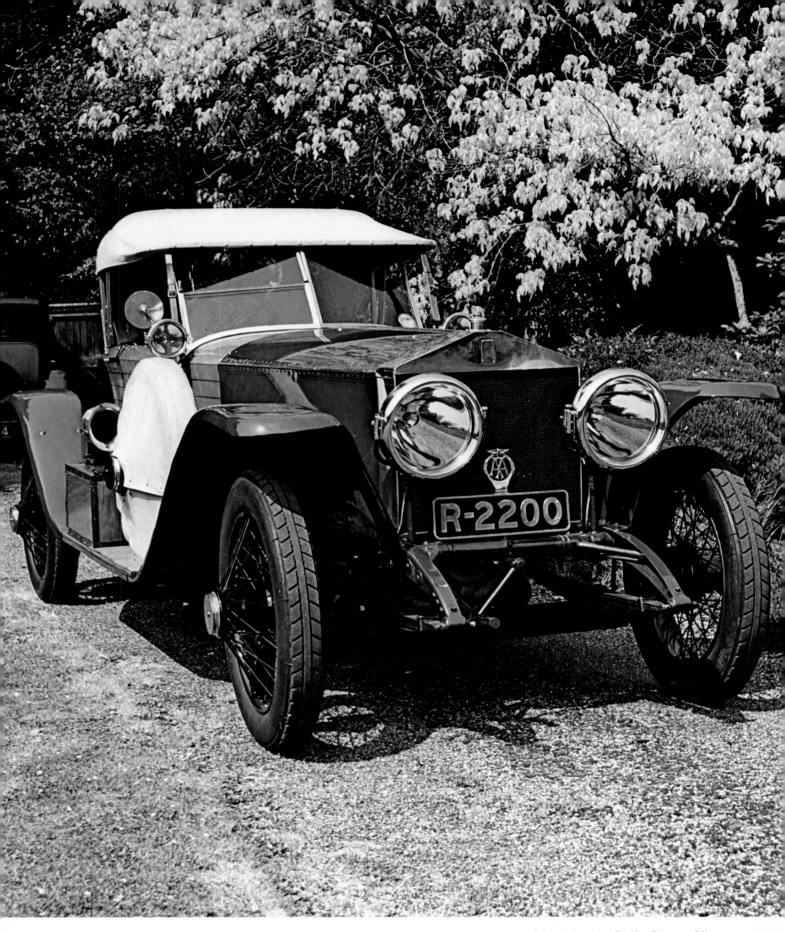

An old original, a Rolls-Royce Silver
Ghost of 1914 with bodywork by
Schebera–Schapiro of Berlin. Most
Rolls cars were instant classics, and
this one's credentials are immaculate.

as highly thought of by the knowledgeable, for rather vague reasons. The 2.0 litre engine was supposed to be supercharged, but it has been said that it needed more than a blower to enable the mixture to thread its way through the labyrinthine passages of the induction system. In spite of its lack of power, it was a handsome beast, long-lived, and worthy. The 4.5 litre was big brother to the 2.0 litre and as such had a family resemblance. It was orthodox in design and had no claim to be recognised as a leader of anything, but was a nice, solid, middle-class representative of its day and must be given consideration.

Rover has curiously reversed its image in recent years, from the 'Doctor's Coupé' of the post-Second World War years to an *avant garde* machine trying to slot in as a poor man's Mercedes or Jaguar. It might even achieve that, if the factory could consistently produce cars.

Singer? They produced some horrors, both mechanically and in appearance, although the dreaded Le Mans was curiously pretty in its own way. This was the car on which all three members of the racing team broke their steering at the same place in a T.T. race. It was proved to be due to a faulty batch of parts from an outside supplier, but from then on they were stuck with a bad name.

Vauxhall somehow landed themselves with the image of pink tinware on soft suspension, rusting to pieces before the instalments were paid, but all that is a thing of the past and some of their modern designs rank with those of any other mass-producer. Until the 1970s, however, there was not much worth writing about after the 30/98 went off the production line in 1928. There followed a 50-year gap in General Motors' British stable, and not many protagonists are likely to push for the inclusion of those lost models like the Wyvern, Velox, Cresta, Victor and Viscount.

But what of those companies whose claim to fame rests on their having introduced some novel component to the motoring world, rather than some complete concept of transportation? If we start at the front of the car and move back, credit can be given for some of the changes, if not for all of them. In the early days of motor racing, for example, the bore of an engine was limited by the regulations while the stroke was unrestricted, encouraging designers to make their engines taller and taller, until one appeared with a stroke of 280 mm. This was nearly three feet high and its driver had to peer around the sides to see

One of the few exceptions to the rule that Rover never made a good car. The latest 3500 hatchback sheds their 'auntie' image, hopefully for ever, with good looks and handling to match.

Lagonda's 1930 3.0 litre may have looked pretty, but the firm produced very little of merit and this model was never particularly popular.

where he was going. Should such a car be cherished? It may have been horribly impractical, but it could be said that it represented a milestone in motoring design.

Moving back, we arrive at the transmission, where time has only proved that there is no justice in this world. From the very early days, there was something called a 'Système Panhard', in which a friction clutch behind the engine drove via a gearbox, a cross-shaft and chains, which drove the rear wheels; but it was Panhard's partner, Emile Levassor, who evolved the system, so why not the 'Système Levassor'? Later, the ingenious brain of Louis Renault made a much bigger step forward, when he threw away the chains in favour of a shaft to the rear axle, together with a differential, but this system, now used by the vast majority of the World's cars, is not known as the 'Système Renault'.

Mind you, there have always been odd men out. The British Frazer-Nash, for example, scorned the Renault transmission system (by then adopted by everyone else) and continued to use chains right up until 1939. But this car, with all its crudities, would not be denied immortality by anyone with a grain of emotion about the automobiles of the past.

Interestingly, very little happened in the area of automobile transmissions after Messrs. Levassor and Renault had made their mark; not, at least, until the late 1930s, when automatic transmission arrived on the scene. Here, too, there has only been one basic design, copied since by all and sundry. Manufacturing methods have changed over the years, bringing us clutches instead of bands, sintered parts and impregnated paper instead of thick, friction material, but the main design continues along very similar lines. Should the first one on the scene therefore be immortalised?

Rear axles have not changed

much either, since the arrival of the hypoid bevel a long time ago. Apart from a late stand by Peugeot, the worm soon disappeared, while Frazer-Nash and Trojan tried to make do with no differential at all. The rest conformed.

Brakes improved over the years, perhaps in spite of Bugatti's opinions. Rolls-Royce took the gearbox-driven servo from Hispano, so that one had to accept delayed-action stopping, but new braking methods are surely not enough to justify automotive immortality, even if it is important to be able to stop.

And what about detail changes? The steering wheel replaced the

Citroen's Light Fifteen, whose novel features in 1934 included monocoque body construction and front-wheel drive. The later, six-cylinder version, became famous in the hands of Inspector Maigret.

tiller; solid tyres became pneumatic; the tubeless tyre pushed out the tube; the radial robbed the crossply of its glory; Cadillac introduced electric starting in 1912. But all these were routine developments, hardly worthy of special praise, despite being essential for the progress of mechanical propulsion.

Genuinely major changes have happened to bodywork, especially once those people whose business it was to clothe motor car chassis stopped bending bits of aluminium or mild steel around a wooden frame and nailing it on – a crude method at best. One of the biggest changes in the history of the motor car was wrought by the American firm of Budd Bodies, who perfected a way of stamping body parts out of sheet steel and welding the pieces together. This led to the monocoque, to which the engine and other mechanical parts were attached, so eliminating the chassis (except for a few specialist firms, many of them, curiously enough, in the United States, birthplace of the Budd method). For reminders of this revolution in Europe, one might turn to Morris or Citroen, who were the first to use it on the eastern side of the Atlantic. Unfortunately, the E-type Morris of 1938, which ought to be immortal, was inclined to rot away, leaving one to select the Citroen Light Fifteen which also employed front-wheel drive, a very novel combination for a mass-produced car at the time.

Centre
This 1890 Peugeot was fitted with a steam engine by Serpollet.

Bottom
If neither petrol nor steam will do, how about electricity? This device, the *'Jamais Contente'*, achieved 100 km/h in the hands of Jenatzy in 1899. Electric cars don't seem to have advanced greatly since then.

If rarity is a measure of appeal, this first-ever Moskvitch should qualify. If it looks rather like a pre-Second World War Opel Kadett, that is because it was built with dies 'acquired' by the Russians during the conflict.

Should we include the first machine to manage without a gravity-fed fuel tank; the first windscreen wipers; the first mechanical direction indicators; the first air conditioning? And what of steam cars, which have been almost forgotten, but which held all the early World Land Speed Records in 1898/9, finishing up at 60 mph, a fantastic velocity for the 19th century. Steam conquered electricity to raise the record to 75 mph in 1902, but now it seems that electricity will vanquish petrol, if the prophets are right. Even if nobody can change *your* mind, an examination of the candidates and their contributions to the progress of performance, comfort and safety can be nothing less than fascinating.

The plan in this book is to divide automotive history into three distinct periods: before August 1914, taking us up to the point at which production ceased in most countries for five or six years; from late 1914 to 1939, when most of it stopped again; and from 1939 to the present time. On the face of it, this might seem illogical, there being more years in the later periods, but this is not entirely the case. The first cars appeared in 1886, giving us 28 years up to 1914; the period from the First World War to the Second is similar in length; and, while the last period is admittedly long, it might be said to have produced rather less of immediate interest. The number of makes has steadily declined in recent years, so that there are now fewer manufacturers that at any time since 1900. They make many more cars, of course, but we are not concerned here with quantity, only with particular examples whose merits admit them to the ranks of mechanical immortals. There have been over 4,000 makes since it all began, but only 158 exist today, and some of those produce so few vehicles as to be manufacturers in name only.

A good example of a latter-day classic, the Jaguar E-Type set new standards in silence and performance for production sports cars.

2 Pre-1914: Basic Beginnings

Sorting sheep from goats is simple compared with the task of deciding which cars were significant in the years before 1914, when there were several hundred makes on the market. If 'several hundred' sounds a bit vague, it is no wonder: there were 40 manufacturers active in Switzerland before 1914, yet not one survives today; there were 100 makers of light cars in Britain even before 1904; and the United States boasted 84 different steam cars before the First World War, while the same country produced 250,000 cars as early as 1912.

This chapter is concerned with ordinary cars for ordinary people, or at least those ordinary people who could afford four wheels. How can ordinary cars be classic? We have already been into that, of course, and vehicles like the Model T Ford or the much later Mini have revolutionised the life (and the language, in some cases) of many people. Such machines must have their place, if one can only decide which ones are the most deserving.

But in the pre-1914 period, we must first deal with the cyclecar, which was a phenomenon of the times and cannot be ignored, although whether it is worth remembering is another matter. They were defined as motor cycles with four wheels (chain or belt driven) powered by engines developed for two-wheeled machines, almost invariably air cooled and with one or two cylinders, although a few speed-crazy fools had four cylinders. We cannot possibly list all 300 marques, but the cyclecar was a milestone, in the progress of the mechanical vehicle and cannot be dismissed. Why anyone should want to keep one, other than in a museum, is hard to imagine, but people do keep curiosities, so why

The first Daimler of 1886, a carriage from which the horse has bolted (unlike the Benz, which started life as a motor-car).

Steam had its short day. Here a Stanley Steamer shows how it was done, in silence and elegance and without that smelly exhaust.

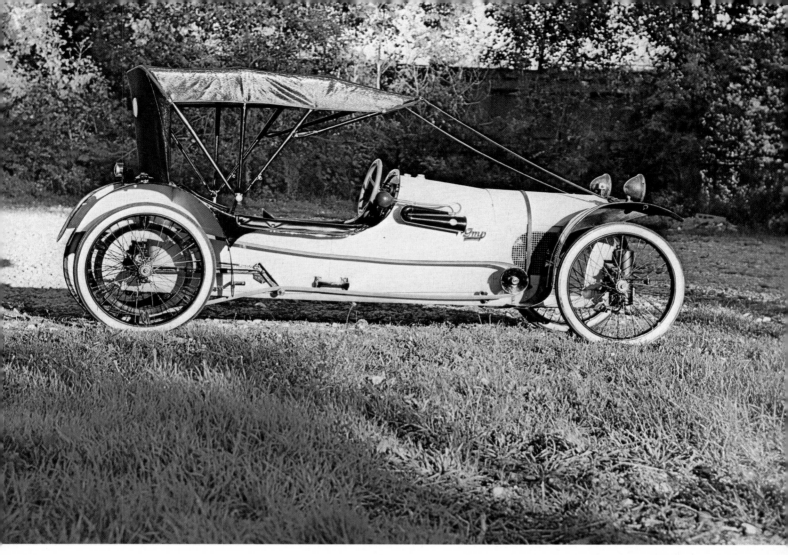

This rakish device is a 1913 Imp cyclecar with an air-cooled, vee-twin engine, friction transmission and belt drive. Its wheelbase was just 8 ft 4 ins and it weighed 600 lbs.

The Swiss Ajax of 1908, which was popular as a taximeter cabriolet. It had a four-cylinder, 3,420 cc, 20 hp engine.

not a relatively harmless cyclecar? Two of the best known were the Bedelia and the Tamplin, so these might be included as representatives of the era and as examples of what seemed like a good idea at the time.

The Bedelia could only have been French, from around 1910. In its original form, it was like an extended bathtub, with two occupants sitting one behind the other. It was the original back-seat driver's car, as the person in the rear seat had the steering wheel and most of the other controls, including the gear lever. The steering did not take advantage of any of the new ideas, like Ackermann's (which had only been around since 1818), but used centre-pivot steering like a horse cart, which made life uncertain to say the least. Various

23

engines could be provided, with one or two cylinders, and it was an exciting form of transport in which the driver could not see where he was going, while his passenger could see but did not want to. And this was said to be one of the better examples of the cyclecar. The driver's vision, incidentally, was much improved on the French army's version, in which a stretcher was placed over the front of the vehicle with its occupant naturally lying flat. It looked like something

This extended bathtub of 1910, known as a Bedelia, is now in the Turin Biscaretti museum; the 'passenger' sat in front and shared the driving.

invented by a drunken cartoonist, but worked well as an ambulance.

The Tamplin was a British equivalent of the Bedelia, and it became relatively civilized, with side-by-side seating for two – as in a motor car – and with the engine under the bonnet at the front. But the Carden version, designed by Captain Carden, was originally more primitive than the Bedelia, with a single-seat body and the engine behind the occupant, the mighty power unit being a single-

cylinder affair of 482 cc. The Tamplin/Cardin was also called a Sheret, six alternative engines were used and there were one, two and four-seat versions. What 700 cc did with four people is not disclosed, although it was perhaps no worse than an Austin Seven. The Carden looked like a child's pedal car, and the astonishing thing is that they sold at the rate of 40 a week.

A remarkable amount has been written about the cyclecar, but two are enough. Moving on to the orthodox vehicle, one must take

The Cyclecar was fortunately short-lived, or the people who rode in them might have been more so. This Tamplin of 1920–21 resembles a child's pedal car.

A real trap for the unwary, the 1920 Carden was like a four-wheel bicycle and just about as difficult to control, but it sold well.

Lest we forget, this is how it all began, with Karl Benz and his 1885 motor tricycle, with spindly wheels, chain drive and absolutely no creature comforts.

account of the first two machines by the venerated Messrs. Daimler and Benz. Admittedly, there were earlier attempts, but these two are generally acknowledged to have built the first proper motor cars, even if one was a three-wheeler. Karl Benz is always said to have driven his tricycle in 1885 and Gottlieb Daimler his car in 1886, but the Mercedes-Benz museum in Stuttgart credits both men with the same date (1886), which must be some kind of political statement. The remaining examples of these cars are carefully preserved, and

Which way does it go? By 1891 Gottlieb Daimler had progressed to four seats and a fold-down hood — that's him in the rear (right) seat, along with Wilhelm Maybach.

they should be mentioned, even if their history is so well-known as to be tedious, including the saga of Frau Benz's garter-elastic, which ultimately held the trembler coil together.

Such very early machines, whether horseless carriages or cyclecars, were so primitive as to be of little interest except to historians, but if we consider what was available only a few years later, progress was astonishingly quick in every aspect of design, control, and roadability. Although the Germans invented the motor car it is true that the French made it work, so that people like de Dion-Bouton, Peugeot, Panhard, Renault, Levassor, Bollée, and others must be given some credit, if only because some of the names survive on vehicles being made to this day.

The alphabet dictates that we must start our quest in Italy, however, with the wares of Alfa Romeo, who first appeared on the scene in 1910. Like their rivals at Fiat, they originally used initials – A.L.F.A. standing for Anonima Lombardo Fabbrica Automobili – until Nichola Romeo took over in 1915. Right from the start, Alfas tended to be sporting cars, although their first model (the 4.1 litre 24 hp) was not as worthy as their second, the 2.4 litre 12 hp, later made as a 15 hp and as a 15/20 hp. The 12 hp of 1910 was the nearest Alfa ever came to making plebian transport. A four-seater with touring or limousine bodies, it had a front-mounted, four-cylinder, monobloc engine driving the rear wheels via a three-speed gearbox and shaft. The engine had a compression ratio of 4:1 and could propel the touring model at over 50 mph. With semi-elliptic springs all round and artillery wheels, it was an example of plain, sensible engineering, although only 330 were made in five years. We now think of Alfas as having twin overhead camshafts, but this early device had side valves.

Amédée Bollée could actually provide us with an exhibit dating back to 1878, in the form of a steam car, but it was too primitive and no

An early Benz of 1900, a two-cylinder racer called the 16 PS with all the features of its day, including no brakes and chain drive.

A heart-shaped 'radiator' opening hides the air-cooled engine of a 1913 Morgan Runabout. This had the same design of sliding-pillar, independent front suspension used on Morgans to the present day.

Léon Bollée was an honoured name during the pioneer days of motoring. This 16/20 hp tourer from 1913 was one of his larger models.

Looking a little over-dressed, even for 1910, this Buick four-cylinder ohv featured white wheels and tyres.

An 1889 Daimler Phoenix, and this particular one did rise from the ashes. For 40 years it ran a saw-mill until restored in Britain.

example now remains. It did have the engine in front, so anticipating a fashion which has lasted 100 years. There are examples of the 1896 Léon-Bollée Tri-Car still running, and in all of them the passenger once again sat in front of the driver and closest to the accident. It might be worth having one for curiosity value, and they do still manage the run from London to Brighton each year in the British event for pre-1904 cars. The engine was behind the driver's seat, the flywheel brushing his right leg, and the drive was by belt to a single rear wheel. There are good reasons for commemorating the Bollées – father and son – as son Léon invented the term *voiturette* to describe his car and this was adopted by everyone to describe a light car. His engine was a single-cylinder, motor-cycle-type, 650 cc unit, but had the weakness or nuisance of hot-tube ignition, along with a three-speed transmission. In their day – before 1900 – Léon's little three-wheelers were the fastest petrol-driven devices, yet the more-or-less orthodox, four-wheel car that followed was not as popular.

CGV was another early make, this one seen on a ladies outing in 1905, with the party suitably dressed to fight the elements.

William Morris, the clever, cut-price motor merchant, bought Léon's old factory at Le Mans some years later and made Anglo-French hybrids called Morris-Léon Bollées, which were British cars assembled in France, but the company failed.

Buick must be included too, and although they later tended to serve the upper end of the market, the early Buicks (1903) were, like Cadillacs and Oldsmobiles, under-floor engined devices with epicyclic transmission and two speeds. These cars were remarkably alike, except that the Buick had overhead valves and its two-cylinder engine was bigger, at 2.6 litres. They went on to grow into luxury saloons and sporty tourers like so many others, and only these examples remind us of their early beginnings. Some early Buicks still run in Veteran car events and they make an interesting comparison with early vehicles from Europe, enabling one to see how different solutions to the

28

The long and the short of it, M. Bouton (left) and his partner, Count de Dion, who played such a big part in developing the motor car.

same problems were being found, even at that early period in the science of making motor cars.

Also from the United States, Cadillac once built cars for basic transport, although they now have a name for luxurious transport. Their first models, from 1903, included a single-cylinder, 1.5 litre car which, in 1908, passed a rather novel test in England: the Royal Automobile Club supervised the dismantling of three complete cars, whose pieces were jumbled up and re-assembled; the cars then ran round the Brooklands race track without any mechanical mishap and the company were presented with a trophy to mark this early demonstration of standardisation. The car was the Model A, by the way, which had an underfloor engine and two-speed planetary transmission.

Alexandre Darracq was one of the many gentlemen who came to the motor car business by way of bicycles and motor cycles and he founded Gladiator, Millet and Perfecta before getting around to using his own name in about 1899. His first car was actually a Léon-Bollée built under licence (and called a Darracq-Bollée), but he introduced his own car in 1900 with a 785 cc, single-cylinder engine. As usual, however, this was a crude machine and best ignored.

In 1901, the good Mr Darracq produced his Type N, with a front-mounted engine of 90 mm × 100 mm, still one-cylinder but now of 636 cc. This engine had mechanically-operated inlet valves, high-tension ignition, drip-feed lubrication, and was connected via three-speed transmission to a pro-pellor shaft and rear axle, the company following Renault's lead and eschewing chain drive.

With a weight of just over half a ton and decent brakes, the N could top 30 mph and was reliable, too. It

De Dion were in there at the beginning, too. This is a 3½ hp *voiturette* in 1900, driven by H. W. Egerton in the 1,000 Miles Trial.

proved very popular among the masses, becoming one of the very first quantity-production cars in the world.

One of the most famous pioneering names was that of de Dion-Bouton, who were building cars by the thousand as early as 1900. Their single-cylinder, rear-engined model was an example of mechanical simplicity, having a variety of displacements and power outputs, but usually supplying about 5 bhp from 500 cc at 1,500 rpm. With water-cooling from a front radiator, high-tension ignition and de Dion's own carburettor, the engine had an automatic inlet valve located above the exhaust valve. The separate gearbox contained two, constant-mesh ratios, with an ingenious system of expanding clutches to select first, second or neutral by means of a lever mounted on the steering column. Steering, by the way, was by handlebars rather than a wheel.

The chassis was made of brazed steel tubes, with semi-elliptic springs at the front and, naturally enough, a de Dion rear axle, which was an early – and enormous – improvement on chain drive. With a variety of body styles to choose from, including some enclosed ones, the car generally weighed around 800 or 900 lbs and could do 24 mph.

Some of the multifarious Swiss cars might be worth considering, but there are so few survivors from so many models that one or two makes will have to represent them all: we simply must have an Egg, although we do not, of course, want a bad Egg. This firm appeared in the 1890s, but their interesting models dated from around 1906. Their creator, Rudoph Egg, lived in the mountains near Zurich, with the result that all his machines were characterised by an ability to climb steep hills. His Excelsior of 1906/07, for example, was a splendid device.

Just across the border in Italy, one can hardly ignore the early efforts of the company which was to become Europe's most influential in so many ways, the giant Fiat empire, which now includes both Lancia and Ferrari and who make something like 80 per cent of Italy's cars.

Fiat were about in 1899, in this case with a 3½ hp runabout with tiller steering, chain drive, but with a front radiator.

Ford sold this 1904 Model A complete with tonneau, double-tube tyres and brass rails. It had a flat-twin, 8 hp engine under the driver's seat.

Fiat began in 1899 and, within two years, were offering for a sale an 8 hp phaeton with roof, this being a car which would easily have passed for a much more modern machine. With a vertical, two-cylinder engine of 1,082 cc mounted in the front and producing 10 bhp to drive the rear wheels via a clutch, gearbox and chain, it could top 30 mph. There were two seats under the roof, but no windscreen to keep out the draughts, while two even more hardy souls could perch behind the roof on an exposed rear seat, suitable for footmen or servants. Early examples had coiled-tube radiators and tended to overheat, but this was quickly overcome on later models with a honeycomb radiator. Maximum engine revs were 800 per minute and the car provided leisurely transport at a time when the horseless carriage was evolving into the sophisticated device which we now call a motor car.

The Swiss designer Martin Fischer should have an honourable mention, if only for his remarkable gearbox of 1913: this consisted of a large drive wheel with four, internally-toothed gears. The big gear was connected to the propellor shaft; the small gears were the variable ratios, selected by means of a shaft (from the clutch) which was universally jointed and could therefore be swung about to mesh with any one of the small cogs. For reverse, a second pinion was brought in between the one on the end of the clutch-driven shaft and the teeth of first gear. Fischer patented this design and used a picture of it as his company logo.

His innovation did not stop there, either, and his 33CV Torpedo was fitted with an engine whose sleeve valves were also worked by a complicated system

Hey there! Ford's 1906 Model N, a 15 hp four-cylinder, made horses turn their heads. The N sold in large numbers and was the immediate predecessor of the famous T.

of gears and shafts, driven by the five-bearing crank. With a bore and stroke of 85 mm × 120 mm giving the four-cylinder unit a capacity of 2,723 cc, maximum power was 33 bhp at 1,200 rpm.

Fischer also fitted quick-change, artillery-type wooden wheels, with central nut fixing, which was well ahead of its time. And his cars had glove boxes in the dashboard – the first to do so?

Across the Atlantic Ocean in the United States, production of cars was in full swing by about 1903, the self-propelled devices finding immediate favour in the land of opportunity and private enterprise. Many of the pioneer names are still with

Henry Ford himself on his first car, the Quadricycle of 1896, with cycle wheels, tiller steering, and in his favourite colour – black.

us, including Ford, who take the credit for putting the world, or a large part of it, onto wheels in 1908. The car with which they achieved this was, of course, the archetypal Model T, which remained in production for 18 years. It used a 2.9 litre, four-cylinder, monobloc engine with water cooling and a peculiar, epicylic transmission which required the driver to exercise 'considerable dexterity on his pedals. Starting the engine, incidentally, involved jacking up one rear wheel and spinning it, but the

car endeared itself to millions, made Henry Ford a wealthy man and changed the course of American history. It was slow, but economical (30 mpg), cheap to buy and virtually indestructible.

The British make of Humber is usually thought of in a luxury context, but there were some mundane Humbers in the early 1900s, among them the 10/12 tourer of 1905, a robust, four-seat runabout with orthodox construction. It had a four-cylinder, side-valve front engine cooled by water, artillery wheels suspended on semi-elliptic springs and a windscreen.

Lancia confuse matters somewhat, because their first model was

Another early car, the Lutzmann, was really a Benz Victoria. In 1894 it could be had with 5 hp instead of 3 for £1 extra.

called an Alpha, which had nothing whatsoever to do with the company of that name, but was only so-named because it happens to be the first letter of the Greek alphabet. Produced in 1907, it was the only early Lancia mundane enough to be included in this chapter, with a 2.5 litre, four-cylinder, side-valve engine, a four-speed gearbox (un-usual for the time), shaft drive and three-quarter elliptic rear springs – Lancia unorthodoxy right from the start. Later cars, although just as innovative, became bigger and either more luxurious, more sporting or both.

The name of Bill Morris has already been mentioned, in con-nection with his Léon Bollée in-

A pioneer motorist, Mr Alfred Harmsworth, wearing the right clothes aboard his Lohner Porsche 28 hp, with electric motors in the hubs.

A period shot of Bill Morris himself (later Viscount Nuffield) in his 1913 Bullnose Morris outside the showrooms of his agents in London's West End.

volvement, but the man is better known as the founder of Morris Motors, of course, and their Bullnose Morris must be included as one of the steps on the road to motorising the public at large. It appeared in 1913 as the Morris Oxford and it was, in many ways, the British equivalent of the Model T Ford. It was a simple, reliable car with a four-cylinder, water-cooled engine, three-speed gearbox and artillery wheels – just what the public wanted. Before the First World War, it had only two seats, but a four-seater tourer appeared after the Armistice, along with various saloon bodies. It was one of the first cars to run without much in the way of service and without needing to be fiddled about with to keep it going.

The American firm of Oldsmobile were among the pioneers, and can lay claim to having the first-ever vehicle in mass-production, the Curved Dash Runabout of 1903. This was very much of a horseless carriage, with the driver and his companion exposed to the weather and with tiller steering, but its very simplicity was one of its virtues. The engine, similar to a Cadillac, was a single-cylinder, 1.6 litre unit driving the rear wheels through a two-speed planetary transmission and chain. It sold well as a town car, and some people even undertook long-distance journeys, mostly for publicity, but it did not enjoy the long life of the Model T, being superseded by improved models with better amenities.

In any representative sample of early French cars, there would have to be at least one Panhard-Levassor, as René Panhard and Emile Levassor – with their front-engined car, which appeared as early as 1891 – set a trend which was to influence the whole future of the motor car. Their first model was really too primitive, but the B1 of 1898 had a four-cylinder engine built under licence from Daimler and supplying 12 bhp from 2,412 cc, enabling the car to proceed at over 30 mph. Engine speed was controlled by a centrifugal regulator with both lever and pedal

America's first production car was the Curved-Dash Oldsmobile of 1903, which shows its horse-and-cart origins.

Oldsmobile had this smart tourer by 1909, apparently completely without weather protection.

operation, the clutch was a leather-cone type, while the gearbox had four forward speeds and one reverse. Final drive was by chain.

Among the BI's novelties was aluminium bodywork and a special brake controlled from a steering-wheel-lever and intended to stop the car running backwards down hills. It seems that the normal brakes were fairly efficient in a forward direction, but none too certain in reverse.

In 1912, the company produced a

Panhard were in the running by 1893, with the unusual feature of smaller front wheels, which aided the turning circle.

Where it all started in Britain. The first petrol-engined car to be imported there was this 1895 Panhard.

Opposite, top
An early Swiss car, the Ideal of 1902, with a single-cylinder engine of 785 cc, 5.5 bhp, two-speed gearbox and rack-and-pinion steering.

From Panhard (who used to claim that they were the oldest car makers in the world, a title which could be disputed by Mercedes or Peugeot), we come to one of the less conventional of those myriad Swiss manufacturers, Popp. Lorenz Popp lived in Basle and was financed by Eduard Burkhardt, the Swiss agent for Benz cars. In 1898, he decided that he could improve on their products, however, and produced two of his own models, one with two seats and one with four.

The Popp 7 hp featured a mid-mounted, water-cooled engine with two cylinders in parallel and mounted horizontally; with measurements of 92 mm × 120 mm, the capacity was 1,595 cc and the power output 7.6 bhp. Inlet valves were automatic, but the exhaust valves were actually operated by a chain-driven, overhead camshaft – in 1898!

The engine was by no means the most revolutionary feature, however, that title being claimed by the transmission, which operated by means of belts to a countershaft and chains from countershaft to rear wheels. The belts were tensioned or slackened by means of a lever, which slid the whole engine unit backwards and forwards on rails. This acted as the clutch, while alternative pulleys provided two forward speeds and a reverse gear.

Despite all this innovation, the crudities inherent in any motoring machine of the 19th century were present: steering was by vertical column and wheel via chain and sprocket to a rack and pinion; braking was achieved stage-coach-style, by shoes applied directly to the rear tyres.

Peugeot started even earlier, in 1876, and the same family remain in

15.9 hp tourer with lines so modern that it might easily have been mistaken for a car of the 1920s. Powered by a 2,614 cc engine built under licence from Knight, it produced 22 bhp at 1,200 rpm and had shaft drive to a rear axle. The engine consisted of two blocks of two, with 80 mm × 130 mm dimensions and sleeve valves, which made it very quiet by the standards of the day, if a little smokey. Options included water heating for the passengers and a brass gauge recording the distance covered in kilometres, while the cars came with windscreen, canvas roof, lights and horn fitted, although braking was by drums fitted to the rear wheels only, which must have made life exciting when attempting to bring this $1\frac{1}{4}$ ton car to rest from its maximum speed of 40 mph.

Opposite, lower
Peugeot was another pioneer, as in this 1892 'vis à vis' with hood. It had a twin-cylinder vee engine, three-speed-and-reverse gearbox and double-chain drive.

High if not handsome, this is a
Peugeot racer during the 1911 *Coupé
Automobile*.

High if not handsome, this is a
Peugeot racer during the 1911 *Coupé
Automobile*.

control of the company to this day,
having presided over four major re-
arrangements in the past century.
In 1978, they became the largest
makers of automobiles in Europe,
their empire now including
Chrysler's European operations as
well as the whole of Citroen.

Armand Peugeot was born into
an old ironmongery firm of that
name, which was responsible for
most of France's pepper and coffee-
mills, a by no means inconsiderable
undertaking in a country so concerned with culinary matters.
Armand studied in England and
went home to make bicycles – the
firm still make them – and, later,
motor cars. To make matters
slightly complicated, Peugeot sold
woodworking machinery to
Panhard et Levassor, but Peugeot
himself preferred steam to petrol
and turned to Léon Serpollet for his
first engines. He was not pleased
with the results, however, and went
back to Levassor for a petrol
engine, fitted to a car with which he
then undertook the longest car
journey then achieved: he accompanied the entrants of an 1891
bicycle race, all of whom beat the
car's average speed of 9.5 mph.

But Armand was not satisfied
with Levassor's engines, either, and
from 1896 made all his own. By
1903, the name of Peugeot was
already well known in what passed
for motoring circles in those days.
Their model for that year was the
3.6 litre 18 hp Double Phaeton,
with four cylinders in two blocks of
two and about 20 bhp at 1,200 rpm.
With decent, worm-and-nut steering and mudguards designed to
keep the wind, dust and mud off the
occupants, it was ideal for travel on
the unmade roads of the time and
could manage 50 mph.

Peugeot's real classic among ordinary cars, however, was the 6 hp
Bébé two-seater of 1913, which – as
all the world knows – was designed
by none other than Ettore Bugatti.

Louis Perret's Peugeot at Clermont-
Ferrand in the Press Cup race of
1907.

38

A Bébé Peugeot, designed by Ettore Bugatti, with unusual closed coachwork and the front seat at the back, as it were.

This was a cheeky-looking little car in which two large men were hard-pressed to sit side-by-side without bending the body, but it had much charm. Some historians suggest that it was conceived in 1902 and redesigned by Bugatti in 1912, but none dispute that it came from his pen.

The engine was an orthodox, water-cooled, 856 cc monobloc, side-valve unit with what the Americans call a T-head, that is to say with a camshaft on either side, one for inlet, one for exhaust. In many ways it anticipated the Austin Seven by ten years as the first 'mini' car, unless we give that title to the Wanderer Puppchen (doll) which was a contemporary of the Bébé. The German car, however, had a bigger engine (1,145 cc) and seats one behind the other, so the claim of the Bébé is the stronger as it was more like a proper car. It was no racer of course, but drivers had 10 bhp to play with, only slightly less than the much later Austin Seven. The Peugeot also had an unusual transmission arrangement, consisting of concentric propeller shafts each of which meshed its own teeth on the crownwheel. The Bébé had only two forward speeds, although in 1914 it gained a three-speed transmission.

There were some 50 Peugeot models before the First World War, so there is a wide choice, but the Bébé was the truly classic one, not only for the jewel-like quality given it by the designer, but because it was the first in a long line of miniature cars, culminating in the famous Mini which was to give the English language – and many others – a new word.

Moving North to the Paris region brings us to Renault, which was founded in 1898 by the brothers

Louis Renault with his racer, during the 1902 Paris–Vienna, which his brother Marcel won at an average speed of 39 mph, beating many more powerful machines in the process.

39

Marcel Renault at the wheel of his 30 hp before the Paris–Madrid of 1903, which was stopped at Bordeaux after many crashes, including that which killed Marcel himself.

Louis and Marcel and which is one of many French and German motor manufacturers to have survived through nearly 100 years. Unhappily, Marcel was killed while competing in the infamous Paris–Madrid race of 1903, which was halted at Bordeaux after a great many accidents. Marcel had won the light-car class of the Paris–Vienna event of 1902 with a 16 hp Renault – much lighter and smaller than the cars of his rivals – but the racers do not really fit into this book.

Louis Renault was the power behind the company and, as we have seen, was the first to use the now-orthodox system of engine, clutch, gearbox, shaft and rear axle with differential. His first, primitive models were not particularly interesting, but there is no doubt that the little twin-cylinder, 1,100 cc AX, introduced in 1906 and produced for many years thereafter, was a real classic. When, in 1977, Renault organised a run from Paris to Vienna to commemorate their 1902 race victory over that route, there were more examples of the AX than of any other model taking part; they all completed almost 1,000 miles without major problems, including a climb of the Arlberg pass.

The AX did nothing sensational, but chugged along at 40 mph without any bother and was still utterly reliable, even after the passage of 70 years. It seems to be the sort of veteran car that is quite usable, even if the two-wheel brakes call for caution in traffic. The simple, reliable specification enables it to keep running.

Renault have always liked small cars and, in 1910, produced an 8 hp, 846 cc model, with two cylinders of 70 mm bore × 110 mm stroke. The water-cooled cylinders were cast in a single block with side valves, magneto ignition, gravity lubrication and Renault's own carburettor. It had the dashboard radiator

Louis Renault, brother of Marcel, here seen on the tragic Paris–Madrid race of 1903. Louis (whose car featured the familiar rear radiator) retired on hearing the news of his brother's fatal crash.

layout which graced all Renaults until the 1920s and which made routine maintenance very simple. A leather-cone clutch took the drive to a separate, four-speed gearbox and then by shaft to the rear axle. The driver had three pedals which, as on modern cars, worked the clutch, accelerator and brake, except that the footbrake operated on the transmission, wheel braking being achieved by an external hand lever. The whole car was very light, managing 28 mph on less than 10 bhp.

Rover are another firm now associated with more expensive devices, but in 1911 they produced a 12 hp with no special peculiarities but with a design considered good enough for re-introduction after the First World War; it stayed on the market until 1925, so people must have liked it. There was a two-cylinder, sleeve-valve version, but most people opted for the four-cylinder, 2,297 cc one, which gave 22 bhp and was a good example of what British manufacturers were up to at the time.

Finally to one of the world's first attempts at a stripped-down basic motor car, the Le Zèbre Type A of 1909 to 1914. It was designed by Jules Salomon to carry one or two people from A to B and nothing more. There was a single-cylinder, 630 cc engine under the bonnet with side valves, magneto ignition, gravity fuel-feed, a total-loss oil system and only 6 bhp, driving through a two-speed gearbox to a rear axle. The pressed-steel frame members and tubular cross braces were all bolted or rivetted together, suspension was by semi-elliptic leaves and the wheels were wooden. Windscreen, hood, lights and a wicker basket for the luggage were all listed as optional extras.

Everything inside the car was kept as simple as possible, with no instruments or accessories and only the very basic minimum of controls. But the car was light (only 780 lbs), would travel at 30 mph and looked much larger and more expensive than it was, this straightforward marketing ploy resulting in ample sales.

Above
Vauxhall – now part of General Motors – were British pioneers, with this 1903 single-cylinder 5 hp.

Below
Early cars (posing?) on the Auvergne Circuit used for the Gordon Bennett race of 1905. A Renault 'leads'.

3 Pre-1914: Putting on the Style

Writing about luxury cars from the pre-1914 era may seem, perhaps, a contradiction in terms, as most motor vehicles of that time were so primitive in terms of comfort and noise level as to virtually preclude such a description. Fortunately, there were some exceptions and it is with these that we must concern ourselves here.

An alphabetical approach is always logical, so that we must start with a curiosity from west of the Atlantic Ocean, the American Underslung. This came from the American Motor Car Co., a firm with a life of just two years, and not to be confused with the American Motor Carriage Co., the American

Cyclecar Co., or any of the myriad other firms using their country's name at the time. The first American Motor Car product appeared in 1906 and was quite orthodox; the Underslung arrived a year later, with axles on the 'wrong' side of its springs in order to make the whole car lower. This gave the machine a rakish appearance, rather similar to that of many modern replicas of vintage cars.

Still in the United States, the Autocar was made by a firm who still manufacture trucks. They started in Pittsburg, Pennsylvania, in 1897 and moved across the state to Ardmore in 1900. What is their claim to fame? Well, they made the

Opposite
The 1906 Autocar Model X Runabout was built in Pennsylvania, USA: gear change, clutch, spark and throttle were all controlled from the steering column. Autocar became part of the White Motor Co and nowadays they make heavy trucks.

Two cylinders, water cooling and jump-spark ignition were features of the Autocar Model X engine, which had 102 mm bore and stroke. This immaculate example resides at Hillcrest Motors in California.

Low-slung cars, with their inherent handling advantages, were a feature of many designs by the American, Harry C. Stutz. This four-cylinder American Underslung was designed by him in 1910, before he formed his own company.

first, multi-cylinder American car with shaft drive in 1901. By 1905, large two and four-cylinder cars were being made with other peculiarities, in that not only the throttle and spark were controlled by levers on the steering column but also the gear-change and clutch. They were such a challenge to drive that they simply must be of interest to any collector. The Autocar has been described as the first shaft-driven car anywhere, but this cannot be true as Louis Renault used a shaft on his prototype of 1898.

Returning to European regions, the alphabet brings us next to the Austro-Daimler marque, made in Vienna from 1899 to 1934, after which the company merged with Steyr and later with Puch. Austro-Daimlers could hardly boast a more aristocratic background, some of their models being designed by the legendary Dr Ferdinand Porsche, who is better known for the cars made under his own name, but who was also responsible for such immortals as the Auto Union racing cars, various sporting Mercedes and the Volkswagen Beetle.

Austro-Daimler were the Vienna branch of the parent Daimler company, of Canstatt in Germany. Originally, the new plant was run by Paul Daimler, son of the founder, but Dr Porsche took over in 1905. At this point, however, it would be interesting to digress from the main theme to consider a little-known story of how at least one Austro-Daimler car might have carried a different name. To explain this, it is necessary first to recount the well-known story of how the Daimler car came to be called a Mercedes, thanks to the Austro-Hungarian consul of Nice, Emil Jellinek, who appointed himself unofficial agent for Canstatt Daimlers and drove one of their 24 hp cars into last place on the 1900 Nice–Marseilles race.

Jellinek hid his identity under the nom-de-plume of Herr Mercedes, and called his car a Mercedes Special, the name being that of his daughter. After the race, he de-manded from Daimler a better car for his rich friends and the company obliged with a machine featuring a pressed-steel frame, honeycomb radiator and mechanical valves. This 35 hp machine eventually won the Nice–Salon–Nice race of 1901, so delighting Jellinek that he asked the Emperor Franz Joseph for permission to change his own name to Jellinek-Mercedes.

All this is merely to introduce to the story of Jellinek's other daughter, Mercedes' sister Maja. One of the earliest Austro-Daimlers was blessed with her name, but it did not catch on for some reason and the world never got a Maja model. In many ways, it would have been even more logical than the Mercedes affair, as Jellinek's residence in Vienna must have brought him even closer to the Austrian factory than to Canstatt. Austro-Daimler produced a num-

The Czar of Russia, no less, about to ride in his Delaunay–Belleville with some suitable companions of blue blood.

ber of designs before the arrival of Dr Porsche, among them a four-wheel drive, cross-country device for the Imperial and Royal Technical Committee of 1902–05. Designing vehicles for heavy loads later became a speciality of the Austrian works.

The products of Dr Porsche himself, however, were the real classics, particularly his Prince Henry, over which we will gloat in the next chapter. Before 1914, Porsche's main contribution was the 16/18PS, a simple design with side-valve engine and chain drive. In 1911, a team of these swept the board on the Alpine Trial, which included the high passes of the Austrian and Italian Alps. In honour of the victory, a 16/25PS was introduced, called the Alpine. It had a 2.3 litre, four-cylinder, side-valve engine producing 30 bhp. Subsequent developments included 20/30PS and more luxurious 35/60PS models.

The next make to come under scrutiny are Berliet, more par-ticularly the American licence-holders of that company, Alco. The American Locomotive Automotive Company of Providence, Rhode Island, to give them their full title (they later dropped the word 'Automotive') made cars until 1913. In the early days, they produced steam engines as well. Their American Berliets, however, were very good cars, including a 54 hp, 9,505 cc, chain-driven model which was raced for many years, winning the Vanderbilt Cup in 1909 and 1910, with one Harry Grant at the wheel on both occasions. From 1907 onwards, shaft-drive cars could be had, many of them becoming taxis. There was also a 60 hp six-cylinder job, which offered high-quality coachwork in either open or closed form. In theory, an Alco should be identifiable by its locomotive badge, if it were not for the fact that Berliet also used it in France and still do so on their trucks.

As a companion to this early originality, there was the Brush, an English machine from a company operating between 1902 and 1904. These now have rarity value, but there is at least one surviving. The 1904 Brush had four cylinders and an engine from a French company called Abeille, who made both engines and tractors. Chain-driven, the Brush could be of 12, 16 or 20 hp.

David Buick came from Scotland and travelled to the New World as a child. He founded the automobile manufacturer that still bears his name in 1903, but sold out to William Durant in 1908 and died a poor man. Durant's firm, General Motors, went from strength to strength, which is probably the only reason Buick's name lives on. The pre-GM cars were – as we have seen – very limited, with under-floor, flat-twin engines and planetary transmissions; later ones came with four cylinders and a

Lancia were ahead of the times with this closed, luxury saloon Theta as early as 1913. The driver, however, sat in the fresh air.

Rare Austro-Daimler 27/80 from 1912, during the period when Dr Ferdinand Porsche was one of the firm's directors.

Daddy of them all, a 21.0 litre Métallurgique with aero engine, still in use on British roads today, after 70 years.

choice of 2.7, 3.3 or 5.2 litres. The most luxurious of the pre-1914 machines appeared in that very year, however, with six cylinders and electric lights. Buick's advertising slogan at the time was 'When better cars are built, Buick will build them' which sold a lot of cars for them. The six-cylinder, incidentally, was called the B55 and its engine produced 48 bhp.

Staying west of the Atlantic, Cadillac made their share of pioneer motor cars, beginning in 1903. There was no Mr Cadillac, the name being selected by the firm's founder, Henry M. Leland.

Cadillac's earliest, single-cylinder car was reviewed in the last chapter, but his more prestigious products are of greater concern here, like the 30 hp, four-cylinder of 1906, a design which continued until 1914. By 1912, this had not only electric starting, but electric lights as well and was a very driveable motor car.

Crossley is a fine old English name which is remembered for the splendid tourers in which First World War staff officers rode about waving at the troops. They had a rather appealing badge with a Maltese cross in a circle, which is somehow more memorable and impressive than many of the other car badges we see. The company began as engine builders, but made cars from 1904 to 1936. The First World War staff car, the 20/25, was a four-cylinder and is the best-known and best-loved model, and there were other, large luxury models in the pre-war range, most of which did not come back after hostilities, when big cars were no longer selling, although the 20 had a four-cylinder engine of 4.5 litres with an orthodox layout and was rather desirable.

Daimler come next, but the products of Gottlieb Daimler of Canstatt have been dealt with, as have those of his colleagues in Austria. As the subject in hand is that of luxury cars, however, it is

Opposite, top
This Brush roadster was designed by
Alanson P. Brush, who had earlier
been responsible for the original,
single-cylinder Cadillac car.

Opposite, lower
Among the first British manufacturers
were Brown Bros of London, who
produced motor tricycles as early as
1899. By 1905, they had advanced to
this 18/20 hp tourer.

only natural that we should include
the British Daimlers. Until 1909
these were mere copies of their
German name-sakes, but the two
companies went their own way after
that date and there were over 40
different British Daimler models
before 1914, providing plenty of
selection.

The company trademark for 23
years was a trail of blue smoke
created by the use of sleeve valves,
which provided the luxurious silence with which we now associate
the name.

An Englishman, Charles Knight,
designed the sleeve valve, which
had two sleeves wrapped round the
cylinders; by turning and moving
up and down these operated the
induction and exhaust processes.
Knight failed to sell the idea in the
USA but it caught on elsewhere and
Minerva, Mercedes and Panhard
all used it. Daimler called it 'The
Silent Knight' and modified the
design to work with a single sleeve.
Peugeot and Voisin in France also
took up Knight patents later and
made them work well.

The high and dignified Daimler
had the fluted radiator that is with
us still, if only as token indentations
on a Jaguar. All sorts of equipment
was available and the car was cum-
bersome, slow and thirsty, but not
without its charm. It could be a 12,
15, 20, 22, 23, 25, 26, 30, 33, 38 or
40 hp. During the First World War,
Daimler went over to making aircraft and munitions and there were
no more cars until 1919.

A De Dietrich would be a pleasant addition to any gentleman's
stable; the company ran under
different names from 1897 to 1935
and eventually sold its cars as
Lorraines after a spell as Lorraine-
Dietrich. The first half of the
name was taken from the area where
their Luneville factory was situated,
and the double-barred cross was their
emblem. However, the 1904 De
Dietrich was the first with 'proper,'
mechanically-operated inlet valves
and therefore reasonably modern in
concept.

The company, which made railway carriages, went into the motor
industry by making Bollées under
licence, before they developed their
own design. Their later ones were
perhaps a bit like Panhard or
Turcat-Méry cars, but then all early
cars had similarities. It was in the
years after pioneering and before
standardisation that there was so
much individuality, which is what
this book is all about. The best De
Dietrich had a front-mounted,
four-cylinder engine of 13.0 litres,

One of the USA's most important
manufacturers of electric cars was
Baker of Cleveland, Ohio. This is their
1910 model, complete with buttoned,
leather upholstery.

with chain-drive, a wooden chassis strengthened by flitch plates (as used by everyone except Mercedes at the time) and a tubular radiator with its handsome badge.

Delage is sometimes thought of as a car of the 1930s, but the company was very active from 1905 onwards. Louis Delage learned his trade at Peugeot and started by making the usual sort of small car with a proprietary engine, but he was also a racing man, competing from 1906. Perhaps this is what

gave all his production cars a sporty image, even those with leanings to luxury. Delage won Indianapolis as early as 1914, with a 6.3 litre car with the rather original feature of a gearbox with an overdrive fifth gear behind a four-cylinder engine. There had been a 3.0 litre in 1911 with 80 mm × 149 mm motor which also had the five-speed gearbox, so it was nothing new to him. Both were desirable cars, although the larger one was a bit too much of a racer. Both also had horizontal

valves worked by pushrods, which is a little difficult to envisage.

Delaunay-Belleville has such a lovely ring about it that the name alone is enough to justify a place in eternity. Connoisseurs insist that the marque was at its best before 1914 and slowly declined after that. The Delaunay-Belleville model called the SMT (Sa Majesté le Tsar) for Nicholas II of Russia, must surely be the most desirable. It was a six-cylinder 70 hp and the odd thing was that it was chain-

car in which the Archduke Franz Ferdinand of Austria–Hungary was assassinated at Sarajevo, the event which sparked off the First World War, and the actual car can still be seen in the Vienna Military Museum. Keen historians can make the slightly longer trip from Vienna to Sarajevo, where there is a museum dedicated to Gabriel Princip, the assassin, who is revered as a hero in his native Serbia, and who has had his footprints preserved in the concrete on the spot where he stood to shoot.

Gräf & Stift supplied cars to the Austrian Imperial Court and were makers of standing. The firm is still going, making buses and trucks, but the choice models from pre-1914 were four-cylinder, side-valve engined cars of between 4.2 and 10.0 litres, the firm being inclined towards large engines.

Kissel came from the United States – from Hartford, Wisconsin to be exact – and existed from 1906 to 1931, and rather than the model known as the Kissel Kar we might look at one of the handsome, 1914 six-cylinder tourers, which had the oddity for those days of a 'square' engine (121 mm × 121 mm). It also had electric starting in 1913, only one year behind Cadillac, plus wire wheels with centre-lock hubs, roof, windscreen and all the modern conveniences, so that it was a refined and elegant carriage.

So, too, were the early products of the Lanchester brothers, who made many contributions to the technical advancement of the motor car by applying scientific methods in an age when most people relied on trial and error. Unfortunately, the Lanchesters lacked the necessary business acumen with which to turn their ideas into the commercial successes which they deserved.

The Lanchester 25 hp of 1912 was a typical example of their quality machines, being every bit as good as the contemporary Rolls-Royces about which one hears so

much praise. The Lanchester's in-line, four-cylinder motor was 'all square' with bore and stroke of 101.6 mm, giving a capacity of 3,299 cc and the ability to revolve at up to 2,000 rpm. With pressure lubrication, dual magneto ignition, horizontal ohv and Lanchester's own wick carburettor (which worked by evaporation), this unit gave just under 40 bhp and provided a top speed of 53 mph.

The whole engine was set back into the passenger compartment, so that occupants sat one on either side of it, which must have helped the handling. There was a torsional vibration damper on the front of the crankshaft and a very advanced transmission system with a three-speed, epicyclic gearbox controlled by friction – rather like a modern automatic. Cantilever springs were used all round, providing a very comfortable ride, while there were brakes on both the transmission (foot operated) and the rear wheels (lever operated), needed because the whole machine topped $1\frac{1}{2}$ tons.

Marmon were American, from Indianapolis, and existed from 1902 until 1933. They were famous for making one of the few 16-cylinder cars ever produced, but that came much later. In the pre-1914 period, a more typical product was their Model 32, a 5.2 litre roadster of most peculiar appearance with the rear axle and gearbox married into what came to be called a transaxle. It had a big, four-cylinder engine and in 1911 was the only model listed. Although Howard Marmon's earliest cars used air-cooled vee engines and other such oddities, his Model 32 was quite orthodox apart from its transaxle. Incidentally, when the 500-mile race was first run at Indianapolis, Marmon won with a special, and they also competed in many other races, winning 25 of them in 1910. At that time most makers went in for racing as the best method of proving their wares.

Detroit provided the next make: Maxwell, which led a chequered existence between 1904 and 1925. They started life as Maxwell-Briscoe, and became part of the

driven when all their other models were shaft-driven. But the whirring of the chain added to the majesty of this giant limousine, with its great, round, locomotive-like radiator. The firm actually made locomotives and boilers long before 1904 (when their first beautifully built car appeared at the Paris show) so the radiator needed only a smoke-stack to complete the picture.

A Gräf & Stift simply must be included; this, of course, was the

With four cylinders and no less than 7.0 litres, the Packard '30' stayed in production for six years.
This version, originally sold in 1912, had every modern convenience—so long as the weather stayed dry.

What was in the basket? Tools, perhaps. The car is a 1904 tourer from the unlikely-sounding firm of Alldays and Onions Pneumatic Engineering Co Ltd, of Birmingham, England.

Below
The engine of this 25 hp Lanchester tourer is actually mounted between the front seats, which must have dampened any amorous goings on. The car, produced in 1912 and featuring a three-speed, epicyclic gearbox, typified the unorthodox designs of the Lanchester brothers.

short-lived United States Motor Co (which included Stoddard-Dayton and Brush) until this collapsed in 1912. Mr Briscoe then left to pursue his own career, leaving Maxwell to pick up the pieces, which he did.

Most of his cars were four-cylinder machines, but he also made a few sixes, one of which was built to take seven passengers in a 10 ft 8 ins wheelbase car that weighed over 1½ tons. The Maxwell 50 of 1914 had a 6,242 cc engine with side valves and dual magneto/coil ignition operated by a dry battery. With 50 bhp, the car could only manage about 45 mph, but it did have lots of room.

The company, whose advertising slogan was 'Perfectly simple, simply perfect', were taken over by Walter Chrysler in 1923 and their own cars were eventually replaced by Chrysler and then Plymouth products.

Belgium is not a country which has produced many cars, although a number of modern manufacturers do assemble cars there nowadays. Their two most famous home-produced names were probably also their best: Métallurgique and Minerva, both very much in the luxury bracket. Métallurgique were eventually swallowed by Minerva, so there was some connection between the two; and being swallowed by the Roman goddess of Wisdom and Art must surely have done something for a motor car.

Métallurgique started in 1898 and died in 1928, and one desirable model was the 38/80 hp saloon of 1914 with a distinctive radiator

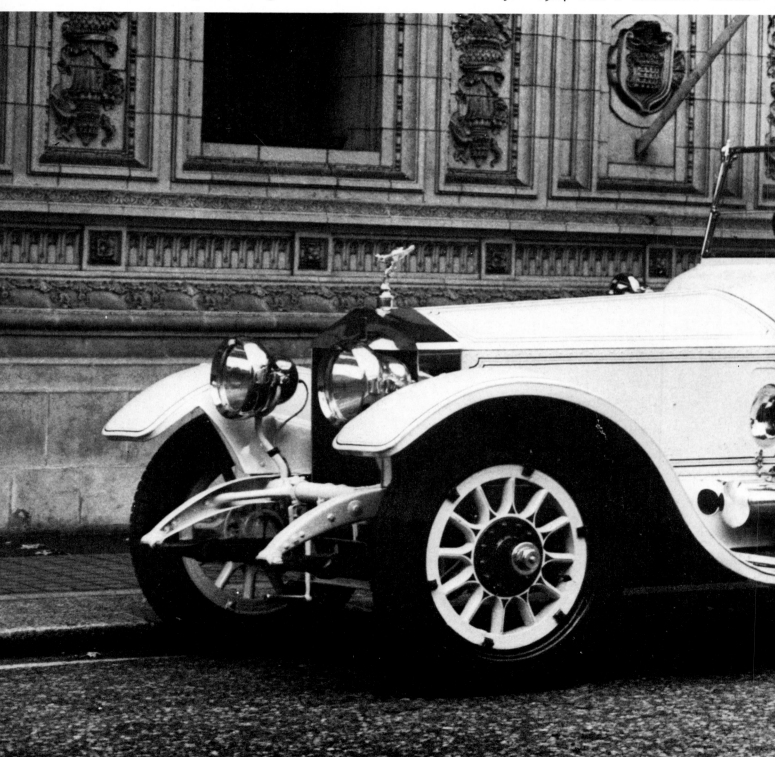

designed to cut through the air. The early ones were too crude, with twin-cylinder engines and chain drive, but this model had a four-cylinder, inlet-over-exhaust engine (Americans called it an F-head) and a four-speed gearbox. The closed, limousine coachwork was most impressive with a high, peaked roof, opening windscreen and railway carriage door-handles. Métallurgique might even have borrowed the Maxwell slogan: 'Perfectly Simple and Simply Perfect'. Métallurgique cars, made at Marchienne au Pont, were exported to England and were built in Germany under licence by the Bergmann Electric works in Berlin. During the First World War the Germans took most of the machine tools and the company never recovered from this blow.

Minerva supplied cars to at least three kings, which is recommendation enough. The 'goddess' began as a bicycle maker, but soon progressed to swift, silent cars with Knight sleeve-valve engines. The 1913, 26 hp tourer offered all the most desirable requirements.

The interior of at least one 1903 Mors must have been fantastic. It was described as Louis XV style on the 'ceiling', with a Morocco leather holdall comprising clock, barometer, thermometer, manicure set, notebooks and looking glass, plus an electric telephone to the driver.

Packard existed from 1899 to

An example of quick development. This 1920s Silver Ghost (a model born in 1907) is a long way from the crudities of 1900 or so.

their sad end in 1968, and to represent this marque, a six-cylinder Model 48, with 7.25 litre engine would be appropriate. It had acetylene lighting and competed in price with Rolls-Royce.

Another oddity from the period was the Paige-Detroit of 1908. Of all the 'Paige' companies, Graham-Paige, which lasted until 1941, is the most familiar; it began with Paige-Detroit, becoming Paige-Linwood and Paige-Larchmont on the way. The early Paige-Detroit, however, had a three-cylinder, two-stroke engine of 2.2 litres and a two-seat roadster body. Later, the engine was changed for a normal four, so that the early one has real rarity value.

In 1907, there arrived the car which might be said to have dominated the luxury car market before the First World War. It was listed only as the 40/50 hp when it was

This British-built, Wolseley Cabriolet 24/30 gave its occupants the best of both worlds in 1913, with 'all-weather' coachwork.

introduced, but soon acquired the name that was to make it famous: Silver Ghost. It came, of course, from Rolls-Royce, who continued to make it until 1925, such was its state of mechanical perfection at a time when most other cars were crude, horseless carriages.

The Silver Ghost was a big car, with a wheelbase of up to 11 ft 11 ins and an engine which started life at 7,036 cc and was increased in 1909 to 7,428 cc. This was a six-cylinder unit, with the cylinders mounted in two blocks of three, and it had side valves, a feature that no doubt contributed to the silent smoothness for which the car is remembered. Power outputs were not, of course, revealed by the company, but were thought to be around 48 bhp at 1,250 rpm, sufficient to enable the car to cruise at 62 mph in overdrive top (fourth) gear while still covering almost 18 miles on every gallon of fuel.

There were two separate electrical systems (one battery, one magneto), two methods of controlling

the fuel/air mixture (one manual, one automatic) and the oil system delivered extra lubrication when the throttle was pushed down. It was a magnificent engineering masterpiece for 1907.

After all this elegance, we can go down-market a little and consider a Schact, an American car made from 1905 to 1913 in Cincinnati, Ohio, by a company who carried on making trucks until the Second World War. The early cars were motor-buggies, owing much to the horseless carriage, but American connoisseurs still like them. They had big, carriage-type wheels, 12 hp twin-cylinder engines hiding under the driver's (and only) seat and chain drive. Later Schact models were much like anyone else's.

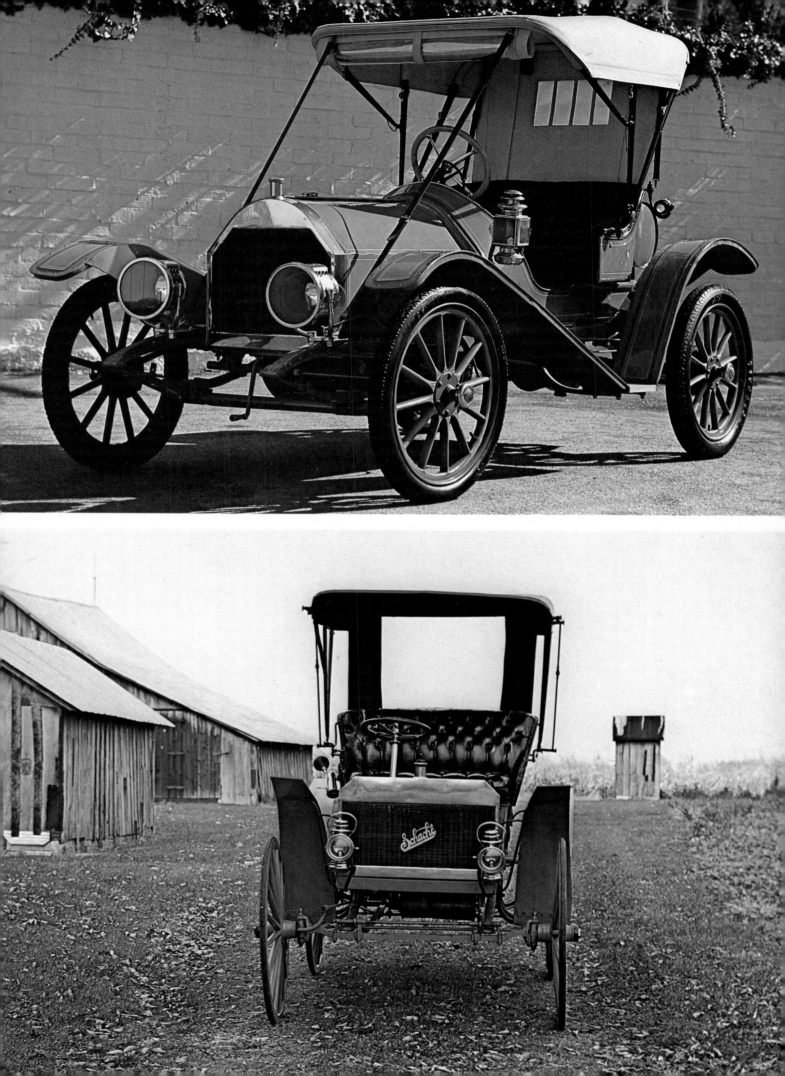

4 Pre-1914: The Quest for Speed

Sporting cars are, of course, more exciting than either the ordinary machines or the luxury cars. In actual fact, driving an open car tends to be noisy and tiring, but let us not spoil the dream by being too practical in contemplation of some nerve-tingling rides.

For anyone who likes big, lusty bangers, the pre-1914 era is cer-

Opposite, top
A most imposing Alfa Romeo of 1911, the 24 hp Spider complete with everything except brakes!

Opposite, lower
A Bugatti of 1910 (the Type 13), which has lost the rear end of its coachwork to become a sort of pick-up.

tainly a golden and heroic age. Nothing can match the sheer size, noise and drama associated with the chain-driven monsters of the early age of the motor car. And with brakes an unknown quantity, fitted only on the rear wheels, their ability to stop was about on a par with their willingness to start on a cold day. The giant Métallurgique now owned by James Fitzpatrick is a prime example: it needs an assistant with a crowbar as long as a man is tall to turn the engine over before it will fire up on the trembler coil.

However, a realistic starting point would be the first Alfa Romeo, the 24 hp (which came back after the First World War as the

20/30, or the 20/30 ES Sport). Alfa began assembling French Darracq cars at the Portello Works in Milan in 1906, using Italian workers and French engineers, until – in 1909 – Cavalier Ugo Stella, managing director of the Societa Italiana Automobili Darracq, Milan, decided to make a new car to suit the Italian market.

On 1 January 1910, therefore, the factory management was changed to all-Italian and no more French units came from Suresnes. The company name was also changed to

If it moves, race it. A racing steamer from Serpollet in 1903, driven by Le Blonde on the *Circuit des Ardennes* in June that year.

Delage's 1911 *Coupé de l'Auto* winner, with a horizontal-valve, 3.0 litre, four-cylinder engine and a five-speed gearbox with overdrive top. Note the unorthodox exhaust arrangement.

Anonima Lombardo Fabbrica Automobili. The 24 hp, in two-seater sporting form, had revolutionary features like a monobloc engine instead of separate cylinder castings, shaft drive in place of chains, and a rather superior rear axle. It had a four-cylinder, 4,084 cc, 45 bhp engine with forced lubrication by pump, two valves per cylinder, a four-speed gearbox, and right-hand steering, as did all sports and racing cars until much later. The two-seater was the 'Corsa' or racing model, with a bolster tank behind the driver and (for racing) four spare tyres strapped one on top of the other at the rear. According to contemporary reports, after severe road testing in the autumn of 1910, it 'met the favour of many Italian and foreign gentlemen who selected it for the excellent engine pick-up and the accurate handicraft of the running parts.' It had its baptism of fire in the 1911 Targa Florio, when the head tester, Nino Franchini, led the race for two of the three laps of the Madonie Circuit 'until he was forced to retire when made blind by a mud splash'. This sounds a rather unlikely reason for retiring, a bit like the official excuse of 'sparking plug failure' when one can see a big-end sticking out of the engine. Some 200 of these cars were made and they went on for several years, partially-completed models being hidden during the war and produced again afterwards. The pre-war ones had 'Alfa Milano' on the badge with the Milanese cross and the Visconti snake; the postwar ones had 'Alfa Romeo Milano', as Nicola Romeo took over in 1915. The earlier cars had side valves as the classic Alfa dohc did not come until 1914. A total of 680 of the 24 hp and 20/30 models were made from 1910 to 1920 (including 100 hidden in parts during the war), and 124 of these were Corsa or ES Sport models. Many of these had no

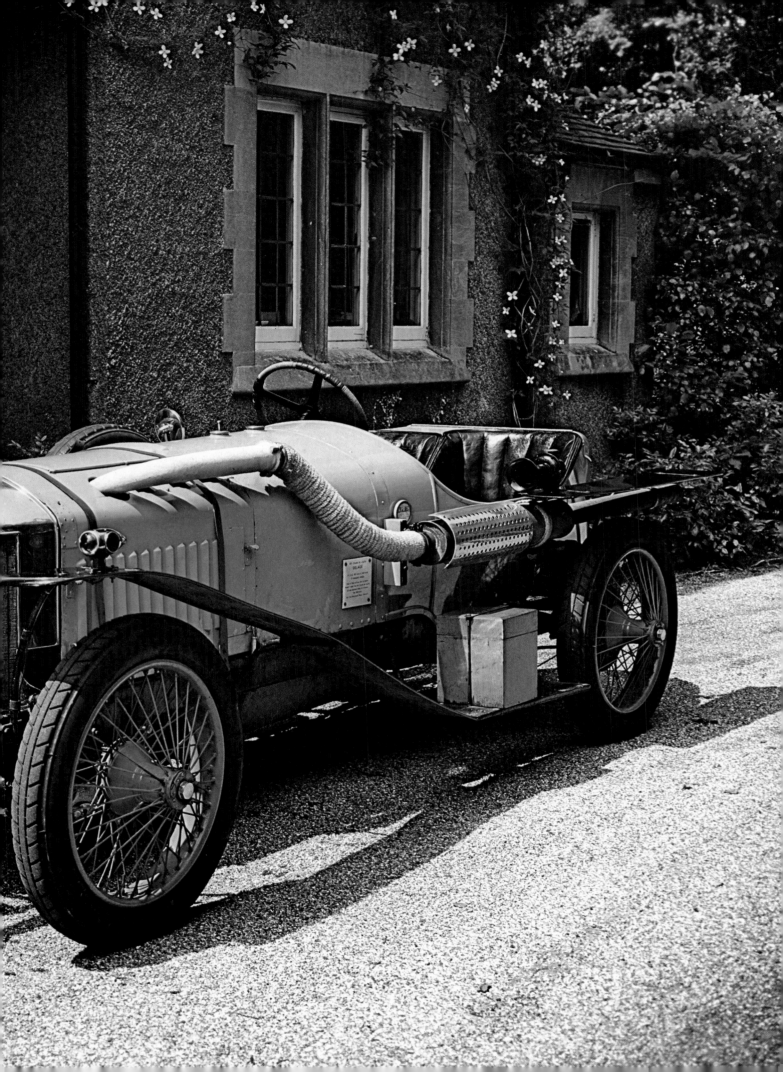

Mr Bugatti's 'Black Bess', a 5.0 litre machine of 1912 with chain drive, here seen at Le Mans, with pointed back and front ends to cheat the wind.

windscreen or weather protection at all and had wooden-spoked artillery wheels with detachable rims.

After Alfa, who better than Austro-Daimler, who had been building racing and road cars from 1901 onwards, although their early efforts were merely copies of the Canstatt Daimlers. Their first truly significant product appeared in 1910, when Dr Porsche designed for them a 5.7 litre, five-bearing, four-cylinder engine with five valves per cylinder (one inlet and four exhaust) operated by a single, overhead camshaft and producing 95 bhp at 2,300 rpm, all of which took the 22/80PS, as it was known, to 88mph, an unheard-of performance for a non-racing car. With an early form of streamlining included on the body design and chain drive (shafts were considered too weak for so much power), this machine was designed for the 1910 Prince Henry Trials and it duly swept the board, taking the first three places overall and five places in the top ten.

With no Prince Henry Trials the following year, Porsche turned his attention to the Austrian Alpine event, creating a team of 60 mph, 2.2 litre, side-valve, 16/25PS cars with shaft drive. These took the

The Chadwick Six Runabout of 1908 with eye-catching, two-seater 'spider' coachwork, rear tank, enclosed chain drive, but no windscreen.

first five places and the team prize. After such resounding successes, it was only natural that the road-going 22/80 tourer should become the Prince Henry, and the 16/25 the Alpine model, both of these road cars being true classics by any definition.

Next comes an even more famous name, that of Bugatti, although the early date does limit the choice of car rather severely. Ettore Bugatti began designing for other people – like Baron de Dietrich, Mathis and Deutz – in 1900, but the first Bugatti under the name of the

patron did not come until 1910, when a 1300 cc, ohc model appeared at the Paris Salon. This Type 13 was not in the sporting class, any more than the Bébé Peugeot which Bugatti also designed. One of his first sporting cars was a 1914, 5.0 litre, four-cylinder, chain-driven affair and it is said that 'a few' were made; certainly they ran at Indianapolis in 1914 and 1915 (without winning). But

A 130 bhp Clément-Bayard of 1908 with an overhead camshaft engine. In spite of an enormous engine of 13,963 cc, Clément could do no better than fourth in the 1908 GP.

Shaft-driven Clément-Bayard of 1911, with six-cylinder engine and dashboard radiator. Some of these were exported to Britain as Clément-Talbots.

valve engine.

Unkind people have suggested that Bugatti stole his first ideas from Isotta Fraschini, whose 1908 *voiturette* was similar to the very first Bugatti (the Type 10), but that need not diminish one's enjoyment of a 'Brescia', as it was a close-to-100-mph machine in spite of its small engine.

For a contrast to the Bugatti, how about another chain-driven monster, a Clément-Talbot 50/60 hp of 1911, which, although sold in England under that label, was really a French Clément-Bayard? But whatever its name, the most desirable car would be an English-built version, like those which were raced with giant engines of up to 16.0 litres, without very much success: although placed in two Grands Prix, including the first one in 1906, they did not actually win anything.

The daughter of Adolphe Clément, the man who started all this confusion over names, married Charron, the cycling champion of France, who, with two friends in the cycle-racing world – Girardot and Voight – founded the first car agency in the world. Up to this time (about 1900) people had bought direct from the manufacturers. There was a Charron car and also a CGV, the name being made up from the three men's initials. Charron actually managed the Clément-Bayard factory until he

perhaps a so-called 'Brescia' Bugatti would be the one to choose. This did not really appear until after the war, but it had been designed before hostilities commenced. The 'Brescias' were 16-valve versions of the four-cylinder Type 13, enlarged to 1.5 litres and called Type 22, taking the name 'Brescia' when they won the first four places in the Italian Grand Prix for *Voiturettes* at Brescia. It was in these cars that the English driver, Raymond Mays made his name at Shelsley Walsh hill-climb and elsewhere in the years after the

This was claimed to be the world's first straight eight, although it was really a marriage of two fours: the CGV of 1902.

First World War. Various Bugatti hallmarks, like the horseshoe shaped radiator, the reversed, quarter-elliptic rear springs and the fragile semi-elliptic front springs with their odd attachment to the chassis appeared on this model. The Types 22 and 23 were actually long-chassis road models with the 16-valve engine, the only true 'Brescia' being the short-chassis racer which was still a Type 13, albeit with a 16-

The car which almost started W. O. Bentley on the road to fame and fortune. It is a 1910 DFP, which he imported and raced.

fell out with his father-in-law and went back to selling CGVs in Paris. These were sold in England as Charrons.

The big chain-drive Clément-Talbot was related to the 1908 GP car, which was described as the fastest car in that race, reaching a maximum of 104 mph. It was designed by Sabatier, an overhead camshaft was used, and it was obviously a very exciting machine to drive.

For our next car we turn to a certain Alexandre Darracq, a draughtsman who worked for Hurtu, who made sewing machines and later cars. In 1891 he began to build bicycles, and sold the business in 1896 to an English firm who demanded that he made no more bicycles. But the agreement specified nothing about bicycle parts, so Alexandre fitted up a big works at Suresnes, near Paris, with the best American machine tools and started a cut-price parts business. By 1898, he was making cars as well as cycle parts, motor-cycles and tricycles. He retired a millionaire in 1912.

His first cars were Léon-Bollées built under licence, and then came his own 6.5 hp model. He also ran what must have been the first school for racing drivers. He did not drive in races himself, but his cars were in all the big events from 1900 to 1907. His Flying Fifteen, which was good value for money in 1914, was a 3.0 litre, four-cylinder sold from 1904 onwards. Darracq offered at least six different models each year until 1914, when there were only three, and most of them were worth their price, except for those with rotary-valve Henroid engines. These came in 1912, the year Alexandre opted out.

The DFP had its place in history as the car which Walter Owen Bentley drove and for which he acted as agent in England before making his own car in 1919. The

The American Charles Duryea in the car of his own name which won the Chicago race of 1895.

Top
A massive Fiat 24/32 hp of 1905 with four-cylinder, 7.0 litre engine, 75 km/h top speed and only a transmission brake.

Centre
The well-known American driver, Ralph de Palma, at the end of the French Grand Prix of 1912, with his Fiat and a good supply of spare tyres.

Bottom
This shot epitomises the Targa Florio, the round-Sicily mountain race. The car is a big Fiat 28/40 on the 1907 event.

Top
An early Ford model racing in the days before front-brakes.

Centre
The great tall cars, with 200 mm strokes were brought about by the formula rules. This Fiat was typical of the time.

Bottom
A Hispano-Suiza racing car of 1910, fully road-equipped apart from mud-wings.

initials stood for Doriot, Flandrin et Parant and this trio, who made small cars, were virtually put out of business by the First World War, so any choice of DFP models must lie between the 12/15 (which the Bentley brothers ran in races) and the later 12/40, into which aluminium pistons were introduced. The 12/15 was a 2.0 litre with a four-speed gearbox and a 55 mph maximum speed, which Bentley was said to have improved to 89 mph, a suspiciously enormous increase. The other model, the 2.0 litre 12/40, was the one in which he finished sixth in the 1914 T.T.

The Belgian Excelsior company made their best sporting model after the First World War, the Albert I Excelsior. However, dealing with the pre-war period, we must go for an earlier car, being careful not to confuse it with the Swiss car of the same name, dealt

A Hispano leads a typical, tall-engined Peugeot at the start of a Spanish race in 1910. The canopy was to keep off the sun.

with under the Egg name in an earlier chapter. One of the advertising stunts performed by Excelsior was to make a run from Brussels to St Petersburg (now Leningrad) at an average speed of 50 mph, with racing driver Christaens at the wheel. This must have been a considerable feat over the roads of 1913, even though Christaens used a racing model of the kind in which he had taken sixth place in the 1912 *Coupe des Voitures Legères*. However, a sporting example of the pre-war Excelsior was the Type Adex, made from 1911 onwards, with either a 3.0 or 4.0 litre engine, overhead exhaust, and side inlet

Henry Ford in one of his competition appearances (left) urges on his clutch-and-gear-less '999' against Harry Harkness' 40 hp Mercedes-Simplex at Grosse Point, Michigan in 1902.

This Briarcliff tourer was one of the most popular versions of the 1909, four-cylinder model made by Lozier, of New York State.

valves, reversing the usual inlet-over-exhaust formula. They were fours and sixes respectively, and there was also a 9.0 litre six.

After Excelsior, we come to the Fiat company, who offered an enormous variety of choice, although the one to have was really a racing car, the dividing line in 1911 between a racer and a sporting car being rather fine. The S74 was a spartan, open two-seater with no weather protection, chain drive, brass outside levers, bonnet straps, bolster tank behind, and artillery wheels. It had no wings, running boards or anything to break up the wind along the sides except for the four, stark wheels. Three of these ran at Savannah, Georgia, in the American Grand Prize of 1911, a 400-mile race which Bruce-Brown won at 74.75 mph. He also won the first half of the French GP the following year, when it was run in two parts over 956 miles.

The S74 was described as a 'grosso bolide', weighing 3,306 lbs with a four-cylinder engine in two blocks of two, with 10.0 litres capacity and 190 bhp at 1 600 rpm. The factory description of this stark machine read: 'There is practically no bodywork: the two seats are fixed directly to the chassis and behind them is mounted the fuel tank.'

From the Fiat racer to a different type of car: a machine of legend in the 1920s, the immortal Hispano-Suiza, made in France and Spain and designed by a Swiss. This was the car of which Michael Arlen wrote in *The Green Hat*: 'Open as a yacht, it wore a great shining bonnet; and flying over the crest of this great bonnet, as though in proud flight over the heads of scores of phantom horses, was that silver stork by which the gentle may be pleased to know that they have just escaped death beneath the wheels of a Hispano-Suiza car, as supplied to His Most Catholic Majesty.'

High-flown nonsense? Maybe, but a Hispano was the apotheosis of

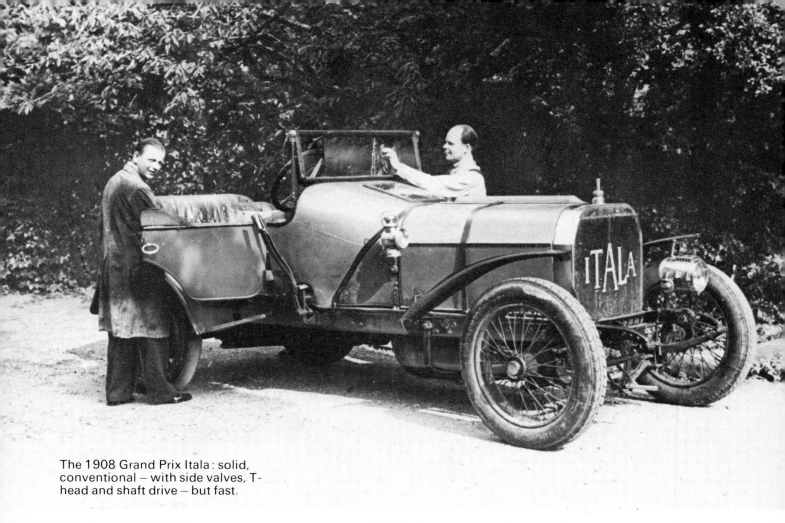

The 1908 Grand Prix Itala: solid, conventional — with side valves, T-head and shaft drive — but fast.

Cagno's Itala being weighed before the 1908 *Coupé Florio*, organised by Count Vincenzo Florio. What a massive brute it was.

A Lion-Peugeot, with one of the impossibly tall engines of the middle 1900s, which forced the driver to look around the bonnet.

the sporting motor car. And the one to pick from the pre-1914 era was the Alfonso, named after Alfonso XIII of Spain, the king mentioned by Michael Arlen. It was a sporting two-seater and won the *Coupé de l'Auto* race in 1910. The Alfonso Hispano was made for several years and in more than one version, and several still exist, first choice being one with a 3.6 litre, four-cylinder engine, cylinders cast in pairs and a T-head. This production model was much less spartan than the Fiat, with long, swept wings joined by a running board, windscreen, lights, horn, starting handle, hood, and spare wheel. But it was beautiful and functional and looked much more modern than its year of introduction. Top speed was quoted as 72 mph.

It is appropriate that Isotta-Fraschini should follow Hispano as the two companies made cars very similar in concept and tend always

Centre
The Nice–Salon–Nice race of 1901, with the winner (Werner) covering 392 kms in 6 hrs 45 mins with his Mercedes.

Below
The Mercedes 90 hp racer of 1904 with Baron de Caters at the wheel.

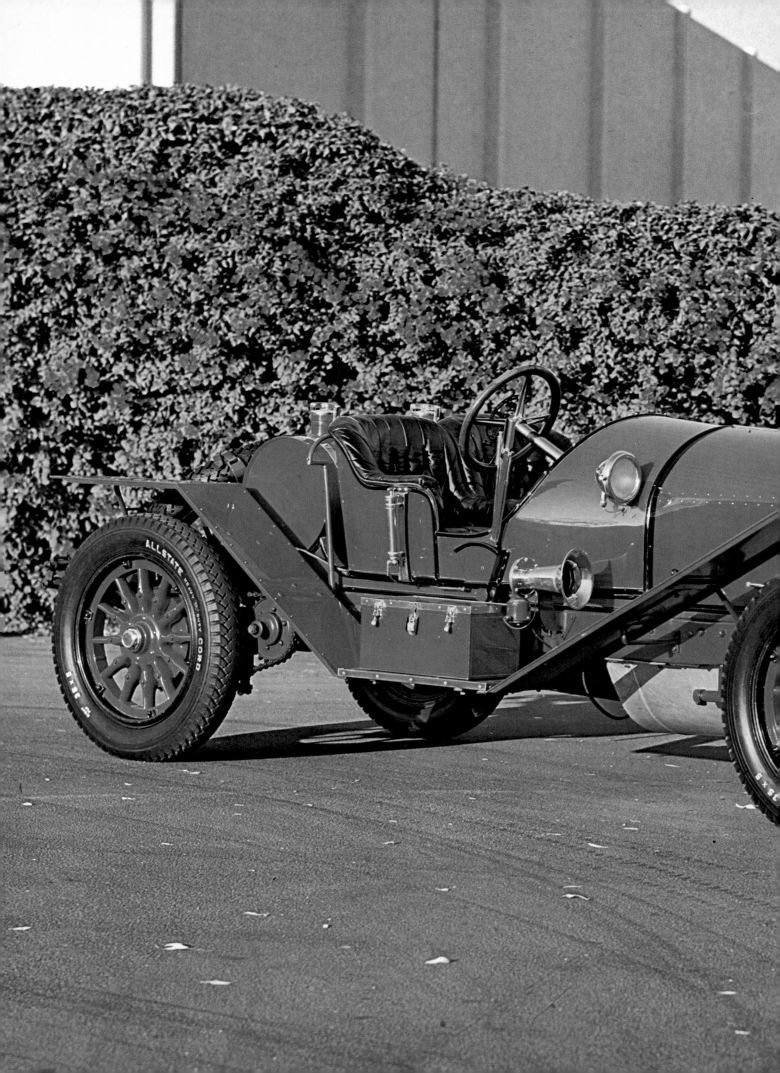

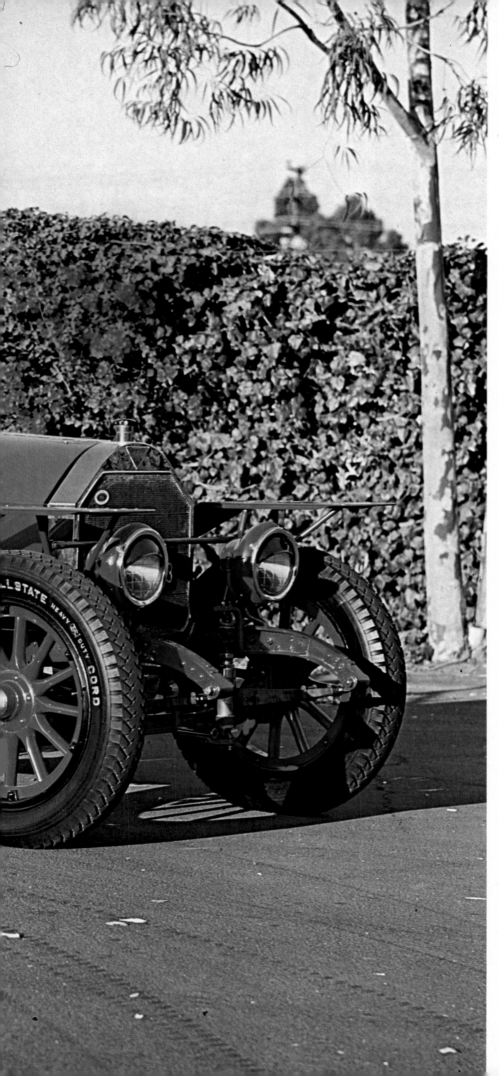

Simplex of New Jersey, USA, introduced this 10.0 litre, 75 bhp car in 1912. The four-cylinder, T-head design was said to be the last chain-driven American car.

to be bracketed together. The Isotta name, like that of their rival Rolls-Royce, is compounded of the names of the partners, Cesare Isotta and Vincenzo Fraschini, whose company was in business from 1900 until 1949. Their 10.8 litre KM, a 16-valve, ohc four-cylinder with four-speed gearbox and discreetly covered chain drive, was notable. Its 140 bhp engine and dual magnetos gave it an 85 mph top speed. It also had four-wheel brakes, unusual in 1914. Radiators were V-shaped or pear-shaped, photographs of the time showing the two types; the pear shape was perhaps more handsome, if less efficient. The TM of 6.2 litres was similar to the KM and there was also a shaft-driven model (which was a little tamer) and a 7.2 litre racing version which ran at Indianapolis without distinction.

Itala followed the Hispano/Isotta pattern in building some vast and expensive machines, although in a different idiom. They started as racers, and never used chains, which for this period was a curious combination of facts. The well-known Matteo Ceirano, who was involved in so much motoring history and with so many makes, was party to this one too, even if only up to 1906. Itala won both the Coppa Florio and the Targa Florio, and were famous for their victory in the Peking-Paris race of 1907. The cars were patronised by royalty. In 1914, they offered a choice of 11 models, including three with rotary-valve engines which were best avoided. Best were the 11.0 or 12.0 litre models, brought in from 1908 onwards, especially those with saloon coachwork. An example of the 1908 Grand Prix Itala is now owned by Cecil Clutton, a 60 hp car complying with the 1908 formula of 1,100 kilograms maximum weight and a maximum bore of 155 mm. It is very spartan and still very quick.

Lion-Peugeot, which started life as a separate marque in 1906 and

The first modern motor-car, the
Mercedes of 1901 with four-cylinder
35 hp engine, pressed steel frame,
gate gear-change, honeycomb
radiator and electric ignition.

Count Zborowski (of racing
fame) about to start his Mercedes in
the Paris–Vienna race of 1902.

merged with the 'other' Peugeot in
1913, are often recalled for some
extraordinary racing voiturettes.
They were freaks, ending up with a
280 mm stroke engine, which made
the engine so tall that the driver
could see nothing straight ahead
and had to peer round the machinery. If such early racers are
set aside, the vee-twin series from
1910 onwards were worth consideration. These came in various
sizes from 1.7 litres upwards, and
there was even a vee four touring
car in 1911. This had a four-speed
gearbox, but the twins could be had
with either shaft or chain drive.

There were several early
American sporting cars. Lozier
were a quality US marque from
1905 to 1917, when they were put
out of business by competition from
others in this field, like Cadillac.
Two years after production started,
they gave up their driving chains in
favour of shafts, and the resulting
car was more modern as well as less
brutal. They were successful in

Below
A four-cylinder, 35 hp Mercedes racer
of 1901, very advanced apart from its
chain drive, which the designer
thought more reliable for high power.

Opposite, bottom
Carl Schmidt in his NSU for the 1909
Prince Henry Trial, run over 1,200
miles from Berlin to Munich by way
of Budapest, Vienna and Salzburg.
Just to finish, as this car did, was
regarded as an achievement.

Barborou on his lightweight
Mercedes (1903 Paris—Madrid) with
a basket-work seat for the crouching
mechanic. Even the lamp-brackets
were drilled.

racing around 1910, winning the National Stock Car Championship and the Vanderbilt Cup, and finishing second at Indianapolis, which is a good pedigree. But the racing Lozier was hardly a suitable road machine, and the 50 hp, 9.3-litre six was preferable – its various two-seat roadster and torpedo bodies making it near to ideal. This one had a T-head with cylinders cast in pairs and a four-speed gearbox with a geared-up top. The body types included the Briarcliff sports tourer, Lakewood torpedo and Meadowbrook two-seater.

Mathis was a well-respected Franco-German name in motoring history. They were made in Strasbourg, which was in Germany when they began production in 1898 but became French after 1918. Bugatti at Molsheim similarly changed countries and their first cars were sold as Hermes. Emil Mathis worked with Ettore Bugatti on the design of the Kaiserpreis Hermes in 1906, but the first true Mathis came in 1910. There were various models, including a 1.8-litre four-cylinder, sporting two-seater,

which – even as early as this – had pressure lubrication. The Mathis ran as a German car in the French *Coupé des Voiturettes* in 1911, and put up a good time at the English Sheisley Walsh hill climb in 1912.

In Germany, Mercedes produced the prototype of the modern car in 1900/1901, with a pressed steel frame, honeycomb radiator and a gate gear-change, plus mechanically-operated valves. This was in fact the first car with the Mercedes name, though made by Daimler (under circumstances already related) as the 35 hp, 5.9 litre model. Some historians say that Daimler adopted the Mercedes name in 1902, but the official company history lists the date as 1900/1901. One reason advanced for Herr Jellinek's adopting the name of his daughter Mercedes for his car is that Panhard-Levassor held the licence to make Daimler engines in France, and sued him for breaking their monopoly, which sounds reasonable enough. Daimler died in 1900, Benz left his company in 1903 and both Jellinek and Maybach had left by 1908.

Benz adopted the name Parsifal for cars which became Benz-Parsifals, and Mercedes, for some unknown reason, called theirs Simplex, so they were Mercedes-Simplex from 1902 to 1904.

The three-pointed star is supposed to indicate the threefold mechanisation of transport on land, sea and air. Gottlieb Daimler apparently sent his wife a postcard with a guiding star drawn over a picture of his house in Deutz, and said this would one day mark the ascendancy of his work. His sons later suggested this as a trademark for the firm and, in June 1909, the board registered both three and four-pointed stars, but used only the three-pointed one. Much later, when the Daimler and Benz firms joined forces in 1926, the names Mercedes and Benz were arranged in a circle around the star, with the Benz laurel wreath incorporated. Benz had used a badge with a gear-

Opposite, bottom
The legendary Lautenschlager and his Mercedes racer during a tyre change at the French Grand Prix of 1908.

A 1912 rival to Vauxhall's 30/98, the Mercer 35 Raceabout featured a 4.8 litre, T-head motor producing 55 bhp and a top speed of 75 mph.

The pits really were pits dug at the roadside in 1908. This Mercedes driver is making a tyre change during the French GP at Dieppe.

Lautenschlager's Mercedes in the 1908 French Grand Prix at Dieppe, which he won at 69.05 mph.

wheel around the words 'Original Benz' from 1903, and the wreath from 1909.

What is now known as the Mercedes 60 was officially the Simplex Phaeton of 1903, but both the 60 and the 90 are listed in the official history as Mercedes Simplex racing cars, whereas in a model chart issued by the company museum, the 60 appears as a production model. Both 60 and 90 had four-cylinder engines. There was parallel development from 1886 to 1903 of Daimler and Benz models, and the Mercedes 60 was much like the Benz-Parsifal racer of the same year, both having four cylinders and 60 bhp. A true story that has been told many times concerns the Mercedes 90 team cars for the 1903 Gordon-Bennett race being destroyed by fire and the company drawing on customers' 60s to replace them. Jenatzy drove a car borrowed from Gray Dinsmore and won the race. The 60 engine had inlet-over-exhaust valves and produced a 70 mph maximum in 9.23 litre tourer form, or 80 mph if it was a 9.29 litre racer, with 65 bhp at 1,000 rpm. There was a difference of one millimetre in the stroke, which is hard to understand.

Opel (this is a 10/20 hp) took four places in the top ten on the Prince Henry Trial of 1909, which ran from Berlin to Munich by a roundabout route taking in Budapest and Vienna.

The American young man's dream in 1913, a Mercer 35J Raceabout with monocle windscreen, wire wheels and everything that the girls liked.

Fritz Opel leads the way in the 1903 Frankfurt touring car race. In a 10 hp car bearing his own name, Opel won.

This 1907 shot shows Carl Jörns winning the *Kaiserpreis* in the Taunus Mountains, using a very early Opel.

Top
The first in a long line of Vauxhalls which led eventually to the famous 30/98, this is a 'Prince Henry' C-type.

Centre
Heinz von Opel in his 8/24 streamlined racing car which set records in Berlin in 1921. On this occasion, it did 128.84 km/h.

The next obvious choice is the young American's fancy of 1911, the Mercer 35T Raceabout. This was a basically ordinary car which was carefully screwed together so that it could be used for competition as well as on the road. It had a large, four-cylinder, side-valve, T-head engine of 4,789 cc with a bore and stroke of 110 mm × 126 mm and a camshaft on each side of the block. With pressure lubrication (of 13 pints of oil), pressure cooling and pressurised petrol feed, it was a sturdy and reliable unit giving about 55 bhp at 1,650 rpm. The Raceabout was guaranteed to do 70 mph and to cover a mile in 51 seconds, but many of them could easily better those figures.

The engine and gearbox were separate, but were mounted to-

Ferenc Szisz, who partnered Marcel Renault to victory on the Paris–Vienna in 1902, also won the 1906 *Grand Prix de l'ACF* at Sarthe with this Renault.

Above
The *Grand Prix de l'Automobile Club de France* at Amiens in 1913, won by Boillot on this 90 hp Peugeot.

One of the world's first six-cylinder production cars came from the British company of Napier. This is their 1909, 30 hp with the crew suitably attired.

gether on a sub-frame within the pressed-steel chassis frame. The two, rigid axles were suspended on semi-elliptic, leaf springs and Hartford friction shock absorbers, while drum brakes were fitted only to the rear wheels.

Made by the enthusiastic Roeblings family in Trenton, New Jersey, it was described by the company as 'the most talked-of car in America' and its light weight, monocle windscreen, bolster fuel tank and rear-mounted spare wheels all contributed to its racing-car feel, which must have had more than a little to do with the fact that Mercer sold over 500 of them during their four years of production.

There were few British cars in the sporting category during this period, apart from exceptions like the Clemént-Talbot, but the great Napier would conveniently live in company which included Mercedes, Itala, Isotta and Hispano. Napier were famous as the makers of the first six-cylinder

Girardot's Panhard-Levassor for the Gordon Bennett Cup of 1901 was a typical design of the period, complete with chain drive.

83

production, car and manufactured a glorious racer/tourer of which at least one still exists in England. They had been active for nearly a century in other forms of heavy engineering when they came to cars in 1900, with the famous Selwyn Francis Edge as a sort of marketing manager and racing team manager. Their cars were complex and refined and there were many different models, but after 1918 they followed a single-model policy to extinction, although they did bid against Rolls-Royce for Bentley when the latter went broke in 1930. Napier made cars with two, four and six cylinders but one that was outstanding was Montague Napier's T51, or 45 hp; with a 6,105 cc side-valve engine and six cylinders. Even better was the T49 or 65 hp with a 9,652 cc engine. Most Napiers before the First World War had side-valve engines, although there was a 90 hp of 14,491 cc from 1908 to 1910, basically similar except that it had inlet-over-exhaust valves, and produced 120 bhp at 1,800 rpm.

One of the nicest looking two seaters to appear during this era was the Rolland Pilain, derived from a 1,526 cc racing voiturette built for the 1908 *Grand Prix des Voiturettes* at Dieppe. The following year saw the Pilain family introduce a road-going version with a plethora of curved surfaces, low construction and a steeply raked steering wheel whose angle bore more relation to modern trends than to the vertical steering columns and wheels favoured by most road cars at the time.

The Rolland Pilain of 1909 had a 2,211 cc engine of 80 mm × 110 mm, producing about 22 bhp. The four-cylinder unit was a cast-iron, in-line monobloc with side valves, fan-assisted water cooling, magneto ignition and a single, vertical carburettor. The three-speed transmission went via a prop shaft to the rear axle, and suspension was by semi-elliptics all round. With a wheelbase of 8 ft 9 ins and an all-up weight of under 1,400 lbs, the Rolland Pilain could travel at around 62 mph.

How the sports car looked in 1914: a 15/20 Talbot two-seater, with four-cylinder engine of 2.6 litres, outside handbrake, Klaxon and pointed tail.

Vauxhall made the first 20 hp car in the world to exceed 100 mph, here driven by A. J. Hancock at Brooklands in 1910.

Charles Jarrott and his intrepid mechanic starting the 1903 Gordon Bennett on their Napier. They crashed at 60 mph.

Another pioneer make, a Sizaire-Naudin with flags flying in 1908. Note the early independent front suspension.

One way to go racing in 1904. Pelzer on his Serpollet steam racing car under the eye of the law at the start of the Gaillon hill-climb, one of the make's last appearances.

5 1914–39: Mass Production

There is a problem choosing worthwhile, mass-production cars from between the wars, as so many makes sprung up to meet immediate needs, some even surviving until the Second World War. The financial crisis of 1929 sorted out a number of the less substantial firms, but there was still a vast number to choose from and all those which made a contribution to motoring history should have a place in this book. The task of making a choice is so beset with problems that the only way to tackle it is to plunge in with plenty of prejudice and select those that appeal.

The German Adler company must be included, as they made so many cheap cars which were representative of the period. They came into being in 1900 and are still going strong as manufacturers of office machinery, but car production ceased in 1939. The Adler to choose is the Trumpf, which appeared in 1932 and could be had in 1.1, 1.5, 1.7 or 2.0 litre form, with front-wheel drive and independent suspension. The two-door, lightweight coupé sold well in its myriad sizes, and there were special competition models which achieved success in various events, including the Le Mans 24 hour race.

The Austin Seven cannot be omitted, although its importance has been elevated out of all proportion to its real worth. Nevertheless, it was one of the first cars to offer the cheapest kind of motoring for the masses; perhaps the best thing that can be said about it is that it was an improvement on the motorcycle or the cyclecar (although even this might be questioned by some, as the motorcycle/sidecar combination often offered more performance). The 1922 Seven came with a 747 cc engine, three-speed gearbox and four-wheel brakes operated by combination of hand and foot levers. It was slow but economical, and later sports and racing versions did all sorts of incredible things. It had a clutch which was either in or out, inefficient brakes and other shortcomings, but it was good for its time. A rather boring little car, but a reminder of how things used to be. The pick of the Sevens was possibly the Chummy, open four-seater — the original model, not one of the souped-up sporting types. Later

The Adler Trumpf of 1938 was a 1.0 litre car with four seats and four doors, which suited a lot of people and sold well.

Double take from 1928: Austin Seven on left with its big brother, the Twelve (Heavy) on the right. With railway carriage door-handles, the latter just went on for ever, slowly.

'You buy a car, but you invest in an Austin'. So ran the advertising slogan in 1937, when this 1.1 litre Cambridge Ten Saloon was sold.

Sevens had four-speed gearboxes and various improvements, but the Chummy was more endearing than the sardine-tin saloons which followed.

With this British light car, one might pair a French one, the Brasier from Ivry-Port, by a company which had several names in its life from 1897 to 1930 – it was called Georges-Richard, Richard-Brasier Chaigneau-Brasier, and just Brasier. Georges Richard used his own name first, coupled it with that of his designer, and then left the company. Chaigneau afterwards complicated the company history with the fourth name-change. The 9CV itself was unexciting but representative, its 1927 form being a two-door machine rather like a Citroen, with a forepeak to the roof and a built-in trunk on the back carrying the spare wheel behind it. It had disc wheels and a large

A BMW looked graceful even in 1937, when this 45 hp, six-cylinder came on the scene. They called it a limousine, although it was not.

toolbox on the running board, just like its betters. The engine was an orthodox four-cylinder, front mounted and driving the rear wheels. Slightly later came a front-drive, straight-eight with ohc, but its development resulted in the company going out of business.

The British firm of Calthorpe is best remembered for its motor cycles, but there was also a range of Calthorpe cars from 1904 to 1926. After 1919 they stuck largely to a one-model policy, and one would pick their 10 hp Calthorpe Minor, which was designed before the First World War but continued to be made afterwards. The Minor was a four-cylinder, side-valve machine of only 1,087 cc, from which later models were developed. It boasted 25 bhp at 3,300 rpm. The designer was G. W. Hands, a bicycle man, and there was a smart tourer version and some sporty two-seaters.

For something completely different one might sample some of the popular American cars of the period. One of their big companies,

This is the six-cylinder version of the famous Citroen Traction Avant, with air suspension, an elongated wheelbase, and very restricted steering lock.

Opposite, bottom
The Classic Chrysler 60 of 1926 with cow-catching bumpers and the rumble seat beloved of the period.

Chevrolet, had cars on the market by 1911, were the market leaders and produced the cheapest General Motors cars. Perhaps the most representative Chevrolet would be their 1930 Model AD, a 26 hp, two-door sedan, which looked very like a Model A Ford. It was sold under the slogan 'six for the price of a four', and kept ahead of Ford in sales for all but four of the next 30 years. It was called the 'Cast Iron Wonder' – from its pistons of that material – or the 'Stovebolt Six'. The ohv, 3.2 litre, six-cylinder engine produced 50 bhp at 2,600 rpm. In later years there were other models, including a Tourer, a Landau Phaeton (known in the United Kingdom as a cabriolet) an

Opera Coupé (two-door, fixed head), a Sport Roadster (drophead coupé with rumble or dickey seat) or a four-door Club Sedan. The 1932 Phaeton tourer was the rarest, as only 420 were made, all different and with optional extras such as black cloth tyre covers, wood-spoke wheels, detachable trunks, spotlights, bumpers and single or dual side-mounts. This car dominated the American market in sedan form.

There should be a Chrysler to go with the Chevvy, and Chrysler in the 1930s also meant Dodge, Plymouth and De Soto. By 1933, all Chryslers except one model had eight-cylinder engines, but the pick of these was the earlier Airflow, a hideous looking design which made people laugh at the time and lost the company money. Nevertheless, Carl Breer, who was responsible for it, really started something. To get a wind-cheating shape at the rear, he had to move the rear seat forward, which pushed the front seat forward, which pushed the engine forward, and so began a whole new series of problems in terms of handling qualities. The Airflow came out in 1934 with either a 4.9 or a 5.3 litre engine, admittedly an eight and bigger than other cars discussed here, but one must take the motor with the car. The Airflow covered a flying mile at 95.7 mph, a record which stood for 23 years.

From a big American car, a switch to a little British one – the Clyno, at its peak in about 1927. Clyno were, like so many others, originally motor-cycle makers, but they produced a light car to challenge the popular Morris Cowley. The Clyno was in production from 1922 to 1928, the 10.8 hp model for the whole of that time. A smart little tourer version, with a 1,368 cc, four-cylinder, side-valve Coventry Climax engine was one of the best, or one could choose the Nine with its 951 cc, side-valve engine, which appeared in 1928 and was the company's other good seller. The early 10.8 won a great name for reliability, but when Clyno tried to keep up with the unexpected demand, their standards dropped. The fabric-bodied, Nine saloon with the spare wheel stuck on the scuttle side was a nice period piece, and there were other bigger and more complex models, including a straight eight.

Crossing the Atlantic again, the alphabet brings us to Dodge, and their family relationship to the Chrysler Airflow. The Dodge Brothers, John and Horace, supplied Ford with engines before making their own car under the name of Dodge Brothers. As they were mostly fours until then, Walter Chrysler bought Dodge in 1928 to give himself a low-price model range. Just the same, the new owner chose to keep the sixes, including an L-head, side-valve 58 bhp, 3.4 litre unit, fitted to both the Senior Roadster of 1930 with dual side-mounts and a rumble

Opposite
Chevrolet, for so many years General Motors' cheapest American brand, and the world's best selling make, came up with this offering in 1933, with a 3.4 litre engine, free-wheel, rubber engine mounts and synchromesh gears.

Above
Citroen's bid for post-First World War sales was the 10 hp Type A of 1919, of which this is the prototype, with a 1.3 litre, four-cylinder engine, disc wheels, cone clutch and a three-speed gearbox. By 1921, production was running at 10,000 cars per year.

Opposite, top
The Ford 8 hp Model Y, which caught up with Morris in 1935 and offered a £100 Popular version.

Opposite, lower
Ford followed the indefatigable Model T with this 24 hp saloon glorying in the name of the Fordor. Even worse, there was a Tudor (ugh).

seat, and to the 1931, four-door sedan with lengthened wheelbase (up to 114⅜ ins.), which had a real gangster image. These may have looked big cars to European eyes, but they were very basic runabouts in the US. Later Dodges used a 3.5 litre power plant producing 87 bhp at 3,600 rpm and 1932 saw the introduction of free-wheel drive. Dodge did not adopt Airflow styling (used by Chrysler and De Soto) and their sales kept up as a result.

Fiat were well into the swing of mass production by the 1920s, turning out tens of thousands of their 509 model, on which the company designers had made a serious attempt to reduce the amount of servicing required. The 509's dynamo, for example, was driven directly from the end of the prop shaft, so deleting the drive belt; the oil level could be checked by an indicator on the engine; there were no instruments at all on the dashboard – merely warning lights for low oil pressure and lack of charge from the dynamo.

Apart from that, the car was basically conventional, with a four-cylinder, 990 cc engine producing 22 bhp (or 27 bhp on the S version). Drum brakes were fitted to all four wheels, while the accelerator pedal was to be found in between the much larger clutch and brake pedals. Various body styles were available, most of them resulting in a weight of around 15 cwt and a top speed of over 50 mph.

The American car of the 1930s, however, was the Model A Ford. True, it was introduced in 1927 and made way for 'the new Ford' with a vee eight engine in 1932, but before the A there was only the Model T, so the A quickly became Mr America's favourite transport.

Edsel Ford, who was then running the company, declared in 1930

Above
This bathtub on wheels is a Gwynne Eight light car of 1922, with 950 cc, ohv, 24 bhp engine. Simple and honest, it sold cheaply and well.

Below
The Japanese started their copying a long time ago. This may look like an Austin Seven, but the badge says it's a Datsun from 1932.

Looking not at all like its modern successors, this Citroen Type B2 appeared in 1923 with 1.5 litres and 11.9 hp.

that no new car was in the pipeline and predicted that more As would be made than there had been Ts, but the 'secret Ford' was actually already under way for 1932. Ford did not like six-cylinder engines, and decided that – if the four had to go – he would go one better than the opposition and give his customers a 'twin four' or vee eight.

By then, however, the A had done a similar job to the T in serving the nation. It came in many body styles including a two-door phaeton or tourer, the only such body ever made by Ford. Otherwise there were the Victoria (two-door, fixed-head coupé), roadster, sedan, convertible sedan, and roadster pick-up models. The A offered three-speed gearbox, four-wheel brakes, water and oil pumps, more instruments, better seats, and a lockable ignition switch, none of which were found on the T. It was powered by a 3.3 litre, four-cylinder, side-valve engine and sold a million a year. The first mass-produced estate car body was offered on the A.

For a complete contrast, there is the curious little English Gwynne car, which can be confused with the Albert, as Gwynne began by making engines for Albert and then took them over. The Albert had little distinction in its life (from 1920–24) except that its radiator was like that of a Rolls-Royce on a smaller scale, but most things improved when it appeared on the roads as a Gwynne-

Clyno were a nine-year wonder on the British car market and 1926 was their best year, when they challenged Morris with cars like this Royal, with four-wheel brakes and a 1,368 cc, four-cylinder, Coventry Climax, side-valve engine.

Albert. In this form, it won a name for good performance, finish and reliability, but was extremely noisy. It had a 950 cc, four-cylinder, ohv engine of Spanish design, enlarged to 1,020 cc in 1926. Gwynnes disappeared in 1929 as better things came on the market. The most distinctive

Gwynne was their 8, with bathtub tourer body and artillery wheels.

Next in line is the Hudson, which most of the time was also the Essex, related to the Terraplane, and – more distantly – to the Anglo-American Railton, which used the same engine. Hudson began in 1909 and disappeared in 1957, by which time it was part of American Motors. The company started as a subsidiary of Chalmers-Detroit, with a badge declaring that they were dedicated to 'Performance, Service and Value', but they broke

away from the parent company in 1909. In the 1920s, they claimed to be the world's biggest manufacturers of six-cylinder cars and they founded Essex in 1919 to sell cheap, four-cylinder cars to returning soldiers.

Both companies did well until the Depression, but then had to cut model numbers, so that Hudson and Essex became the same except that Hudsons had eight cylinders while Essex cars used the Hudson Super Six. Their nicest effort was probably the 1932 roadster, made

Right
This Minerva 32CV cabriolet did the rounds of European motor shows in 1931. It had a six cylinder sleeve-valve engine and weighed more than two tons — a car in the true Minerva tradition.

Below
Most Lincolns were luxury cars but this tourer was fairly basic: a 1922 vee eight with Leland-built phaeton body and artillery wheels.

Bottom
A pre-war Morgan three-wheeler with the JAP twin-cylinder engine out in the fresh air and most of the occupants out there too.

in the year the Terraplane was born. While the Hudson used the 3,455 cc, side-valve engine, the Terraplane had a slightly larger unit and achieved 80 mph and 25 mpg. As an alternative to the roadster, one could buy what they called a Coach (a two-door saloon), which was a popular body style for both Hudson and Essex. They had a period charm, and ranked with the equivalent Fords and Chevrolets as typical of the 1930s in America.

The little, English Humber 8/18 tourer of 1922–25 epitomised the virtues of carefully-made cars in an age when craftsmen had high standards and goods were not built down to a price but up to a specification. Thomas Humber came early on the scene, making bicycles, tricycles, and then cars from 1901. Humber went in for racing, but recovered from this aberration to concentrate on making middle-class, high-quality cars, even after Rootes took them over in 1929. The 8/18, with its four-cylinder, inlet-over-exhaust (F head) engine of 985 cc and with various peculiarities, like an absence of front brakes and a brake on the transmission, was slow and sedate but 'worthy'. It had a pleasing appearance, and was a pleasure to drive.

From the small-but-elegant Humber, to the American Hupmobile, which was a medium-priced rather than a basic car, but which seemed better fitted to the role of everyday transport than that of a luxury or sporting carriage. True, there were some straight-eight Hupmobiles and their last car was a revival of the Cord in styling, but the Hupp of about 1930 was a workaday vehicle.

The company began in 1908 and stopped making cars in 1940, to work on defence contracts during the Second World War. Their cars built up a reputation for reliability and had quite a following by 1914, although they only made about one-fiftieth the number of cars that Henry Ford did. Up to 1925, they stayed with the four-cylinder engine with which they had begun, but in that year, they announced a straight eight, which we will ignore, and then a six.

The common man's car in 1930 was the 70 bhp 3.6 litre Century Six which came in what Americans called business coupé form. Hupmobile decided to offer seven different engines, which did not help their financial position.

Among the ranks of small cars we must include a Morgan, which could have three wheels or four, and a variety of engines. Morgans are still being made today, of course, and are not very different in basic form, although some have more power and go more quickly; they are just as Spartan and uncomfortable. The four-wheeler, with either a Coventry-Climax or Standard 10 engine, was always much more desirable than the tricycle, as Morgan three-wheelers were inclined to be eccentric and rather easily overturned. There was a hand-throttle instead of a pedal, and some had a two-speed 'gear-box', chain drive, a kick-start, and

Three speed gearbox, wet-plate clutch and recently-introduced front-wheel brakes were features of the post-First World War Morris Oxford, another famous name with a long history. This is a 1.8 litre from 1927, the year when Morris adopted the familiar, flat radiator.

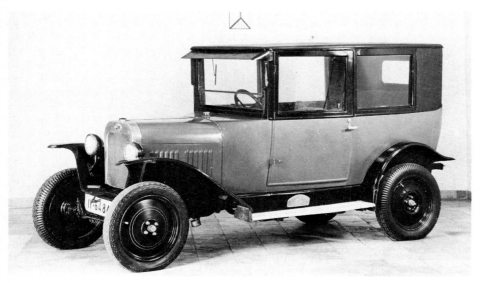

Boxy, little Opel 4/14 Sedan of 1925, with four-cylinder engine, magneto ignition, pressure lubrication, and a three-speed gearbox.

other rather strange mysteries to be solved by anyone new to them. No doubt a three-wheeler Morgan, especially of the Aero variety – with rather more horse-power than there was adhesion from the single, driven rear wheel – had its charms for the young, and it was a special thing in its day.

The 4/4 four wheeler, so called presumably because it had both four wheels and four cylinders, appeared from 1936 onwards, and modern, four-wheeled Morgans have become such a cult that the

company cannot keep up with the demand. The only quaint and exclusive feature common to both three and four-wheelers was (and still is) the sliding pillar front suspension, which dates back to 1910.

A 'bullnose' Morris would have to feature as the standard British transport, just as the Model T and Model A Fords were in the USA. William Morris started, like so many others, as a bicycle mender with a shop in Oxford, and eventually became so rich that he gave

Conventional but popular (which might be Henry Ford's epitaph), the Model A sold over a million a year, even in the middle of the Depression. This 1929 car was typical of the breed, with a four-cylinder, 3.3 litre side-valve engine, three-speed gearbox and brakes on all four wheels.

away millions of pounds to charity, all from making cut-price cars for the masses. His first car was the Morris Oxford of 1913, which is confusing: the Oxford was originally the smaller car and the Cowley the big one, but later

Cowley models became the smaller of the two. Both originally had the 'bullnose' radiator, and later the flat radiator. Collectors now go for either a Cowley or an Oxford from the round-radiator period, which lasted up to 1927. The first Oxford had a White and Poppe engine, while the first Cowley had an American Continental motor, being made during 1915, when there was no British manufacturer of civilian motor cars. The Cowley was, in fact, assembled from American parts, as Morris found he could buy engines for half the price in the US, and, while there in connection with his munitions-manufacturing, did a little car-parts buying at the same time. His man, Hans Lanstad of White and Poppe, stayed in the US to take a close look at how Ford did things.

The early Morrises were simple four-cylinder machines, with side-valves and entirely orthodox construction, and they became ever-cheaper. There were two-seaters with rumble seats, four-seater tourers and various kinds of saloon.

Last year for Hupmobile was 1941, when they offered this 4.0 litre, six-cylinder Skylark. It used the body of an 810/812 Cord (Hupmobile having bought all the dies) mated to the company's own, conventional running gear.

There was nothing extraordinary about them except, perhaps, the exhaust note, which was described as like the sound of tearing calico. The 1.5 litre Cowley or 1.8 litre Oxford from the middle years (about 1925) were the best examples of what people drove in those

Right
Peugeot Quadrilette of 1921, with four-cylinder, monobloc engine, three-speed gearbox and a set of what must have been the tiniest-ever drum brakes.

Centre
The air-cooled, twin-cylinder Rover 8 hp of 1920 lacked refinements, but did well in its day.

days. They were more or less ever-lasting and had one curious feature: completely (well, comparatively) silent starting from a dynamotor which was always in engagement, so that there was no clash of metal on metal as a Bendix drive was operated.

The '£100 car', the little two-seater Morris Minor of 847 cc was offered in 1930. The other '£100 car' was the two-door saloon Ford Eight in 1935, so they did not really compete with each other. This early Minor, by the way, must not be confused with the car of the same name produced in 1949 by Alex Issigonis. Certainly, the '£100 car' had its charms and, with hydraulic brakes and other modern features, was streets ahead of the Austin Seven, although admittedly the Morris came nearly ten years later. Nevertheless, many people now regard the Austin as superior, although it does not stand comparison on a feature-by-feature basis. Far more Austin Sevens have survived and the little, two-seater Morris is now a rarity, but it was a motoring milestone as the cheapest car of its day.

A very minor milestone – and one that does not seem to have led to anywhere in particular – came from the New York Motors Corporation of Moline, Illinois, in 1928. They produced a car called the New York Six whose only claim to fame was a system called Parkmobile, which comprised a four-wheeled, retractable 'undercarriage' to enable the machine to be easily parked. By 1930, the company were making lawn mowers, which was perhaps not surprising.

An American car that really did

The Singer Junior saloon did its best as a hack for the masses around 1930, when people were not so fussy.

Skoda from Czechoslavakia have been around for a long time. They offered this 1,380 cc, Rapid drophead coupé from 1935 to 1938.

appeal to the masses was the Plymouth, a make which appeared on the market in 1928 as a rival to Ford and Chevrolet, the Big Two of the day, whom Walter Chrysler wanted to shake up. The company name commemorated the Pilgrim Fathers (or so it was said) and their advertising slogan – 'the smoothness of an eight and the economy of a four' – was brought about by their use of the 'Floating Power' system, which anchored the engine between a rubber mount at the front and a spring under the transmission at the rear. Early Plymouths had ribbon radiators like Chryslers and the open two-seater roadster was a

The steam car took a long time to beat. Stanley produced this Model 735 in 1920, with a double-acting, two-cylinder engine and direct drive to the rear axle. It looked like a petrol car and could keep up with them, too, cruising at 45 mph, but only 600 were made.

Opposite
Perhaps the most famous Morris ever, the 'Bullnose' Cowley, was introduced in 1915. From 1926, it came with 1.5 litre engine, three-speed gearbox, wet-plate clutch and optional front brakes, an option sensibly taken up by the original purchaser of this car.

particularly attractive design, as was the four-door, four-seater Sedan of 1931. Plymouths were sold in Britain as Chryslers and by 1931 there were eight body styles, plus automatic ignition advance, free-wheel, and constant-mesh transmission for easy gear shifting.

A small British car which was number three in the sales charts of 1928 has obvious claims to be kept for posterity. The marque was Singer, a firm that made bicycles and sewing machines, and the car was the Junior, which had an 848 cc, overhead-camshaft engine, a notable departure from the norm in cheap, small-car production. It was an idea to which Singer stuck until the company was absorbed by others and were reduced to badge-engineering.

The Junior sold mostly in open tourer form rather than as a saloon, at a very low price and with rear-wheel brakes only. Front brakes came in 1927. With its disc wheels and its bathtub body, it may have been undistinguished in ap-

The first car to carry the famous name of Morris Minor appeared in 1929, this 847 cc two seater being a product of 1930. One year later, it became the first £100 car, when a basic version was offered at that price.

pearance, but it was a practical runabout even with only 16.5 bhp. There were two-seater sports versions and one known as the Porlock after Porlock Hill in the West of England, which was so steep that most cars had to climb it backwards. As time went on, the car acquired a fourth gear and then a 972 cc engine, which made it the Junior Special. This vanished in 1932 when the Singer Nine, about

which nothing worthwhile can be
written, replaced it.

Another British car which en-
dured for many years for no obvious reason was the Standard,
ultimately lost in the maze of
British Leyland. Eleven marques of
motor car under the name of
Standard appear in motoring his-
tories, but the only one which made
any lasting impact was British and
appeared in 1903 with a Union Jack
as a radiator badge. These cars – or
at least their engines – were actually
designed by Mr Alex Craig, who
had been responsible for the
Singer. There were all kinds of
Standards, but the car worth remembering was the Nine of 1928
onwards, with a four-cylinder,
1,159 cc, side-valve engine and
often with a fabric-covered body,
as on the Teignmouth model. After
this, there were Big Nines and
Little Nines and Flying Nines and
even some with S.S. bodies from
the forerunner of the Jaguar company, but the simple, square-
rigged, fabric saloon was typical of
the rigours of motoring in 1928. It
could do all of 50 mph and covered
about 40 miles on a gallon of fuel.
The ride was far from ideal, so
much so that one subtle road tester
said that it would perhaps do best as
a town car as it was quite easy to
park. What he meant was that it was
no fun at all on a normal country
road. Still, the Nine was a milestone
of sorts and represented the mixture of minimum comfort and maximum economy which passed for a
light car in those days. To drive one
now would serve to remind us how
good the modern equivalents, like
the Fiesta or Polo, are.

Last of all comes the Studebaker
of fond memory. Henry and Clem
Studebaker started making horse-

Above
The Triumph Dolomite Roadster of
1938 was striking, whether or not the
styling pleases.

Below
Volvo PV651 saloon of 1929: solidity
and safety have always been upper-
most in the minds of the Swedish firm.

drawn wagons in South Bend,
Indiana, in 1852, and it was said
that they made one every seven
minutes. They then turned to electric cars around 1902, with Thomas
Edison as their designer. Gas bug-
gies came later and they then
bought the Everett-Metzger-
Flanders Company, making nearly
8,000 EMF cars which acquired the
unfortunate tag of 'Every Morning
Fixit'. Thus was Studebaker born,
and they lasted until 1966. They
were in money trouble by 1933, but
kept going for a time and actually
produced some of their best cars
during that period. However,
around 1929–30 they were already
making some good-looking cars. In
the 1930s they began to move

down-market, not improving much
on the way. They concentrated on
an all-six-cylinder line, apart from
the cheaper Erskine, which didn't
sell. They offered the choice of a six
or an eight in the President,
Commander and Dictator series.
Through all this time, they retained
wooden-framed bodies when all
other manufacturers had changed
to the Budd, stamped-metal system. The pick of the bunch was
perhaps the President 'Four
Seasons' roadster with wind-up
glass windows, but the best of their
more mundane cars was the only six
they were making at the time, the
Studebaker Six, their cheapest car
and a very worthy representative of
the marque.

6 1914–39: The Coachbuilder's Art

The years between the two World Wars were the heyday of the luxury car. In the 1930s, there were more than 40 coach-builders in Britain alone, offering 70 different styles of body, although admittedly many of them had different names for virtually the same thing. (American terminology was different, with phaeton for tourer, sedan for saloon and so on). By then, the days of tapestry interiors and other eccentric extravagances had gone, but the machinery was reliable, and

electrical equipment offered a whole new bag of tricks.

When it comes to selecting a classic, luxury car of this period, one must usually make two choices, one of a chassis produced by a car-maker and one of coachwork produced by someone else. Later, of course, the welded one-piece body came along, and after about 1938, it was adopted by the mass-producers. Later, even Rolls-Royce, who had never made bodies for their cars, adopted the system.

This Hispano-Suiza may not have been the most energy-effective form of transport for two people, but its body was an outstanding example of the coachbuilder's art in an age when such things were appreciated.

The old art of securing sheet aluminium sections to wooden frames simply disappeared, for the stamped-out body was superior from almost every point of view. Stronger, easier and cheaper both to make and to replace, its only apparent debit was the loss of

individuality conferred by the one-off product.

The mass-producers did learn how to offer alternative body-styles within certain limits, such as convertibles, but each design meant a major and costly change to the body-stamping tools. Later safety laws and a lack of demand practically killed off even this degree of deviation from the straightforward saloon.

In Britain, Armstrong-Siddeley was an old and respected name which lasted from 1919 until 1960, mostly in the luxury market after an initial dabble with smaller cars. The firm resulted from the marriage of Armstrong-Whitworth and Siddeley-Deasy and were the first British concern to produce a new motorcar after the First World War, although they did then persist

in making more or less the same one until 1939. They were famous as aircraft makers as well, and named many cars after well known aeroplanes, like the Lancaster, Typhoon, Hurricane, Tempest and Whitley, all products of the parent company, Hawker-Siddeley. Their cars tended to be massive and heavy and were not known for sparkling performance, apart from one model, called the Siddeley Special, which had a 5.0 litre engine in a sporting body of unusual appearance. But the norm was a big saloon using a pre-selector gearbox and designed to be chauffeur-driven. A good choice would be a 1939, 16 hp model, which looked rather like a Humber (one of their competitors), but more typical of the classic Armstrongs was their so-called Sports Saloon of 20 hp, pro-

The famous, ex-Woolf Barnato Bentley Speed Six of 1930, the car which raced and beat the train from Paris to Nice. With 130 bhp it would exceed 90 mph in standard form.

duced in 1933 with their first overhead-valve engine of 3,190 cc. There was a cabriolet version which was better looking, the saloon being rather upright and severe; this was part of the company image, however, together with double side-mounts and a regal radiator crowned by the Sphinx.

After Armstrong-Siddeley we come to Bentley: either the 'proper', Cricklewood-built Bentley now known as a Vintage Bentley and made up to 1930, when Rolls-Royce bought the company; or what was unofficially known as a Rolls-Bentley and built at Derby. Members of the Bentley Drivers'

Club, who favour the original, W. O. Bentley designs, rather look down on the later cars, which were sold under the slogan of 'The Silent Sports Car', and certainly there was nothing very silent about the older machines, whose engines ranged from a 'baby' of 3.0 litres to one of 8.0. The Speed Six twin-carburetter version of the 6½ Litre and the 8 Litre both featured engines built with the robustness of locomotives, with formal saloon coachwork of the period. Or, if something more modern is sought, there were the 3.5 litre and 4.25 litre Rolls-Bentleys of the 1930s, with modified Rolls-Royce, ohv engines and twin SU carburetters. Individuals tended to put very heavy bodies on to the original Cricklewood cars and over-burden them, and much the same thing happened with the newer cars, which is why the engine was en-

larged from 3.5 to 4.25 litres. As a matter of interest, and in spite of the Bentley Drivers' loyalty to the man's own products, W. O. Bentley himself described the first 3.5 as 'a very nice motor car', so that no-one need feel ashamed of being seen in one.

There was an enormous variety of Bentley body-styles from the various coach-builders, ranging

From the famous motorcycle manufacturers, the Brough Superior was a limited-production British car of the mid-1930s, with an American engine, usually a Hudson six or straight-eight.

Another candidate for the Ugliness Award, this monster with *sedanca de ville* limousine coachwork is one of Dr Ferdinand Porsche's less memorable efforts – a Lohner Porsche made by Austro-Daimler.

The fashionable, streamlined shape was used by many makers in the 1930s. This Austro-Daimler of 1934 is an eight-cylinder ADR8.

WH 7238

from sporting two-seaters to giant limousines. The lighter, more sporting types were first choice, preferably the later, overdrive model with its direct third gear and geared-up top, making it less liable to run its bearings in continuous high-speed running. They were among the most handsome cars ever built and very refined. However, a driver did have to put up with vibration from the stiff springing and with a delay in brake-servo operation as the cable wound itself up.

The next name in alphabetical order is Bugatti, who normally made a very different kind of car to those under discussion. But the giant Bugatti Royale, of which only six were made, was most certainly a luxury car. The Schlumpf collection in France holds a large

proportion of the total production of this 13.0 litre monster. Stopping this 2½-ton, 100 mph vehicle was entrusted to cable brakes as on other Bugattis. A Royale took some believing when one saw it, with an engine 4½ feet long and over three feet high, despite which the proportions were so good that it was not grotesque.

We might settle for a Type 57SC which, although relatively small with only an eight-cylinder, 3.3 litre, supercharged engine, was the ultimate in road cars. It was fitted with some fanciful, beautiful and bizarre coachwork, in which the passengers were confined to a small cabin while the mechanicals took up most of the chassis.

Buick began in 1903 and are still going as part of General Motors. The 1930s produced some memor-

able Buicks, particularly the straight-eights, which appeared in 1931. The company kept up with all the latest developments, offering all-synchromesh transmission with the straight-eight. There was a cheaper Buick called a Marquette which lasted for a couple of years (1929–30) but was not in the class of car we are discussing. There were, however, two particularly appealing models from the pre-1939 period: notably the 1931 Model 8-90L which, with its 104 bhp engine, was to last for 22 years, pulling a vast Pullman of a car with twin side-mounts, peaked roof, external luggage grid, and wire wheels. And in 1939, they introduced the giant, Roadmaster four-door, Streamline Sport Phaeton, offered only on special order. The Series 90 used a 5.6 litre engine and there were also

smaller, 50 and 60 series versions. The cars could have velvet rear carpeting, mohair trim, window blinds and footrests. They were elegance personified. The later Roadmaster was in a different genre, sharing a new, 5.2 litre engine with the Limited and Century lines, still an eight, but with aluminium pistons, and fitted within a 131-in wheelbase. The top specification included the Dyna-flash engine, the all-coil suspension which made the Buick ride famous, and perhaps the optional semi-automatic transmission.

From Detroit to England for our next luxury car, which was made only in small numbers from 1935–39 and used American engines. This was the Brough Superior, marketed by George Brough, who made what was sometimes called the Rolls-Royce of motorcycles. Most Brough cars made were drophead coupés with two-door bodies and Hudson straight-six or eight engines, and bodies built by the English coach-builder Atcherly of Birmingham. They were very handsome, with a Jaguar look, but were a shade too heavy to compete with Railton, who used the same Anglo-American formula. However, Brough scored on appearance, with adequate if not sparkling performance, and quality construction. One car was made towards the end of the company's life with a body from Charlesworth, who also built for Alvis. This had saloon coachwork and a Lincoln Zephyr 12-cylinder engine from the US.

Cadillac ran from 1903 and are still going strong. From the 1930s, the one to choose was a 1930 or 1931 Series 355, when they were using the 95 bhp vee eight with a 134-in wheelbase and some attractive body styles. Cadillac was the GM flagship and had synchromesh from 1928, although only on second and third. It also had a vee engine when others (except La Salle) thought a straight-eight was the thing to have. Body styles included a handsome sedan with four doors, running boards, white-side-wall tyres and dual sidemounts; a more sporting Model 341B Convertible Sedan from 1929, which was a car in real Hollywood style; or a 1930 Series 353 (same engine as the 355) roadster, with chunky artillery wheels, sidemounts, rear trunk, swivelling spotlamps and the rest. They had a solid look, very masculine and had the power to pull their weight, plus an excellent gear-shift.

British Daimler could match the US Cadillac, in style if not performance, and in the 1920s and 1930s they had an enormous range of models with very sober and upright coachwork, much favoured by the British Royal Family. Later ones (from 1930) had a pre-selector gearbox and acceleration retarded even more by a so-called fluid flywheel, which was like a torque converter with the stator (or middle element) missing, so that there was no multiplication of torque. On acceleration, there was a great stirring of oil and generation of heat but not much forward movement. It had a sleeve-valve engine, an arrangement inherited from the pre-1914 car, until the appearance of the ohv Straight Eight of 1935. This had the virtue of being a small-production model and had majestic, upright coachwork and an imposingly long bonnet to hide its 3,746 cc engine, and was not as inclined to produce smoke as the sleeve valve units. It looked rather archaic, but Daimlers were like that, preferring dignity to high performance.

Delage lasted from 1905 to 1954 and almost their entire production consisted of luxury cars of one sort or another. Their heyday was the 1930s, however, at a time when they sold their largest and most magnificent creations – cars that were the epitome of all things French, with striking and elegant coachwork. Supreme among the Delage cars of this era was the D8, which came with a water-cooled, straight-eight, monobloc engine of 77 mm × 109 mm and 4,060 cc. The car was introduced at the 1929 Paris show and was sold with a variety of chassis and bodywork, the largest having a wheelbase of almost 12 ft and a weight of almost two tons.

The ohv engines were refined, with the valve springs operating separate rockers to reduce valve bounce, and the sporting, D8S version gave over 90 bhp at 3,400 rpm, which enabled the weighty machine to progress at up to 80 mph. Later versions came with synchromesh gears and hydraulic brakes, and the short-chassis Grand Sport of 1932 could top 100 mph.

Alongside the luxurious Delage company was another French make, Delahaye, who actually took over Delage in 1935, before

themselves being swallowed by Hotchkiss in 1954. Early Delahaye models were rather dull, if worthy, and the best model was undoubtedly the later Type 135, which appeared on the market in 1936. This six-cylinder, pushrod ohv of 3.5 litres delivered 120 bhp and usually came equipped with a Cotal electric pre-selector gearbox, changing being accomplished by means of a miniature lever in its own gate. A 100 mph motor car, it did well in racing and rallying, producing up to 160 bhp in competition form, enabling one of them to lap Brooklands at over 126 mph in 1937.

In America, where the populace have always looked upon the air-cooled Volkswagen Beetle with great favour, there was an early exponent of water-free engineering in the shape of the Franklin Automobile Co., of Syracuse, New Jersey. Their 1928 Airman saloon, an example of which was owned by the famous pilot, Charles Lindbergh, looked like most other sedans of the era. Underneath its conventional skin, however, was an in-line, six-cylinder engine of 82.5 mm × 120.6 mm and 3,874 cc, with cooling by means of a centrifugal fan with scoops and baffles. Each cylinder had its own vertical cooling fins and the whole engine was enclosed in a metal casing, around which the fan circulated air.

The crankshaft ran in seven bearings, each of which was supplied with its own oil feed by a gear pump, while the valves were overhead, operated by pushrods and rockers. There was an electric device on the dashboard for controlling the fuel/air mixture to the Franklin carburettor, this early form of choke making the device easier to start.

At a time when most cars came with contracting brakes, the Airman had Lockheed hydraulic internally-expanding ones, in keeping with company policy, which dictated quality rather than low price. The American public did not seem particularly impressed, however, and sales tumbled until 1934, when the name disappeared. The Airman weighed 1¾ tons and would do 60 mph.

The early Paige-Detroit was discussed earlier, and now we must deal with the Graham-Paige of a later period. The company stopped making cars in 1940, and their last ones were not things of beauty. Their really worthwhile car was a 4.0 litre, eight-cylinder machine known as the Blue Streak, the 1934 model with optional supercharger having a 95 mph top speed. In the 1930s, Graham-Paige made some beautiful bodies, including what they called a coupé-de-ville (or sedanca) and some sturdy roadsters.

The most renowned Hispano-Suiza was the H6B which appeared as early as 1919, being produced at the Paris factory rather than in Barcelona. The faster, sporting version was called the H6C Sport or Boulogne, as it won the Boillot Cup races at Boulogne three years running. It had four-wheel, servo operated brakes, a 6.6 litre, light-alloy engine with sohc, and an easy 110 mph from 134 bhp. On the radiator was the silver stork mascot, which had been the badge of the French flying ace Georges Guynemer and his Escadrille Squadron. The Hispano had everything a rich man wanted from his toys and was faster than its rival, the Rolls-Royce. It had power and style. From 1923, a larger engine of 7,982 cc could be installed in the Boulogne model, which made it even better.

Horch from Germany existed from 1899 and are remembered by motor racing fans for their part in building some of the Auto Union racers. August Horch himself was one of the pioneers of the German car industry, enjoying

A real Al Capone car, the seven-passenger Buick Sedan, a 1928 Model 50 with 4.4 litres and six cylinders.

A straight-eight engine with overhead valves and synchromesh gears were standard features when this Buick first hit the streets of Michigan in 1932.

The first Cadillac vee eight appeared in 1915 with a 5.1 litre engine. They sold 13,000 in the first year.

A thing of beauty and a joy for ever, this 1930 7.0 litre Delage D8 had a handsome double-cowl tourer body and rear Auster screen.

some success in events like the Prince Henry Trials. From 1923, their chief engineer was none other than Paul Daimler, who started the firm on the road to the outsize monsters for which they are best remembered, although Daimler himself left in 1930 before any of them had come to fruition.

In 1932, Horch amalgamated with Audi, Wanderer and DKW to form the Auto Union group, but the individual company names were retained, with Horch always making the luxury cars. In 1936, they introduced the 853, with an sohc, straight-eight engine of 87 mm × 104 mm and 4,944 cc, which produced 105 bhp at 3,200 rpm. With five-speed gearbox and independent suspension all round (including a double-pivot de Dion system at the rear) and hydraulic shock absorbers, it would also go round corners; only the Second World War ended production. Modern features included twin Solex carburettors and ignition by coil and distributor.

Hotchkiss started life as makers of things for killing people, their badge consisting of two crossed cannons even after they had commenced the more peaceful occupation of making motor cars in 1903. Their name lives on in the 'Hotchkiss Drive', the open-shaft system in which the rear axle is located by its springs or by a torque tube anchored at its front end.

They produced typical French touring cars, apart from an abortive 6.6 litre, six-cylinder ohc device intended to challenge Hispano-Suiza in 1924. Most of their cars were fours, however, like the four-seater torpedo model of 1922, with a 3,962 cc side-valve monobloc of 95 mm × 140 mm, which could manage over 60 mph, at which velocity the rear seat passengers must have been grateful to discover that the car came with a second windscreen for their benefit.

To move now to Humber may seem to be coming rather rapidly down the scale, but the firm must qualify in the luxury car class for making so many chauffeur-driven models between the wars. The Snipe and Pullman arrived in 1930, the latter being a long-wheelbase version of the Snipe, with 3.5 litre, six-cylinder engine. Humber did not make classics in the Hispano sense, but workhorses, with inlet-over-exhaust engine and entirely orthodox chassis, but they served many well. During the Second World War, tourer versions of the Snipe, such as Field Marshal Montgomery's 'Old Faithful', made their own niche in history. The tourers were made in thousands, along with the 4 × 4 Command Car, and even a lightweight wireless truck which, with the big, light-alloy-head engine, went very quickly.

An Italian rival to Hispano was the Isotta-Fraschini, active from 1900 until the firm shut down in 1949, when taken over by an armaments company. They raced with success in the early years, but after the Second World War adopted a one-model policy, producing the straight-eight, 6.0 litre designed by Giustino Cattaneo and known as the Tipo 8. A good example of this big luxury car was the Tipo 8A, 7.3 litre of 1930, with a drophead coupé body and a three-speed gearbox which was almost unnecessary, as the car had so much torque that it could be driven everywhere in top. It was beautifully made, like a Bugatti, and used a lot of fuel, which did not matter much to those who could afford such a car, especially in an era when fuel was so much cheaper. Only a few thousand

The car of kings and possibly the ultimate classic: a Bugatti Royale, with 250 bhp, 12.7 litre straight-eight under the bonnet and a truly enormous chassis. Only six were built.

One of these actually won the Monte Carlo Rally in 1936. With a 70 bhp, 3.6 litres vee eight, transverse-leaf suspension on an all-up weight of less than a ton, the Ford offered exciting and often lethal performance for its day. This 'opera' coupé enjoyed a more leisurely existence, however.

Tipo 8s were made, and they were a bit heavy, not handling as well as might have been expected, but one could not have everything.

The Lanchester brothers were respected pioneers of the motor industry and produced many ideas well ahead of their time. They also made some refined and silent motor cars when these were far

Below
The Hispano-Suiza was always a quality car, this being a 1928 *sedanca de ville* on the 32 CV chassis.

Bottom
A British Jensen from the 1930s with an American, 3.6 litre Ford vee eight engine.

from being the norm. Their company was eventually taken over by the BSA-Daimler combine and Lanchesters finished up being what amounted to down-market Daimlers, with engines that were too small and bodies too heavy. The great virtue of the early Lanchesters was that they were designed as motor cars and not as stationary gas-engines installed in horse-carts as seemed to be the case with so many of the pioneer vehicles. Lanchester really made the first British car, and the one to pick out was their 'small' model, called the Twenty-One, which competed with the 'baby' Rolls Twenty but

Opposite, top
A regal Lanchester Twenty-One six-seater, enclosed-drive, three-quarters Landaulette with split screen.

Opposite, lower
Giant American Lincoln tourers were much favoured in the Chicago gangster days, this 1931/32 KB coming with 7.2 litres of V12.

was much better. This was a smaller version of the Forty (which made Lanchester's name) and had a six-cylinder, 3,100 cc, ohc engine, four-speed gearbox and four-wheel brakes in 1925. The following year the engine went up to 3,327 cc and remained so until 1931. It was sometimes called the Twenty-

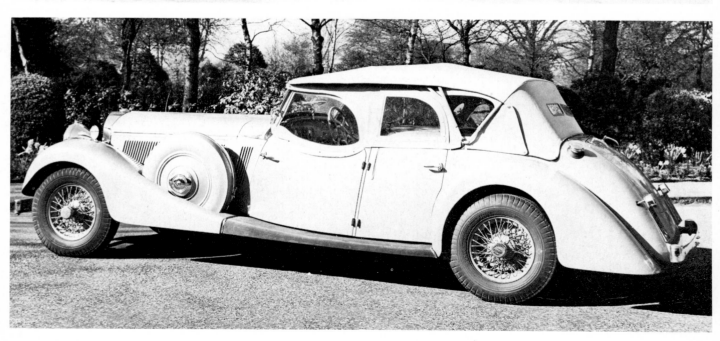

Handsome as well as rare: a 1934
Hispano-Suiza convertible, with 9.4
litres of V12 engine and over 100 mph
available.

Three. One of the distinguishing marks of the Lanchester was a little window in the front of the radiator, through which one could peer at the water-level without the inconvenience of having to unscrew the radiator cap. In general, the cars had perpendicular coachwork, disc wheels and rather a regal air.

The American Locomobile company started with steam cars. Between 1900 and 1929, however, they made high quality, petrol-driven cars, advertising that 'no stock parts or ready-made units are permitted'. This was not still so when they were bought out by W. C. Durant founder of General Motors, in 1922. The Locomobile to have was the Model 48, which was in production for 18 years from

The fabulous 8.0 litre Hispano-Suiza H6C Sport Boulogne of 1928 had an in-line six-cylinder, ohc aluminium engine (developed from the French company's First World War aviation experience) and would pull 100 mph.

1911 and sold as 'The Exclusive Car for Exclusive People' at a price which doubled over those years. It was an 8.5 litre machine with an old-fashioned T-head, putting out 90 bhp and using dual magneto ignition or a coil on later ones. There were solid sedan and sporty versions.

There were some luxury saloons from Mercedes during this period: in 1923, for example, there was the six-cylinder 15/70/100 series, with 3.92 litres and 116 bhp. With the supercharger fitted, one of these cars could top 70 mph, despite being a large, upright machine with a peaked roof, D-back, running boards and side mounts and with ample space for passengers. This model actually appeared before the Daimler-Benz merger of 1926, so it was technically still a Daimler

despite being called a Mercedes.

There were no such reservations about the Type 770 of 1930, however. This was the first 'Grösser' Mercedes, with a 7,655 cc, straight-eight motor producing 150 bhp at 2,800 rpm for normal road use. If the driver was really in a hurry, though, he could engage the optional supercharger and have 200 bhp at his disposal, propelling almost three tons of motor car to over 100 mph. The whole machine was an impressive tribute to the German engineering skills of the era, with a gear-driven ohc, twin magnetos, aluminium pistons, a nine-bearing crankshaft and a gear-driven oil pump. Transmission was by multi-plate clutch to a four-speed, all-synchromesh gearbox with direct third and overdrive fourth gears. The chassis was pressed steel and suspension was by semi-elliptic springs, although late models were fitted with swing-axle rear ends and all-independent suspension.

Naturally enough, Herr Hitler acquired one of these magnificent beasts, although his one boasted armour plating and an all-up weight of around four tons, so that his chauffeurs must have been doubly grateful for the fact that all 770 models were fitted with servo-assisted brakes.

The French Mors (mors is Latin for 'death') was a great name in racing in the pioneer days from 1899 to 1904, but they tended to decline once they gave up competition work. However, they did make some luxury cars from 1918 onwards, with Knight sleeve-valve engines, a good example being the Mors SSS (Sans Soupapes, Silencieuse – Valveless and Silent) which from 1921 onwards had the then-unusual front wheel brakes. The Knight engines were built by the Belgian Minerva firm and with them, the big, heavy Mors could do 70 mph looking very impressive.

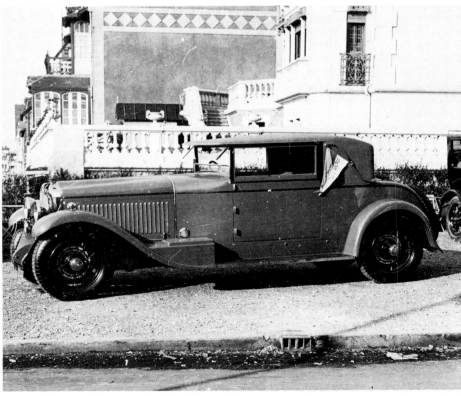

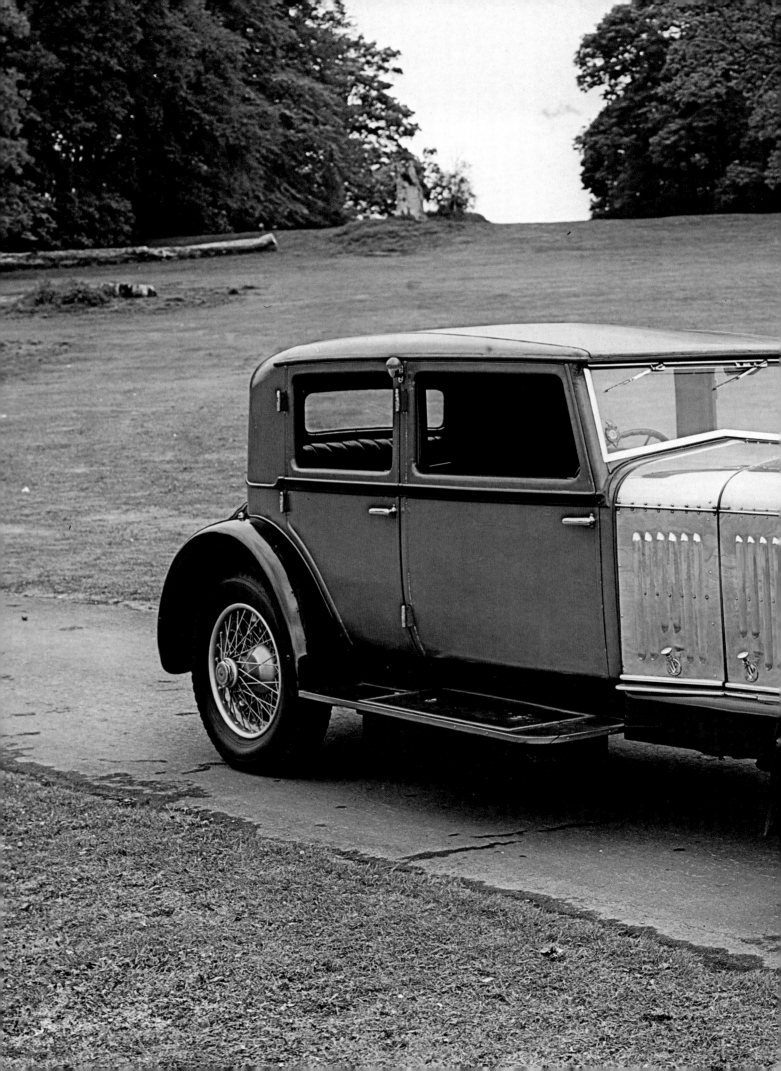

In the late 1920s, the Antwerp firm of
Minerva introduced their 32/34 AK,
here seen in Cabriolet de Ville form,
with 6.0 litres and six cylinders.
Refinement and high performance
were the company's mottos;
sadly they failed to survive the
Second World War.

Eventually Andre Citroen, who ran the company from 1908, used their factory to make his own Type A vehicles, and although some Mors still trickled out, the great name gradually disappeared.

We recommended a Napier sporting model in our pre-1914 selection, but there were also luxury saloons from this famous British firm, which might have taken over the old Bentley concern if Rolls-Royce had not beaten them to it. The pick of their models was the 40/50 T75 with a 6.2 litre, ohc engine. This came out in 1919 and continued until the company ended as motor-makers in 1924. It was a refined machine, with steel cylinder liners in a light-alloy block, dual ignition, and cantilever suspension. Late models had four-wheel brakes to replace the earlier transmission foot brake, low-pressure tyres, and a four-speed gearbox. The 40/50, propelled by 82 bhp, was the only model after the First World War. Unfortunately, the Napier trade

Another great American name, the Packard of 1936 with 39.2 hp, Super Eight engine. This is a close-coupled coupé version.

Below
This masculine-looking Packard of the 1930s has a straight-eight engine of 6.3 litres and 106 bhp.

mark, a water-tower radiator cap, had gone by the time this model came on the market. After car production had ceased, the company continued to make aero engines and powered many World Land Speed Record holders.

The American Packard brothers began, like most early US car-makers, with a single-cylinder gas-buggy in 1899, but – unlike the others – they used an orthodox three-speed and reverse gearbox rather than an epicyclic one. They went on to make a name in the luxury car field until merged with Studebaker in 1954, by which time Packards were nothing but in-glorious Studebakers with the wrong label.

In between those dates, however, they made some splendid cars, including the first production 12-cylinder engine in 1931. This unit, consisting of two banks of six in a 60 degree vee, displaced 7,300 cc and produced 160 bhp at 3,200 rpm. The cylinder block was alloy and,

with side valves, the removable cylinder heads were flat. The crank-shaft ran in four bearings and particular attention was paid to the oil system, with feeds to every part and special temperature controls.

The engine went into a car which, despite being built in Detroit, rivalled Rolls-Royce in its standards of quality and elegance. The Packard Twelve was virtually hand-built, with the result that only 2,000 of them were ever made during the years 1931–34. With mechanically servo-assisted drum brakes on all four wheels, six volt electrics and a semi-floating rear axle, the Twelve could travel at 105 mph. It weighed two tons or more and, with a second wind-screen for the rear passengers, was much favoured for state occasions and official parades.

In 1939, Packard introduced the Six, with a 3.9 litre, six-cylinder engine producing 100 bhp, which enabled them to move down-market a little. Eight body styles

were available, including a formal sedan and a convertible.

For another large car we stay in the United States, going to the town of Buffalo, New York State, where Pierce-Arrow made one of the most up-market US cars from 1901 until they went out of business in 1938, after an involvement with Studebaker. Six-cylinder engines – with a 12.7 litre capacity in 1914 – really built their fortune. They did not even put their badge on the radiator, as they considered every-one should be able to recognise their cars. Another extravagent touch was that cars came with winter and summer bodies – one of each – so that they could be open or closed to suit the season. Truly a manufacturer with style. They also made Americans sit on the wrong side to drive, offering only right-hand steering up to 1920. This was to allow the chauffeur to dismount

A 1933 American Pierce Silver Arrow with a rather special body and a 175 bhp, V12 engine.

onto the pavement more easily in order to let his charges out.

In 1924, with sales falling off, Pierce-Arrow introduced a cheaper six to try and boost sales. This was the Series 80, the first car made by the company to be fitted with front wheel brakes. The advertising men were no less confident, however, the slogan of the day running: 'The Series 80 owner is never embarrassed by having his car mistaken for any other make. Everybody recognises a Pierce-Arrow.' And, indeed, it sold very well.

By the 1930s, Pierce-Arrow were the luxury department of the Studebaker Corporation, turning out large, powerfully-engined machines of great elegance. The Type 41 of 1931, for example, was fitted with a 6.3 litre straight-eight with side valves and a bore/stroke of 88.9 mm × 127 mm, giving 132 bhp at only 3,000 rpm and a restful top speed of just under 90 mph – this on a car with a 12 ft 2 ins wheelbase with drum brakes all round. The water-cooled engine had a completely counterbalanced crankshaft turning in nine bearings, while Pierce-Arrow made their own gearbox and final drive to complement it. Suspension was conventional, with semi-elliptics all round, while the large-bodied cars could often be had with elegant wire wheels.

Western fans, incidentally, might like to know that Pierce-Arrow made their name and their fortune before 1901 by constructing the famous 'Conestoga' wagons used by so many American pioneers during the 19th century.

Among Rolls-Royce cars for the period, one would have opted for the Phantom II Continental. The Phantom II Short Continental Touring Chassis was made to order, and had a higher compression ratio engine (5.25:1 instead of 4.75:1), sometimes with a high-lift

Introduced in 1930, Rolls-Royce's Phantom II had a hypoid back axle, redesigned combustion chambers and other improvements over the Phantom I. This early version lacked synchromesh gears and centralized lubrication, which did not come until 1933.

In some respects, such as its wooden wheels, this Renault 40CV of the mid 1920s appeared archaic. It had a 9.1 litre six-cylinder engine.

Looking quite at home in such
majestic surroundings, this is a
40/50 hp Rolls-Royce Ghost open
tourer of about 1925. Some of these
were produced in America, but
customers there preferred the real
thing from Derby, England.

cam, a high ratio (3.4:1) back axle,
low-raked steering (F type), flatter,
five-leaf springs, and different
dampers. It would do nearly
100 mph on the cheapest fuel,
go at walking pace in top gear,
accelerate away quite happily and
it would cover 14 miles on a gallon
of fuel in the right conditions.
The Continental was made from
1932 to 1935 with a six-cylinder
engine in two blocks of three (the

light-alloy cylinder head being one-
piece) with pushrod ohv, two valves
per cylinder, and a capacity of
7,668 cc. Rolls-Royce never dis-
close power outputs except to say
that they are 'adequate', but maximum revs were 3,500 rpm. Dual
ignition was by coil and magneto
and, like all Rolls cars, it had the
peculiar Hispano brake servo with
built-in lag.

In 1921, one of the most extraordinary vehicles ever to hit the roads
of Europe was revealed at the Berlin
Motor Show. This was the
Rumpler Tropfenwagen (Teardrop
car), in which Edmund Rumpler
tried to put into practice what he
had learned while designing aircraft

for the First World War. The
chassis was formed from a single
sheet of metal, over which was
placed a boat-like body, pointed at
both ends and festooned with a
variety of fins to deflect air and mud
from the open wheels. It looked like
an open boat with stabilizers and a
cabin on top, but it was not intended to be amphibious.

Rumpler's radical thinking
didn't stop at appearances, however, and he commissioned a
special engine from Siemens and
Halske: it had six cylinders, arranged in three banks of two, set in
broad-arrow formation. Each pis-
ton occupied 74 mm × 100 mm and
the total capacity was 2,580 cc,
which produced around 36 bhp at
2,000 rpm, with water cooling,
overhead valves, aluminium pistons and 12 volt electrics.

This power plant was located in
the rear of the car, with a three-
speed gearbox and final drive built
in unit with it, and it drove the rear
wheels via swing axles. Suspension
was by very long, cantilever leaf
springs.

Inside the car, the intrepid driver
of a Tropfenwagen was confronted
by a central steering wheel, with
room for a passenger on either side
of it, and he viewed the night-time
countryside with the help of a
single, centrally-mounted head-
lamp. The front windows were
curved.

All this revolutionary thinking
did not, apparently, make for quick
and copious sales in the Germany of
1921, however, and Rumpler produced a second model in 1924 with
a conventional, 2.6 litre, four-
cylinder engine of 50 bhp. Two
years later, still in search of elusive
sales success, he turned the engine
round and tried front-wheel drive,
but the company folded soon
afterwards.

1914–39: The Age of the true Sports Car

With brief pauses for such minor disturbances as the General Strike in England, the crash of Wall Street in the USA and the Russian Revolution, the time between the two World Wars was a happy one for the sporting motorist. It was the age of Brooklands, of Bentley victories at Le Mans, of young chaps in open two seaters rushing about the roads.

To take a look at the machinery available for fast-driving members of the public during this time, where better to start than with AC cars, who have been in business since 1908 and who kept things very simple between 1919 and 1963 by using the same engine in all their cars: a 1991 cc, six-cylinder, ohc

The British AC March four-seater, sports tourer of 1934 was a handsome machine, with the familiar 2.0 litre sohc six.

unit which they progressively developed from 35 bhp all the way to 103 bhp.

This made its first appearance in the 16, which featured a three speed transaxle of ill repute. The company were taken into serious motor sport when S. F. Edge arrived there in 1921. A special AC achieved a 105 mph flying mile, while another became the first 1,500 cc car to manage 100 mph in 1922. They raced at Brooklands, took a world 24 hour record at Montlhéry (over 82 mph) and were the first British makers to win a Monte Carlo Rally, in 1926.

Financial problems caused a reorganisation in 1929, with the company returning in 1931 with the AC Ace, much the same as the 16 but now fitted with a conventional, four-speed gearbox and with semi-elliptic front springs in place of the

previous cantilever units. This car, too, set a number of records and was a lively, likeable performer with a character all its own. Various options included a pre-selector gearbox, short chassis, extra power and even a supercharger.

Moving up a notch on the performance and price scales, Alfa Romeo cars of this era were completely different. They were always regarded with particular affection in Britain, until the Second World War, when the Royal Air Force was obliged to bomb the Alfa factories, which did not help the love affair.

There were some really delectable Alfas, like the 8C 2900A, which was simply a two-seater version of the 2.9 litre racing car. It was only offered for sale to suitable amateur sportsmen between the years of 1935–39. These 'production' cars actually won the

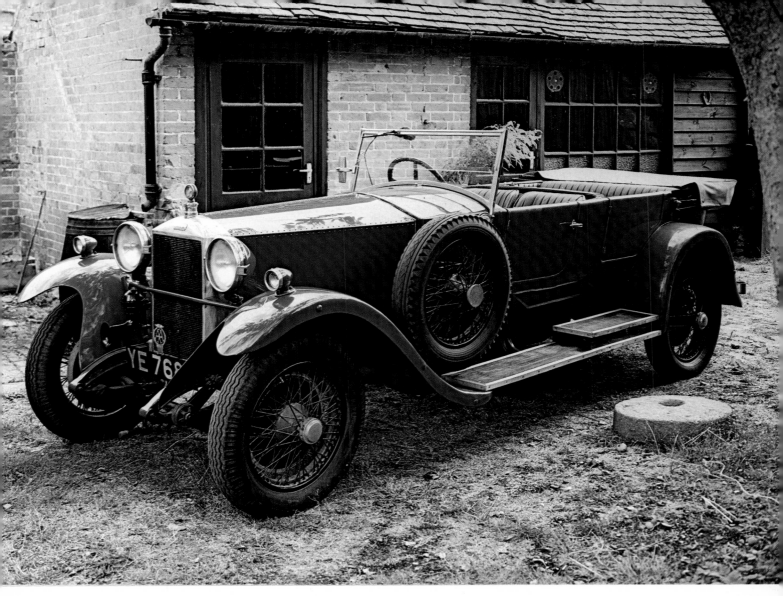

Above
The only model sold in 1927 by
Invicta Cars of Surrey, England was
the 'high chassis' 3.0 litre, this
example being fitted with four-seater
touring bodywork.

A real sports car: Campari in the 1920
four-cylinder, dohc Alfa Romeo racer
during the Targa Florio.

Mille Miglia and the Sao Paulo
Grand Prix in 1936, but only six
of them were ever built. It was a true
sports/racer with 220 supercharged
bhp and a top speed of around
140 mph – hardly beginners stuff.

If one tries to stick with Alfa's
production material, there were
still plenty of classics after the First
World War. The Alfa Romeo RL,
for example, appeared in seven
different versions between 1922 and
1927, one of the nicest being the
Super Sport of 1925, which typified
the Italian sporting car of the time,

135

A road-going version of Alfa's racer: the 1933, straight-eight, 8C 2600 Monza, which was a really shattering experience to drive.

Right
The Earl Howe/Birkin Alfa Romeo 2300 winning Le Mans in 1931.

Right, lower
Nuvolari and Campagnoni on their way to victory in the 1933 Mille Miglia with an Alfa Romeo.

with a vee radiator, vee screen, dashingly-flared mudguards and quick-release wire wheels.

The six-cylinder engine had overhead valves operated by push-rods and rockers, while the crank-shaft ran in four bearings to give 56 bhp at 3,200 rpm. Engine, clutch and gearbox were built in one unit, there being four forward speeds, top supplying up to 80 mph. The chassis consisted of pressed-steel side members with rivetted cross-bracing, suspension being by semi-elliptic leaf springs and friction dampers.

With a $15\frac{1}{2}$ gallon fuel tank mounted on the rear and an all-up weight of well over $1\frac{1}{2}$ tons, the RL needed its pedal-operated, four-wheel drum brakes. Despite its relatively (by Alfa standards) mundane specification, short-wheelbase versions of the RL were raced with success, taking outright victory in the 1923 Targa Florio.

Another production Alfa to achieve sporting fame was the fab-

Above
A truly classic sports car from the years before the Second World War. This 2.9 litre Alfa Romeo raced at Le Mans in 1938, but road-going versions could be had to similar specification, engine from the P3 racing car.

Above
By 1934, Alvis were producing plenty of these – the Speed Twenty, with 2,511 cc, six-cylinder, 87 bhp engine, excellent roadholding and a reasonable price.

ulous 6C 1750, which was introduced at the 1929 Rome Motor Show and promptly walked off with the Mille Miglia three months later. Touring, Sport, Super Sport and Grand Sport versions were built, all fitted with typical Alfa engines: six cylinders, twin overhead camshafts, 65 mm × 88 mm dimensions to give 1,752 cc and, on the supercharged SS version, 85 bhp at 4,500 rpm. The valves were angled at 45 degrees and the camshafts were driven by vertical shafts, while the dry clutch and four-speed gearbox were in unit with the engine. The crankshaft ran in five bearings, with the Roots-type supercharger mounted on its tip.

With a pressed-steel chassis frame, semi-elliptic springs and friction shock absorbers, the SS had exceptional roadholding for its day and could top 90 mph.

In contrast to the very hairy Alfas, Alvis built rather more sedate cars, the pick of these being the biggest-engined model, the 4.3 litre of 1938 in short-chassis, four-seater, touring form. This was a splendid-looking, English machine, even if it did have drawbacks like a vast turning circle, far-from-brilliant brakes, a considerable thirst for fuel, and a coachbuilt body not of top quality. But it was capable of 100 mph at a time when this was rare; it had an imposing appearance, and it was made in small enough numbers to be reasonably exclusive. Orthodox in most respects, the Alvis had a curious front suspension system with a transverse leaf spring, and multiple coil springs to operate its overhead valves. The engine was said to produce 137 bhp at 3,600 rpm and the light touring body made this an effortless machine to drive. With a low axle ratio, it could accelerate smartly, but axle tramp intruded if treatment was too harsh. Several racing specials were developed from this model, and a dry-sump version of the engine was used in military vehicles.

Alvis, by the way, was the first

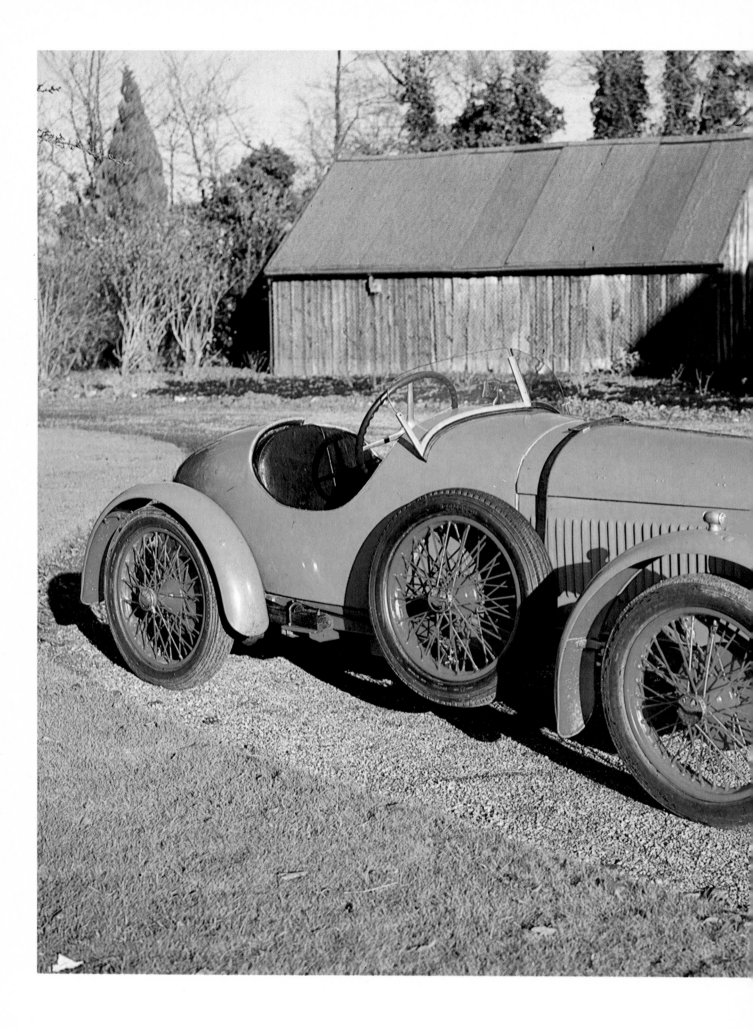

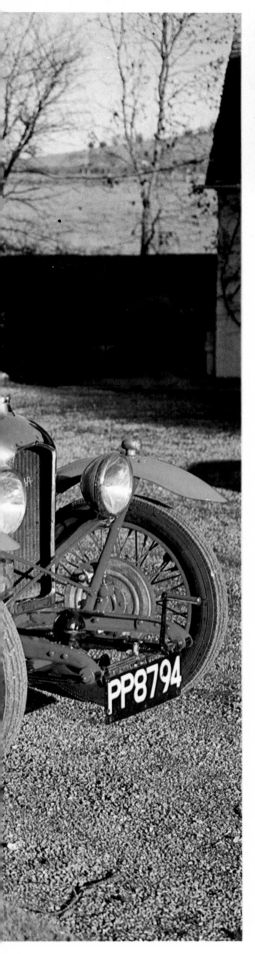

An ambitious design by the Alvis company in 1928, this 12/75 hp had a supercharged, 1,482 cc, ohc engine driving independently sprung front wheels. Despite racing successes at Le Mans and the TT, it never caught on with the buyers.

company in the world to offer for sale an all-synchromesh gearbox. It was made by the German ZF firm in 1931 and used on the Alvis Speed Twenty from October, 1933 onwards. The Germans, having invented it, did not adopt the thing themselves until 1935, when the same ZF design appeared on the Adler Diplomat.

A 1920s equivalent of Ford's modern sporting saloon range was provided by the little French Amilcar, which could be converted from a road car to a racer simply by removing mudguards, lights and other non-essential accoutrements of that type. The 1926 G6 model, whose longevity is demonstrated by the fact that several still appear at British Vintage car races, was a tremendously advanced piece of machinery. The six-cylinder, in-line engine had twin, overhead camshafts, a bore and stroke of 56 mm × 74 mm and a capacity of only 1,093 cc. Despite this, it could

An outstanding small sports car of the 1920s, the Amilcar GCSS Surbaisse was also very pretty.

propel the 1,350 lb car at no less than 109 mph, this performance being made possible by the fitting of a supercharger driven from the nose of the crankshaft, allowing 62 bhp.

Suspension was by semi-elliptic front leaves and quarter-elliptic, cantilever rears, while the brakes followed Amilcar's racing experience and comprised large drums on all four wheels, with mechanical servo assistance. Transmission was by dry-plate clutch, four-speed gearbox and torque-tube final drive.

Racing Amilcars were fitted with roller-bearing crankshafts to give 83 bhp at no less than 6,000 rpm, and proved very successful indeed: the factory claimed 74 wins in 1926, including several *Voiturettes* GPs, while a 1927 version won that year's Monte Carlo Rally. In 1928, the engine size went up to 1,270 cc and competition success continued, but very little actual progress was made on the mechanical specification, the company becoming involved with Hotchkiss before being swallowed up by the Second World War, never to re-appear.

Aston Martin, makers of very English sporting cars, had several models deserving of preservation. The company owed its name to Lionel Martin, who began it, and to the hill-climb at Aston Clinton. In

Kitty Brunell at the wheel of her 1934 'Le Mans' Aston Martin, which she used on that year's Scottish Rally.

the early years, they made relatively small sports cars in tiny numbers. Since the Second World War, they have enjoyed varying fortunes in the hands of several owners and they are now in the very expensive, luxury car business.

The first Astons, in 1922, were heavy and almost without springs, although the cars looked the part, and the company tended to name models after places where they had failed to win races. Owners commented that they could feel every matchstick in the road, but they loved them just the same.

The company first failed in 1925, but returned the next year with a new owner, a pattern which tended to recur right into the 1970s. The engine used before 1936 was a 1.5 litre, ohc unit producing 56 bhp, and this was fitted to such desirable Astons as the International, Le Mans and the Ulster, with varying specifications and states of tune. In their best year, Aston Martin sold

only 100 cars, so they remained fairly exclusive.

The Auburn came from the town of the same name in Indiana, and unhappily the marque died in 1937. There were fours, sixes, eights and a V12, but the obvious choice – the guaranteed 100 mph, 851 Speedster – will be dealt with in another chapter. The Beauty Six which, surprisingly, did not sell particularly well, was nevertheless a memorable car. Introduced in 1920, it had a Continental Red Seal engine, and in roadster form with wire wheels was an attractive car. Although bad sales are not necessarily the sign of a bad car, it did nearly kill the company. E. L. Cord later appeared on the scene and took Auburn onto an entirely new tack, of which more anon.

Bentley only made his own cars between 1921 and 1931, a terribly short life highlighted by wins at Le Mans in 1924, 1927, 1928, 1929 and 1930, all these victories achieved in what were essentially road-going cars. The choice of models lay between the light, 3 Litre of the

early 1920s, the later Speed Six, the 8.0 Litre or the $4\frac{1}{2}$ Litre which (with the 3) made up the bulk of the production, which totalled just over 3,000 vehicles.

The marque was noted for its combination of speed and ruggedness, and was perhaps best typified by the $4\frac{1}{2}$, with its in-line, four-cylinder engine of 4,398 cc, each cylinder having four valves operated by a single, overhead camshaft driven by vertical shaft. This same shaft was also responsible for driving the two magnetos and the water pump, which did not make it too dependable.

Power output started at 100 bhp and was raised to 130 bhp by the time the model ceased production, at which time it could exceed 90 mph in standard form. With a wheelbase of 10 ft 10 ins (apart from eight special cars, which were shor-

The magnificent works of a Bentley Speed Six laid bare. Cars like this, with 180 bhp, won Le Mans in 1929 and 1930 and are now considered the most desirable of the 'old-school' Bentleys.

ter), four-wheel mechanical braking and semi-elliptic springs with friction dampers all round, the chassis was more or less conventional.

There was a supercharged 4½, known as the Blower Bentley, but the designer himself did not approve of this and it was not a great success. Bentley believed that, if

Opposite, top
One of the few high-performance touring cars of its day, the 1924 Ballot 2LT from Paris featured an advanced, sohc engine and front-wheel brakes.

Opposite, lower
Road-going imitation of the Le Mans winner, this 1929 Bentley 4½ litre has touring body work by Van den Plas.

you wanted more power, you should add a few cubic inches to the capacity (following the good old American theory) rather than corrupt the purity of a design by bolting on extras. The Blower car failed to win a race, so perhaps W.O. was right.

We have, in previous chapters, picked out an early Bugatti and a luxury one. Now we add a third, the Type 35, which was one of the loveliest-looking automobiles of all time, both in overall appearance and when one lifted the bonnet to see its gleaming engine with hardly a wire or pipe in sight. With precise steering and super-smooth gear-change, and despite a clutch

The Type 23 'Brescia' Bugatti was introduced in 1910 and continued in production after the First World War. Despite many detail improvements, the design remained largely unchanged in 1926, when the model was superseded.

which is very much IN or OUT, there is nothing quite like a Bugatti. The 35 came in many guises, but all had the straight-eight, non-detachable-head engine with three valves per cylinder. Some were supercharged (Type 35C), or had 2.3 litres (Type 35B) or had other variations. All were drivers' cars par excellence. The model arrived in 1924 and was known by its special wheels, with cast-in alumin-

ium brake drums. It had a roller-bearing engine and was hardly a poor man's toy, but it was a prince among cars.

Nothing could be more different than the bulbous, overwhelming, front-wheel drive, all-American Cord made by the Auburn company. The first version, the L29 with a Lycoming, straight-eight engine, appeared in the late 1920s with all kinds of fancy coachwork. It was a handsome machine, but it failed to sell in large numbers during a period of financial crises in the USA. Cord re-appeared in 1935, with a hideous, Gordon Buehrig body on the Model 810, followed by the 812, which was bigger and even more outrageous. But Cord cannot be omitted from American automotive history and the two-seater convertible was less extreme than the sedan. The engine, like that of the Auburn, was of 4,934 cc in the L29; there was a 4,738 cc vee eight in the 810, which also had an electric gearshift, rather like the pre-selector lever on a Cotal box. However, the Cord transmission was not too good.

The terrible twins, Delage and Delahaye must be dealt with next. There were some six-cylinder Delages such as the 3.2 litre DM of 1926, which some regarded as the best Delage of its period. But there was a more sporting version, called the DMS, whose engine had a re-profiled camshaft, double valve springs, bigger choke, and other modifications which could be complemented by suitably lightweight, sporting bodies.

As for Delahaye, their 1937 Type 145, with 12-cylinder engine and Cotal electric-selection gearbox, was a great contrast to the masculine-looking Delage. This car was very fast, with a 4.5 litre V12, and did well in racing, with 238 bhp and a De Dion rear axle.

From France we must go back to the United States for their ultimate enthusiasts' machine, the Duesenberg, which has often been called the biggest, most expensive and fastest car of its time. It was named (by an American) as the world's finest automobile and the ultimate model was the J. Introduced in 1928, it boasted a straight-eight, twin camshaft Lycoming engine with four valves per cylinder, 6.9 litres, a five-bearing crankshaft with a mercury-filled vibration damper, aluminium connecting rods and pistons and a claimed power output of 265 bhp at 4,200 rpm.

The rest of the car matched the engineering perfection of the motor, with a channel-section steel chassis, six tubular cross-members, semi-elliptic leaf springs all round,

The American Chancellor Miller Speedster of 1928, one of the rare road cars with the Indy-winning engine designed by Harry A. Miller.

hydraulic dampers, centre-lock wire wheels, a wheelbase of up to 12 ft 9½ ins and a weight of well over two tons. Despite its massive size, however, very few contemporary rivals could match its performance, with zero to 100 mph in 21 seconds and a top speed of 116 mph.

In 1932, Duesenberg produced the supercharged SJ, which had more of everything, and was said to reach 100 mph from rest in 17 seconds, and to do 104 mph in second gear.

No bigger contrast is possible than that provided by the eccentric English Frazer-Nash, which was driven by chains and offered the minimum of weather protection. It went on selling in this primitive form right up to 1939, though it was already out-of-date when it started

A magnificent combination of car and scenery: a 1936 Cord Westchester 810 Sedan heads east, with 4,730 cc of Lycoming vee eight driving its front wheels.

The biggest, fastest, most elaborate and most expensive automobile on the American market in 1930 was the Duesenberg Model J. Lycoming supplied 6.9 litre, eight-cylinder engines with twin, chain-driven ohc and four valves per cylinder. It developed 260 bhp at only 4,250 rpm – twice as powerful as anything else you could buy at the time – and would go at 116 mph.

production in 1924, as introduced by Captain Archie Frazer-Nash. From 1910 to 1922, he made the G.N. (Godfrey and Nash) to a similar, but even more primitive formula, with an air-cooled engine out in the open. His Frazer-Nash did at least have a water-cooled engine with a bonnet over it: either an Anzani side-valve unit, a Meadows or a Gough, mounted in a simple, light chassis and driving through a bevel-box, from which a cross-shaft with a separate sprocket and chain for each gear led back to the axle. This crude arrangement gave a lightning-quick gear change,

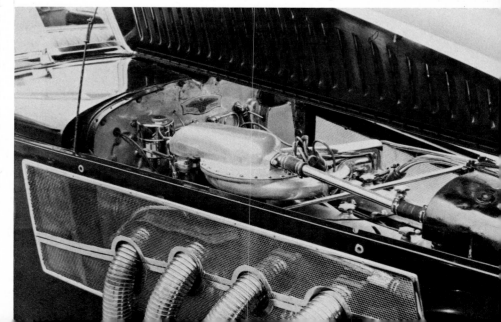

Author James Leasor with his Cord 812 convertible with 4.7 litre vee eight and front-wheel drive – as used by his hero Jason Love in books. As you might expect from so ardent an enthusiast, every part of this car has been immaculately restored.

even though the chains did break from time to time, and the primitive drive scheme has so endeared itself to vintage-car lovers that, instead of being museum-pieces, surviving Frazer-Nashes tend still to be driven on the road. There were a number of models, but the TT Replica had extra prestige and reasonable performance from 1.5 litres, while the Blackburne could even be supercharged if desired.

There were connections between Frazer-Nash and another British sports car of a slightly later date, the HRG, as the G was the same Godfrey referred to in GN. It was only coincidence that his initials also happened to be H.R.G., as the name of the car came from his surname and those of his partners, Halford and Robins. The Herg, as it was usually known, was really a Frazer-Nash which had lost its chain drive. It also used a Meadows engine of 1.5 litres and more or less dispensed with suspension, following the old belief that the only way to make a car handle well on the road was to remove its springs. There were token, quarter-elliptic

Top
Popular sporting vehicle of 1935, a Fiat Balilla with 1,100 cc, ohv, 36 bhp engine. About 1,000 were made.

Above
This extraordinary device is a Bucciali. Built in the early 1930s, it was seen at various shows but was said never to have run on the road.

springs at the front and semi-elliptics at the rear, together with a very open, two-seater body, and an orthodox gearbox and rear axle. It sold cheaply in Britain and its light weight brought worthwhile perfor-mance. It continued in existence with only a few changes – like hydraulic brakes instead of cables – until 1955, but fewer than 250 were made in all, making them real collectors' items.

The Invicta, made from 1925–33, also used engines from Meadows, although the 1.5 litre version was dreadfully underpow-ered and overweight. The cars had rows of external rivets along the bonnet, like contemporary Rolls-Royces, and they were sold as high-performance machines, a claim only justified by the 4.5 litre, low-chassis version, which had underslung springs and a top speed of 95mph. Driven by Donald Healey, who later made himself famous with his own cars, a 4.5 litre Invicta won the 1931 Monte Carlo Rally and took the only *Coupe des Glaciers* awarded on the same year's Alpine, despite which the cars were said to lack roadholding and to turn over too easily when pressed. Nevertheless they looked the part and were typical of their times, with a rugged beauty and all

149

Europe's young men of 1924
hankered after the Isotta-Franschini
Tipo 8A with its 7,372 cc, straight-
eight engine giving 120 bhp and
around 80 mph.

One of the better Frazer-Nashes, the TT Replica. They were an acquired taste, with chains instead of a gearbox and called for driver skill.

the right noises.

Another user of the same engine and a maker of cars of similar character was the Lagonda concern, which – although British – was started by an American, Wilbur Gunn from Springfield, Ohio. The name means 'swiftly-flowing stream' in one of the Red Indian languages and the company made their own cars from 1906 up to 1939, including some lovely-looking machines which had an air of 'rightness' like Bentley, Alvis and others. In most cases they were,

perhaps, better in looks than in performance, but this was true of many vehicles of that era. The pick was the 4.5 litre, Meadows engined car, which continued in production up to 1938. Traditionally, it was a four-seat tourer, but there were also saloons. The LG6, as this model was called, used a straight-six, ohv power unit with twin, SU carburettors and a conventional chassis with half-elliptic springs. It was a simple car, and therein lay its virtue.

Of the other Lagondas, the 2.0 litre was a nice looking car but did not have real performance, while Lagonda enthusiasts do not like the 3.0 litre, although it was of similar design. A number of coachbuilders

designed bodies for the 4.5, mostly on Vanden Plas lines. It's top speed was around 95 mph, so perhaps the similar weight but lower power of the 3.0 was its main drawback.

No car could be more different from a Lagonda than a Lancia. While the British car was the epitome of sound, orthodox engineering, Vincenzo Lancia started a company in 1906 whose products

Opposite, top
Donald Healey and the Invicta in which he won the 1931 Monte Carlo Rally.

Opposite, lower
A striking-looking Lancia Astura with convertible coachwork, built in 1937, with a 2.6 litre vee eight and 73 bhp.

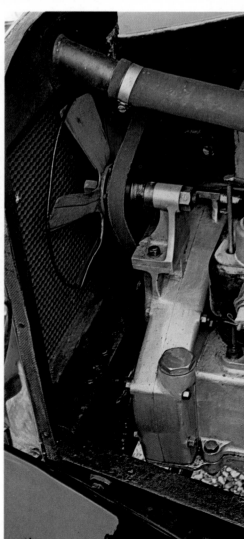

When the Lagonda 11.1 hp light car was introduced in 1913, it was packed with radical, new features: monocoque construction, an anti-roll bar on the suspension and the world's first fly-off handbrake, to list but a few. By 1922, the same basic car was still popular and the engine (right) had been enlarged to an 11.9 hp, of which this is an immaculate example.

Opposite, top and above
By all accounts, it took a brave man to sit in either seat of this car – the SS Jaguar 100 of 1935. With up to 3.5 litres and 125 bhp and a very short wheelbase, it required considerable skill to drive quickly. It proved hard to beat in rallies, however, and sold well.

Below
Looked on as a sports car in export markets because of its superior handling, the Lancia Lambda was never intended as anything other than everyday transport in Italy, many of them being used as taxis.

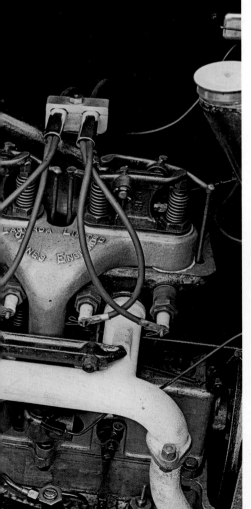

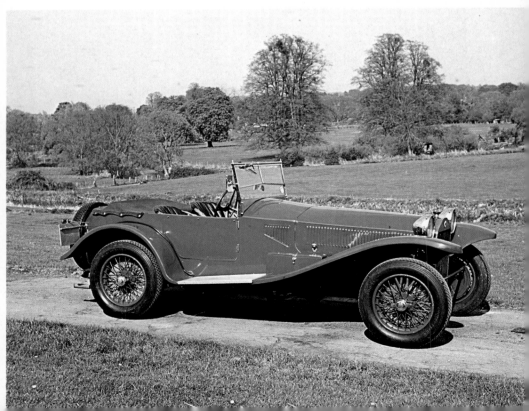

This was the one to have in the late 1920s, if you had to have four seats. The Seventh Series Lancia Lambda with independent suspension and a 2.4 litre, narrow-angle vee four.

Opposite, top
Another Lancia, the Dilambda with a narrow-angle, ohc vee eight engine; over 1,700 were made between 1929 and 1932.

have always been marked by ingenious solutions to problems which other people solved in simpler ways. Some people think Lancia used complication for complication's sake, but the Italian's cars had independent front-wheel suspension in 1921, long before most people had thought of it; a foot-starter in 1913, and their cars were the first in Europe with electric lights. Lancia also pioneered the vee engine, the transaxle (a combined gearbox and rear axle now much favoured by Italian designers) and introduced unitary construction long before Budd in America.

Despite all this, there was only one Lancia worth considering in the classic context, and that was the Lambda, which was produced from 1922 to 1931 in nine different series. The engine progressed from 2.0 litres to 2.4, and then to 2.6, always

as a narrow-angle vee four. The original model produced 48 bhp and weighed only 15 cwt, giving the car 70 mph when others were straining for 55. It was indeed a motoring milestone. Later Lancias could approach 80 mph, yet were considered touring cars in Italy; they were so far ahead of English cars in the early 1920s, that they were rated as sports cars in the UK. In Italy, the Lambda was even used as a taxi (with closed bodywork).

An English marque, perhaps less well-known in other countries despite impeccable credentials, was Lea-Francis, which lived from 1904 to 1953. Around 1930, the 'Leaf' was the car for the sporting young Englishman to have, in particular the Hyper Sports with a Cozette supercharger attached to its 1.5 litre

An unusual Mercedes, a Type 150 with four-cylinder, 1.49 litre, 55 bhp, rear engine from 1934. A curio.

Meadows engine and a vast fuel tank to keep this happy. The first Lea-Francis sports car was the 12/40 of 1925, and there were some less successful models until they produced the Ace of Spades, a 2.0 litre, ohc which ran in parallel to the 12/40 until 1935. The Hyper, with its rear-sloping radiator, was a development of the 12/40 and would reach 90 mph. It won the Tourist Trophy in 1928 and managed to finish well up (sixth and eighth) in the Le Mans 24-hour race, showing reliability allied to lively performance. The 'Leaf' was not made in the numbers of some competitors, nor did it achieve their success, but it was an amiable companion.

During its early years, the Le Mans 24-hour race was confined to production sports cars with four-seater bodywork, a rule which certainly suited the old-established French firm of Lorraine Dietrich, who took second and third places in 1924, first and third in 1925 and swept the first three places overall in 1926. The cars used for these remarkable achievements were all versions of the 15 hp tourer introduced shortly after the First World War. This was a six-cylinder machine with overhead valves operated by exposed pushrods and

rockers, a bore and stroke of 75 mm × 130 mm and a displacement of 3.5 litres. With double oil coolers and twin, Zenith carburettors, this produced 70 bhp at 3,500 rpm and would propel the one-ton car at up to 93 mph. Stopping at Le Mans was achieved with the help of special Perrot-type servo-assisted brakes.

The alphabet now brings us to Mercedes, who seemed always to be in the van of technical progress during this period. In the early 1920s, they produced a 1.5 litre sports car of fairly modest dimensions and even more modest performance, but this was all changed in 1923, when the company became the first to offer supercharging to

Lautenschlager won the *GP de France* in 1914 on this very modern-looking Mercedes. With 115 bhp from 4.5 litres, three of these shaft-driven cars took the first three places.

Below
Le Mans in 1930, with Caracciola leading Birkin in the Mercedes–Bentley battle which ended only when the Merc came to a halt.

The MG every collector wants – a TA like this 1937 example, with semi-elliptic springs and wire wheels.

the general public. To go with the booster, the 1,499 cc engine was upgraded, with the full benefits of Mercedes' racing and aeronautical experience. Twin, overhead camshafts, driven by a vertical shaft at the rear of the block (as on the 1914 Grand Prix racer) were substituted for the single camshaft used previously; the 65 mm × 113 mm cylinders were lined with steel, with welded water jackets.

The supercharger was a Roots-type unit, which forced air through the carburettor. It was engaged by its own clutch, being actuated when the driver applied full throttle, which action raised the power from 25 bhp to over 40 bhp, taking the car up to almost 70 mph.

Also developed from the 1914 GP car was a double-cone clutch, which took the drive via a four-speed gearbox and a torque-tube to the rear axle. Suspension was by semi-elliptic leaves and friction

The first MG was really a modified Bullnose Morris, produced in 1922, seen here with the designer and Morris agent Cecil Kimber at the wheel.

dampers all round and braking was available only on the rear wheels. Quick-release wire wheels completed the picture.

If 70 mph does not sound too exciting, it should be remembered that this little car led directly to the heavy metal of the Mercedes

The Twin-Cam, 3.0 litre Sunbeam was a great joy to its owner in the 1920s, even if the chassis did flex. This is a 1926 model.

38/250, with its howling supercharger frightening the onlookers as three tons or so of very fast car hurtled down the highway. There were few faster cars apart, perhaps, from the big Bentleys, with which they did battle at Le Mans, in Ireland and elsewhere.

The 7.0 litre sports cars of 1929 onwards, culminating in the 1938 540K with a smaller, 5.4 litre engine, were never to be forgotten. They were given one model name in Germany and a different one in England, which complicates matters, but the 27/170/225 SSK (as the factory called it in 1927) had a straight-six of 7.1 litres with 225 bhp at 3,200 rpm using the supercharger, giving a 109 mph top speed.

By 1931, there was a similar-looking machine under the label of SSKL (L for Light), which had a visibly drilled chassis. This had the same dimensions, but produced 300 bhp at the same engine speed, and had a top speed of almost 150 mph! Both models carried twin spare wheels on a truncated tail, and the KL was a real sports racer. The 'kompressor' (the K of the model designation) came in when the throttle pedal was pressed hard and was only supposed to be used in short bursts of a few seconds. The later – and gentler – 500 series had smaller engines of eight cylinders, less power and more luxurious coachwork, but the SSKL was the real classic.

Another hard-to-find car was the English Squire, of which not more than ten were made. They were built to a very high standard of workmanship and used a 1.5 litre, dohc Anzani engine said to produce 105 bhp, driving through a pre-selector gearbox, which was typical of the time (1934–36). Squire's aim was to build the best car of its kind, without regard for price. They were beautiful-looking vehicles with bodies by various coachbuilders in two and four-seater tourer form, and they attained a reputation out of all proportion to the number made.

A much more mundane vehicle was the British Riley, but it sold well and there were three successful sporting versions which looked somewhat alike: the Imp, the Sprite, and the MPH. There was also a Brooklands Riley which was really a racing car, but which was driven on the road.

The company began around the turn of the century and continued until they were swallowed by the Nuffield Organisation. The three two-seat models referred to had varying engine sizes, the Imp using the 1,110 cc Nine, the MPH the six-cylinder 1,633 cc or 1,726 cc ohv unit, and the Sprite the 1,496 cc four. They were all of 1934–6

A Riley Monaco of 1934 which, with its high-cam engine, was way ahead of its time.

vintage and offered good performance with attractive lines.

Stutz came from Indianapolis, home of the famous American racing circuit, between 1911 and 1935. With such a location, they could hardly help becoming involved in motor sport and a Stutz Black Hawk finished second at Le Mans in 1928 and fifth in 1929, which helped sales considerably.

Their best road car, however, was the Bearcat, one of America's fastest sports cars in the 1930s. Top of the range was the Super Bearcat, with a magnificent, straight-eight engine of 85.7 mm × 114.3 mm and 5,277 cc. With twin, chain-driven overhead camshafts, four valves per cylinder, a nine-bearing crank and coil/distributor ignition, it provided 156 bhp at 3,900 rpm and the short-chassis version (with 8 ft 9 ins wheelbase) was guaranteed to do 100 mph.

Electrics were only six volt, while the clutch, three-speed gearbox and semi-floating rear axle were all conventional, but the chassis frame was exceptionally strong, with huge side members and five cross-members, while the brakes were very effective, with hydraulic units on

Opposite, top
An American Stutz 4.9 litre Black Hawk speedster running in the 24-hour race at LeMans, in 1930.

Opposite, lower
A different kind of Stutz Bearcat, dating from an earlier period (1914 on) with four-cylinder Wisconsin engine producing 60 bhp.

Above
Another forerunner of things to come, the SS, which became Jaguar after the Second World War. This was a 2½/2½ litre saloon of 1938.

Below
Re-bodied 1930 Austin Seven by the Swallow Coachbuilding Company of Coventry, England. The firm, owned by William Lyons, became Jaguar.

An Airline saloon, in this case the SS, produced in 1935, before that company were called Jaguar.

all wheels and vacuum servo assistance.

The fine English Talbot car was designed by a Swiss and had French connections. In the 1930s, one could select a Talbot 105 designed by Georges Roesch and produced in London, often with a French Darracq body. It had a six-cylinder, ohv engine of 3.0 litres which ran remarkably silently, with an equally silent start from a permanently-engaged dynamotor which needed 24 volts and a steep hill to work properly; most had Wilson pre-selector gearboxes using the bottom gear band as a

clutch, which became snatchy with wear. The 105 looked like a battleship, did well in racing but was really a touring car.

A tiny corner of posterity might be reserved for the Czechoslovakian make of Z, produced by the splendid-sounding Akciova spoleċnost Ċeskoslovenká zbrojovka of Brno. In 1931, they produced the Z13 with a remarkable, eight-cylinder, 1,500 cc engine. A two-stroke unit, its pistons were arranged in parallel pairs, with each pair of cylinders having two pistons, but only one combustion chamber. A Roots blower helped this complicated engine produce 60 bhp and persuaded the car to manage 95 mph. The company did not survive the Second World War, which was rather ironic, as they started life making armaments for the First World War.

Perhaps not a sports car, but a desirable two-seater Wills Sainte Claire of 1926, with six-cylinder engine and lots of refinement.

8 1939–79: Wheels for the Workers

Alfa Romeo were the first mass-producers to bring twin cam-shafts and five forward gears to the High Street in a shopping car. Their products remained the province of enthusiasts or specialists until the advent in 1954 of the 1300 cc, four-cylinder Giulietta in pretty, two-door coupé form or as a rather boxy but impudent saloon. The shape of the coupé model is one of those classic outlines which has remained undated despite 20 years' production under various names like Sprint, Junior and lastly, the

GTV range. It ranks with the MGB GT as a shape so right from the start that it has just gone on and on. Strangely, the Alfa factory history does not give the designer any credit for the body.

This was the model which brought Alfas into the mass-market, and they have gone from strength to strength in everything but profits, which seem to elude them. Their latest project, the front-wheel drive Alfasud (made at a new factory near Naples in Southern Italy), has been a great

The Italians have joined the small, front-wheel-drive car market, but with added vigour, thanks to lively machines (like this 1973 Alfa Sud) which provide basic transport and better-than-average performance.

success with drivers but a financial disaster. It was introduced in 1971 and has been offered in various engine sizes and states of tune, from the basic, 1186 cc, flat-four ohc up to a 1500 cc version in 1978. The Sud has everything; good looks, performance and handling; it must rank as perhaps the best, mass-

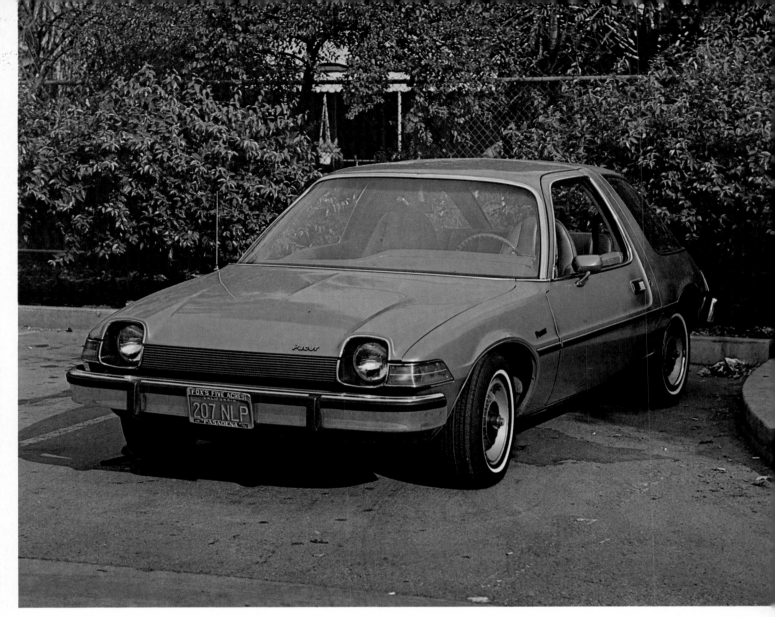

produced small car so far. It is ironic that, although the public love it, it cannot make money for its producers.

American Motors have long been among the less successful companies, although they too have made some good cars as well as weird ones. The less said about the Pacer the better, although it is so odd as to almost qualify as a classic, with its two different-sized doors, swollen-pear shape, and indifferent performance from a relatively large engine. They also made a curious device called the Gremlin, which must have been one of the world's ugliest cars. Also, whatever it may mean in the US, the name in English is that of 'a mischievous sprite alleged to cause mishaps' to quote the Oxford English Dictionary.

The German company, Audi, went through a series of changes,

from producing monsters down to making flimsy-bodied two-strokes, until, in 1965, they came out with a 1.7 litre, four-cylinder ohc machine with front-wheel drive and this set the tone for their modern cars. They have now gone rather up-market with sporting coupés, fuel injection, and special steering arrangements said to provide more safety.

Which saloon to choose? Well, perhaps the Audi 50, which is really a VW Polo, but which is sold only in certain countries. This is the most representative modern small car, although in England, Audi tend to sell quite expensive, large cars, well upmarket of Volkswagen, which is perhaps a factory policy. But the Audi 50 is a little two-door saloon with 1,093 cc and front-wheel drive, a neat and tidy package with 50 bhp at 5,800 rpm from an iron

One that should never have made it? The incredibly ugly – and slow – American Motors Pacer. It may turn out to be a collector's piece by virtue of its looks, or just because it helped seal the fate of its ailing manufacturers.

block, alloy head, and a belt-driven ohc. It will do 88 mph, 37 miles to the gallon, and is a good example of a small economy car which is nevertheless capable of speeds which would confound our grandfathers.

Which is a convenient introduction to Austin, one of the names under which Sir Alec Issigonis's inimitable Mini-Minor was produced. It began in 1959 as the Austin Seven, with a stylized figure seven in the middle (se7en). Austin and Morris were then partners as the British Motor Corporation, which became British Leyland and then Leyland Cars.

The Mini has always been just the Mini to the public who loved it, and not the Morris Mini-Minor or the Austin Seven or the BMC Mini or any of its other titles. It would be difficult to find something new to say about it, as it has gone down so well with its buyers, that it still ranks high in the British sales charts after nearly 20 years of production. It has a terrible ride, is noisy, the driving position is ideal for a monkey but difficult for a human, there is no luggage space, but it still sells millions against much more modern and superior designs. Strangely enough, the Mini made little money for its makers because they pitched the initial price too low, but it should be doing well by now. The much more attractive Italian Innocenti design was never adopted in England, and the original rounded model was better looking than the later variations with long noses and short bottoms.

The Mini must rank with the Model T and a few others as a major step in the development of the motor car. The door-bins fitted to early models (and which were said to strengthen the doors) held four pints of milk or wine, while the sliding windows were fine if you opened the front half and not the rear. Now that Minis are all smart, with winding windows and vestigial bins, they have lost a little of their special quality, but they will still exercise your liver as well as a horse.

Two other Austins must be selected from the galaxy of models: the first of these was the A40, which pioneered the now-universal Hatchback in 1958. It was known as the A40 Farina, and used the 948 cc, ohv A35 engine which also went into the Morris Minor 1000, another long-lived public servant. The A40 looked like a little square-rigger, and the estate version would carry almost anything. It was almost indestructible and many are still running.

Its companion of the day was the Austin-Healey Sprite, the original 'frog-eye' model with headlamps poking out of the bonnet in def-

First of the 'smaller' Armstrong-Siddeley products introduced in 1956 in an attempt to spread their market downwards, the 234 used a four-cylinder, 2.3 litre motor but was bodily based on the Sapphire range. It was not a success.

Bottom
Revolutionary things have been happening at Volkswagen in recent years, with an almost total rejection of their old, air-cooled rear engines in favour of water-cooling and front-wheel drive. This 900 cc Polo is the smallest – and possibly the best – of the new model range.

erence to some US law which would not allow low-mounted lamps. It looked horrid but caught on, with its 948 cc, ohv engine (as in the A40, Minor, and MG Midget). Later versions were badge-engineered MGs, universally known as Spridgets, and are still going strong after an incredible 20 years for those who like wind-in-the-hair and bottom-near-the-ground. Donald Healey, a famous racing driver, lent his name and BMC made the thing. The Austin version expired in 1971 but the Midget and the same company's Spitfire (both now with the same engine) are the only surviving, mass-produced sports cars with soft tops.

Then there was the Bond, which one doesn't like to speak about in public, but which must have its place in the history of the motor-car. The Bond Minicar, Marks A to G, from 1949 to 1967, had three wheels, one in front, and a single-cylinder, 197 cc, two-stroke motor-cycle engine driving the front wheel and steering with it. It reminded one of the original horrors of around 1899, had no rear suspension, but had a devoted following. The wheelbase was 5 ft 6 ins and to park it, one drove the front in, picked up the rear end and lifted it sideways. There was a convention at the time of having no reverse gear as this entitled the driver to operate on a motor-cycle licence without taking a car test. For the very poor, it offered a means of locomotion less comfortable than a bicycle but requiring less effort except when parking.

It is sad that the Borgward left us,

Opposite, top
When it appeared at the end of 1959, this vehicle caused a sensation – the Austin Seven or Morris Mini-Minor, now known universally as the Mini, came with a transverse 848 cc ohv four-cylinder engine driving the front wheels, four gears in its sump, rubber suspension and a supremely practical shape. Alex Issigonis' masterpiece later demonstrated its versatility by winning countless rallies and races.

Opposite, lower
Much loved by collectors despite its crudities and lack of real performance, the 'frog-eye' Austin-Healey Sprite of 1958 had a 948 cc engine, but weighed only half a ton and would do 80 mph.

as it made many friends between 1949 and 1961 when in production. The one to have was the Isabella, in either saloon or coupé form, preferably the TS (Touring Sport), with a 1.5 litre engine producing 75 bhp and almost 100 mph. They did well in racing with developed versions – some with ohc – giving up to 100 bhp; the well-known English-based driver Bill Blydenstein competed with success before turning his talents to Vauxhall. Unfortunately, Borgward ran out of money and the Isabella disappeared, although the engines lived on in racing cars.

Hardly recognisable from this angle, the sole surviving prototype of Citroen's immortal 2CV was nevertheless very similar to the production cars which followed – even those sold today. The concept, by Pierre Boulanger in 1939, called for 'four wheels under an umbrella,' which was pretty much how it turned out.

After leaving Borgward, we come to something really unique in the form of the Citroen 2CV, which has kept rural France on the move since 1949. Pierre Boulanger, who designed the *Deux Chevaux*, was said to have been told to make an umbrella on four wheels which would carry a basket of eggs without breaking them, hence the most comfortable seats in the motor industry – removeable for picnics – and supple suspension. The 2CV may look like a nightmare and sound peculiar – with a flat-twin engine which started with 375 cc and has since grown to a mighty 602 cc – but it is marvellous transport. Although a little expensive to repair when the time comes to reline the inboard drum brakes, it floats along in the utmost comfort, can carry any number of people, a few ponies, grandfather clocks, a bale or two of hay, and be hosed down inside afterwards. Doors and bonnet almost fall off, seats slip out, and it uses about as much fuel as a

Memorable only for its Variomatic transmission, the DAF appeared in 1959. With a system of belts and pulleys providing stepless, automatic transmission, the driver had only to select forward or reverse. Only 600 cc and 22 bhp of air-cooled, twin-cylinder power meant very little performance, however, and it never really caught on.

cigarette lighter. They even have races for them. No family should be without one.

Chevrolet comes next, with the taxing question of which model? It would be easy to choose one of the eternal Chevvies from the 'Good Ole' Days', but the later ones were more of a puzzle, with the company selling two million cars a year in an enormous assortment of models. There was the Chevvy II and the Chevelle, but perhaps the best was the Vega, a sub-compact with four-cylinder, ohc, aluminium engine with cogged-belt drive to its camshaft. It was in no way typically American, except perhaps that the trend when it was introduced in 1971 was to go for smaller cars. It featured coil spring rear suspension, and could be had in many body styles from hatchback coupé to station wagon.

Colts are Japanese cars made by Mitsubishi, but in the US they are sold through Dodge, as Chrysler have an interest. A complicated story, but it represents the modern

Fiat's 1500 revolutionised the European saloon car market when it appeared in 1935 with a short-stroke, ohv, six-cylinder engine, independent front suspension and an aerodynamic body with recessed headlights.

Opposite, lower
A real classic, Fiat's baby Topolino ran until 1948, propelled by 13 mighty bhp from a 569 cc front engine.

development of cars which are perhaps orthodox and unexciting but which are regarded by the public as reliable and fault-free. This policy, shared by Datsun, Honda and Toyota as well as by Colt, has led to enormous sales at the expense of established companies in Europe and the US. All the Japanese makers are learning very fast about styling, engineering and interiors, where they have done some odd things in the past. Colt are one of the newest companies on the scene, with aggressive advertising on the theme: 'Move up to a Colt' They are successful in Britain, although their vehicles are very

The Chevrolet Corvair appeared in 1960 with a 2.3 litre, air-cooled, flat-six engine mounted in the rear – which caused controversial handling. The owner of this 1963 version managed to cope, however.

ordinary rather than something outstanding to move up to. Their Celeste 1400 SR Coupé, which is a cut above the routine saloons but not too rare or expensive, is probably the pick of the bunch. There are seven different versions of this one model, but it offers 82 bhp from 1.5 litres, and 96 mph maximum, which is good for such a small engine in a sizeable car. The styling may not be up to the best Italian standards but it is acceptable.

We must include DAF, whose remaining car is now called a Volvo 66. As the Daffodil, it was the only Dutch car and very individual, with its stepless, rubber-belt automatic

transmission and no manual option. The initials stood for van Doornes Automobilfabriek and it was the first Dutch car after Spyker disappeared in 1925. DAF arrived in 1959 with all-independent suspension and a 600 cc, air-cooled, flat-twin front engine driving the rear wheels. It always looked rather quaint, but the engine capacity went up to 750 cc, then 844 cc, and finished with a Renault 1100 cc engine – even 1440 cc for competition – still with the rubber bands. But the car to have was the original DAF with the smallest engine, which had little power but much charm, and the strange requirement of stopping the engine before reversing.

From Japan we should include a Datsun as a people's car. The Cherry was not extraordinary in any way except that a great many examples were sold and gave good

service. There were more than 20 versions of the Cherry F II, but the 1200, standard two-door sedan, which we would call a fixed-head coupé, was bottom of the range. It was powered by a four-cylinder, four-stroke, 1,171 cc engine driving the front wheels, offering 58 bhp, 93 mph and 38 mpg, despite pushrod-operated valves. This was surprising from such an everyday layout, but the Cherry was a typical example of thoughtful Japanese engineering. The company name came from the initials of founders Den, Aoyama and Takeuchi in 1914, and Datsun is literally the son of DAT. At one time they made the

Opposite, top
A modern-day classic if only by virtue of its size: Fiat's 126.

Opposite, lower
An Englishman's idea of heaven in the mid-1950s? A Ford 100E Anglia and a country cottage.

Right
Post-Second World War Germany
was not the most affluent of places,
so that those who needed transport
badly enough sometimes had to
resort to drastic measures. This is one
such device, based on a four-seater
Isetta bubble car and built by BMW
as the '600' in 1957.

Below
The Hillman Imp of 1965, with only
875 cc, nevertheless managed to win
numerous rally awards, especially in
conditions like this, when the rear
engine was a positive aid to traction.

Austin A40 under licence, which
may be why the Cherry looked
so familiar.

From the orthodox to the really
way-out: Dyna Panhard, which
finished up belonging to Citroen
and finally vanished in 1967. A pity,
because Panhard had been in the
business from 1889 and used to
advertise as the oldest car-makers.
At first they made racers and giants,
until in 1945, with the Second
World War behind them, they
produced, like a rabbit out of a hat,
the Dyna-Panhard. It was certainly

strange, with an air-cooled, flat-
twin, 610 cc engine driving the rear
wheels, to a design by J. A.
Gregoire, the specialist in front-
wheel drive cars. It had light alloy
bodywork to enable it to perform
well enough on 15 bhp, and an
overdrive top gear. Soon it went up
to 750 cc and then to 850 cc (1952)
with more power. It looked somewhat like the Renault 4CV, something which could not be said of the
later, front-wheel drive Dyna-
Panhard 24CT, which was an enormous machine for only 850 cc, yet

Opposite, top
A company who deserved a better
fate, Jowett introduced this car in
1947, complete with torsion-bar
independent suspension all round,
aerodynamically-shaped, unitary
body/chassis, light weight, good
handling and a top speed of 80 mph,
with a 1.5 litre, flat-four engine
driving the rear wheels.

Opposite, lower
The hideous Metropolitan, built at the
Austin works in Birmingham for the
American market and sold through
Nash between 1954 and 1956. This
convertible, with its A40 engine, was
a huge success in the USA.

The latest heir to the Mini birthright is Ford's front-wheel drive Fiesta, produced all over the world with various engines. It first appeared in Britain, with motors ranging between 957 cc and 1,296 cc.

would do 100 mph. Special versions of this won the Monte Carlo rally and did well at Le Mans, and it must be the car with the most performance from the smallest engine. With room for five people, nothing else like it has ever been made, which surely qualifies it as a classic.

The giant Fiat company put most of Italy's inhabitants (and those of a good many other countries) on wheels. Their classic designs were the pre-war Fiat Topolino (Mouse), the postwar 600 and – in later times – the 127 and 128, all of them in the small car class which Fiat dominated before they moved their sights up a bracket or two. The Mouse returned around 1948, along with the new 500 with an air-cooled twin behind it, but this did not sell well – at first. The 1955

model 600 with 633 cc was more of a proper car, but millions of new 500s eventually littered the Italian roads. Despite being very much a minis-cule car, the 500 had full-size characteristics and was no toy, while the 600 was in some ways more orthodox and therefore less enjoyable.

Ford of Britain, although their various Anglias, Prefects, Escorts, Consuls and Cortinas were all very worthy cars and served many people well, do not have any special char-isma. There is no doubt that the best postwar British Ford is the Fiesta, which is superior in every way to the older models and is more than likely to join the Model T as a special chapter in the Ford history book.

The old, side-valve models slog-ged along, powered racing cars and

did many other marvellous things, but – much as the 100E and the later 105E may be loved – the Fiesta has more panache and style about it than any of the earlier Fords. The Fiesta comes in many varieties and engine sizes, and, although it has yet to challenge the rally crown of the Escort and looks pretty much like any small Fiat/VW/Peugeot, it has a distinctive character lacking in some of its rivals.

Ford of USA offer an enormous choice in the post-1939 era, but their sub-compact Pinto (like the Chevrolet Vega) sums up a motoring era. The Pinto put Ford ahead of Chevrolet, and was pretty much of a committee car, with a four-cylinder engine and a rather ordinary specification of drum brakes and three-speed gearbox, but the two-door sedan had a handsome air

about it, clean and uncluttered, and is worthwhile not so much for what it did but what it was. After all, this is not intended to be a selection of the world's best automobiles, but of those that had something loveable about them or represented a new development or a change in public tastes, such cars being significant monuments of their time.

An odd one to slip in here would be the German Heinkel, later the Trojan in England. This was made from 1955 onwards with two wheels in front, one behind and a 175 cc air-cooled engine driving the rear wheel. It was very small and could be parked nose-on to the pavement; the door, which was the front of the motor-car, swung outwards with the steering wheel and column to disgorge the inmates onto the footpath.

It felt most unsafe but served well as an economy vehicle, a hangover from the super-economy machines which served hard-up Germans after 1945. Now that they are so prosperous, it seems unbelievable that they should once have wanted what were virtually cycle-cars, but the Heinkel reminds us of what used to be.

Also from this period, we simply must have a Hillman Minx, which went on for 34 years and made a come-back for a further three years (1967–70) as the New Minx. It first

Intended as a semi-GT car, the Ford Mustang was an immediate best-seller when it appeared in 1964. In less than 18 months, they sold over half a million examples, the cheapest version using a 120 bhp, six-cylinder engine. This 1973 model has vee eight power, however.

began in 1932, but a representative model would come from about 1956, with 1,290 cc ohv engine, which was both bigger than the earlier models and smaller than the later ones. The Minx was one of the first successful, popular, light cars with reasonable performance, comfort and economy and deserves to be preserved. Perhaps it was never brilliant, but it pleased most of the customers, was a commercial success and was the absolute archetype of what people drove in its day. Hillman became part of Rootes, then part of Chrysler and finally part of Peugeot/Citroen, so they are no longer with us. The Minx had a normal, water-cooled engine up front, driving the rear wheels and it just went on and on. There was also a trendy looking thing called a Minx Californian with lots of gimmickry, but this was not typical.

We would like to include a Holden simply because it is Australian and there are so few Australian cars. That big country is hard on machinery, so any local product must be tough and reliable. Holdens came from America's General Motors in 1948 and were

Above
Ambitious for 1954, the Panhard Dyna Saloon had all-alloy bodywork and easily removable engine/ transmission and back axle units. It could top 80 mph with six people.

Below
When it first appeared in 1956 with 845 cc and 30 bhp, the Renault Dauphine found instant favour with the public, despite criticism of the rear-engined handling.

Above
Developed secretly during the Nazi occupation of France, the Renault 4CV appeared in 1944 with a rear-mounted, four-cylinder ohv engine, all independent suspension, hydraulic brakes and three forward gears. This was its fastest version, the 760 cc, 38 bhp 'Sport'. When 4CV production ceased in 1961, over a million had been made.

Below
France's latest breed of small, family saloons include such devices as the Renault 5, with three doors, supple suspension and the ability to travel minor roads at high speed.

Opposite, top
The ideas of Alec Issigonis have done much to shape the future of basic motor cars. This is his Morris Minor of 1949, with side-valve, 918 cc motor, monocoque bodyshell, rack-and-pinion steering and torsion-bar independent suspension. It set new standards in passenger-car handling and was Britain's answer to the VW Beetle, selling over a million. The headlamps on later variants moved into the wings to meet US rules.

Opposite, lower
One that almost made it. Immediately after the Second World War, dozens of Americans tried their hand in the automobile business, most without success. The Playboy Motor Car Corporation of Buffalo, New York, produced 97 of these compact, three-seater convertibles fitted with 2.6 litre, 40 bhp Continental engines and automatic transmission.

Below
Pretty but unsuccessful, Studebaker's compact car of the early 1960s was the six-cylinder Lark, which could be had (like this 1962 version) as a convertible. It didn't save the company, however.

developments of a Buick which failed to make the market ten years earlier. With a fairly dreary specification of straight-six, 2.2 litre engine and three-speed gearbox with column change, they didn't look too good. Later Holdens looked smarter, although there was an unfortunate Vauxhall influence from the British end of General Motors. The best was probably the 1966 Premier 3.0 litre sedan which was pretty basic but was Australia's own (more or less) and would survive the conditions and come up smiling.

Back in America, Hudson represent a style that is no longer with us. The name goes back to 1909 when J. L. Hudson, who ran a department store in Detroit, put up the cash. Later they tied up with Essex (whom we have seen before), but the 1950 Hornet which did so well in US stock-car racing might be the one to look for. This had a 145 bhp, six-cylinder, 5.0 litre engine, and was the last one which sold well, although it was not too beautiful.

Later ones were much like the products of Nash, with whom they amalgamated to become American Motors. The 1951–54 cars were said to be the ones to have, although none would win a beauty contest. Hardtops and convertibles rated best, while earlier 'step-down' models with a low centre of gravity (from 1948) were much sought-after, despite having pre-Second World War six and eight-cylinder engines.

Jowett are included on merit for being ahead of their time. We are talking, of course, of the Javelin, which disappeared when Ford bought Briggs, the old Yorkshire firm who made bodies for Jowett. They had made peculiar economy cars for years, but in 1947 they introduced the Javelin, a streamlined, advanced-looking, four-door saloon with fastback, flat-four, 1.5 litre, ohv engine, monocoque construction, torsion-bar suspension, and light weight. It gave 80 mph and 30 mpg and should have been a winner, but it lasted only until 1954

Right, top
Early attempt at motor car manufacture by the Japanese – a 1958 Subaru 360, with a rear-mounted, twin-cylinder engine and torsion bar suspension. From this, they could only improve – and they have.

Right, centre
The Aronde was one of Simca's most popular cars, well over a million being sold during a 12 year production run which started in 1951. Apart from the engine – a 45 bhp, 1.2 litre unit based on that of the old 8Cv – it was all new, with unitary body plus coil and wishbone front suspension. In 1953, one achieved 100,000 kms at an average speed of 100 km/h.

Right, bottom
The first post-Second World War design by the Standard Motor Company of England was the four-cylinder, 2.1 litre, ohv, wet-liner Vanguard, with unitary body construction and a three-speed gearbox.

as an example of how a small firm can show the big ones how things should be done.

From Mazda of Japan, there was one outstanding design, the Wankel-engined coupé which appeared in various guises. Mazda began in 1931, but the first Wankel-engined model came in 1964. We could choose a 110S or the later RX series with twin rotors, which were still being made long after most companies had given up the Wankel as impractical. Many were sold in the US. The RX 3, for instance gave well over 100 mph, zero-to-60 mph in just over ten seconds, and up to 18 mpg. It had a 982 cc engine rated as equivalent to 1,964 cc, producing 110 bhp.

Nash left us in 1957 after a life of 40 years. They used to build big straight-eights until the six took over in 1945, the best being the pre-1954 Ambassador Six. One could not say it was a good-looker, with all four wheels half-hidden under its skirts and rather shallow windows, but it was the smart thing in 1950 and should be listed among the milestones of motoring. One that we would *not* have wanted was the Nash Metropolitan, made in England by Austin, with an A40 engine and a track so narrow that it

looked as if it would topple over and probably did. It had no access to the boot from outside, and often came in convertible form. It was a mistake.

From Opel of Germany, the Manta coupé of around 1972, although not significantly better than the current ones, was a good example of a particular type. It was, of course, a General Motors product and, like most Opels, was a good seller. In that year, Opel outsold Volkswagen on their home territory. There were all sorts of bodies and engines to make many models from as few parts as possible, but the best combination was the Manta with a 1.9 litre, ohc engine. It was plain and simple, attractive to look at, went well and had room for four in a two-plus-two configuration.

R is for Reliant, and they made a classic economy car, the Kitten, which did not sell as well as it should because the price was too high and some of the early ones were badly made. It had a glass-fibre, saloon or estate body and a miniscule, 850 cc engine, which – in such a small car – gave adequate performance with good economy. They also made a three-wheeler, but the Kitten was a better bet. The engine was based on the old Austin Seven dimensions.

There is just space for a Renault, preferably a 4CV, which is almost forgotten but has a special place in history as it was designed under the noses of the German occupiers by people who were supposed to be working for them. This 760 cc, rear-engined, four-cylinder mini-car with all-independent suspension sold a million between 1945 and 1961 and was a little marvel until the rust got at it.

Armstrong-Siddeley have gone, after
serving motorists since 1919. This
Sapphire 346 was their ultimate
development, with 4.0 litres and
automatic gearbox only.

9 1939–79: Luxurious Touring

Alvis make a good start in the luxury-car class, although they never quite achieved their pre-war reputation with the post-1945 cars, which had Alvis' own bodies instead of being clad by coachbuilders as in the old days. There was virtually only one model before Rover brought them into British Leyland in 1965. This came in various forms, the under-powered TA14 of 1946 getting a 3.0 litre engine, to become the TA21 and then the TF21. The coachwork changed but the mechanicals were the same and the cars became heavier. One of the better-looking models was the 1953, drophead coupé version of the Grey Lady saloon, which had scoops in the bonnet top, spats on the rear wheels, and clean lines. It was supposed to do 100 mph, 20 mpg and zero-to-50 in 11 seconds, which shows how heavy it was, but it could hold up its head as a luxury car.

We have encountered Armstrong-Siddeley before, and, like Alvis, they never quite made it to the top after the Second World War, although their Star Sapphire was a good quality car, which did not disappear until they merged with the Bristol aeroplane company in 1960. The Sapphire arrived in 1953, with a 3.5 litre engine. It lasted five years in various forms with different engines, before the introduction of the Star Sapphire with the bigger (4.0 litre) ohv, 140 bhp engine and a regal appearance. There was even a limousine. Somehow it did not catch on and lasted only two years, but it was very much in the luxury idiom, suitable for chauffeur-driving, and a pleasure to have in one's fleet of cars.

Sadly, Bentley have also more-or-less disappeared, although some Rolls-Royces are still made with Bentley radiators. There is cur-

How few luxury car makers are left. Alvis lasted longer than most, with eye-catching carriages like this Grey Lady of 1954.

rently a choice of many varieties, including the modern Corniche or Camargue, but the Continental or Flying Spur was the ultimate in quiet, refined, fast travel with suitable accoutrements like a cut-glass decanter and glasses to ease one's passage. All the post-1959 cars had the 6.0 litre vee eight engine but differed in wheelbase and track and the late T2 was the best of all for handling and ride. Bentleys today have little to do with the glories of their past, with automatic transmission as standard and plenty of refined silence and comfort, but they are hard to match as luxurious transport even if their mechanical specification is not the ultimate. The Rolls-Royce theory is that they take the best of everything and refine it, which is why they use an American transmission from General Motors.

Only one model of the German BMW range really fits into the luxury class, unless we go back to the old vee eight 502 of 1953, which sold in small numbers. In more recent times, there has always been a large 3.0 litre, four/five seat saloon augmenting the more sporting cars but still providing high performance. It used to be the 3.3L, which was a long-wheelbase version of the 3.0 litre (with an engine developed from the old 2.5 of 1968) and had comfortable seats, rear footrests, and every convenience for the director/passenger it was aimed at. At the same time, top speed was around the 130 mph

Above
BMW have come a long way from this bulbous, Bavarian 502, with a vee eight engine of 2.6 litres and 100 bhp.

Below
The BMW 633CSi with fuel injection is a really svelte beast, with a 3.0 litre, six-cylinder engine offering 200 bhp.

Early days for Bristol, their 400 being
no more than a modified 2.0 litre
BMW, with their six-cylinder, ohv,
pushrod engine of 85 bhp. One was
third in the 1948 Monte Carlo Rally,
but they were generally intended only
for fast touring use.

mark, with good handling for rapid overall progress. The coupé was for the sportsman, the 3.3L for the man who wanted to travel almost as fast but in comfort and with someone else driving. Sensible.

The Bristol company have been divorced from the aircraft makers since 1960, although car-making began in 1947 with the 400, which some think was the prettiest of all. Since then, they have grown heavier and fatter and with bigger engines have changed into quite a different sort of car. But the current 603 S2 is as good as any of the

The evolution of Bristol Cars has led to their 603, with Chrysler vee eight power and everything screwed together by hand, as befits an aircraft company.

luxury models with big American engines. Otherwise one must go back to the 1973 411, with 6.3 litre Chrysler vee eight and Torqueflite auto transmission. It was a very limited production model, carefully made to aircraft standards.

Postwar Bugattis were not exactly thick on the ground, but there was a Type 101 based on the pre-war Type 57, which was the ultimate apart from the Royale, but without the latter's elegant appearance. The 101 had a Cotal pre-selector gearbox with a little electric switch to choose the gears.

There must, of course, be a Cadillac in any luxury-car parade, and it is only a matter of picking a model. We can no longer have a 12 or 16 cylinder car and the rest are less individual than they used to be, making use of common GM parts,

but there was the expensive Eldorado Brougham of 1957. This had air suspension, which didn't last long, while the Fleetwood Brougham of 1973 had 7.7 litres producing 'sufficient' horsepower, plus, of course, power assisted steering and seat-adjustment, and every kind of aid to comfort and convenience. The argument goes on for ever about whether Cadillac is superior to Rolls, and we had best keep out of that one, but the American car is a very silent and superb machine, whose appearance has varied from elegant to hideous over the years. Around 1953 they were probably at their worst, while some of the early 1970s versions were more restrained.

The Checker Motors Corporation of Kalamazoo, Michigan, have always been famous for their

Opposite, top
Bristols were developed from BMWs, but this Series VI 411 of 1975 uses a Chrysler vee eight.

Opposite, lower
Post-Second World War Bugattis are rare, but this 1951 drophead coupé Type 101 still looks right.

Below
Cadillac went all peculiar in 1967 and produced a front-wheel drive car, the Fleetwood Eldorado.

taxi-cabs, selling very few private cars by comparison with their domination of the taxi market in the USA. All Checkers were noted for their quality of construction, annual mileages of over 400,000 being reported by some satisfied customers, but the company's chief claim to fame rests with their Aerobus Limousine – the longest car in the world. This vehicle is 20 ft 5 ins long, with a wheelbase of

15 ft 9 ins, figures with which nothing else can compare. It has eight doors and room for 12 people, being designed mainly to satisfy the demand by large hotels for a limousine in which to transport customers to and from the airport. It is powered by a Chevrolet vee eight and styling is not a word that could be applied to its bodywork: the rounded lines of this and all other Checker cars have hardly changed since 1959, when they first appeared.

Of all the French cars, the big Citroens were the real magic carpets, with their sophisticated suspension that became a plumber's nightmare if it went wrong. The top model was the 2.3 litre, DS23 Injection Electronique, based on the old DS of the 1950s but evolved 20 years later. This one had 130 bhp under the shark-nosed bonnet and ran wonderfully. DS engines were always noisy and tractor-like, but superb suspension made these excellent long-distance cars, provided the driver remembered the instantaneous operation of the tiny brake button, mastered the single-spoke steering wheel and coped with the idiosyncratic gearchange system. An automatic was evolved by Borg-Warner but by the time it was ready the car was almost out of production.

Delage and Delahaye we have already encountered, but they made very few postwar cars. These were not much changed from pre-1939, but the French scene has not been the same since they left. There was a 1949 D6 3.0 litre saloon (which looked rather like a Bristol) and Delahaye went on to 1953–54, with the Type 235 offering 152 bhp from the old, 3.5 litre engine, but still without hydraulic brakes! French taxes killed them off, more's the pity.

Someone once counted 146 new makes of American car introduced in 1914, but the only one surviving today is Dodge, which belongs to Chrysler. Eyebrows may be raised at the idea of a Dodge as a luxury car, as Walter P. Chrysler introduced the make as his cheap, four-cylinder line when he bought Dodge in 1928. However, they soon moved up to sixes, then eights and

Buick's 1963 rival to the Thunderbird was this convertible Riviera, which looked far nicer than the Ford product.

something called the Luxury Liner between 1939 and 1941, before Pearl Harbor stopped production of civilian cars. The Luxury Liner offered one of the first automatic transmissions, called Fluid Drive. Better still, the 1955 Dodge Custom Royal was a smart, two-door, hardtop coupé with three-tone paint and a 4.5 litre engine which followed the famous Red Ram and offered 193 bhp. There was an even rarer model called the Dodge La Femme, which came with matching rain cape, umbrella, boots and handbag, in the days when it was women who had the handbags. This was hardly or-

dinary and permits Dodge to move into the luxury class. There was even a 1958 Dodge with electronic fuel injection, still a novelty in the States these days.

A rare car from France, was the Facel-Vega, which deserved a better fate. Not very lovely to look at, with funny reversed angles and spindly, fake wire wheels, it was propelled at some speed by a 4.5 litre, Chrysler vee eight engine. Manual or auto were available and later engines grew to 6.3 litres with 390 bhp and 135 mph. They ran from 1954 to 1964 in small numbers, made by Facel SA at Pont-à-Mousson, a firm which also made bodies for

companies ranging from Ford through Panhard to Simca (who initially sold Fords). Facel Vegas were undoubtedly fast, luxurious and costly, jet-set toys. The only one to avoid was the company's swan-song, the little Facelia, a scaled-down version fitted with either a 1.6 litre engine of their own confection or a 1.8 Volvo. This car brought them to their knees.

An English car with benefit of an American engine, which (alas) did

not have a long life despite its merits, was the Gordon-Keeble. Powered by a vee eight Chevrolet of 4.6 and later 5.4 litre size. Fewer than 100 cars were ever made, and although the various companies concerned existed from 1960 to 1967, production happened only in 1964–5. This machine had a glass-fibre body by the celebrated Williams and Pritchard (who do much work for the racing fraternity) and looked handsome. It is more sought after now, a dozen or more years after its death, than it was during its lifetime, and with the reliable American engine and unrustable body it was a good and exclusive Grand Tourer.

Humber was for many years the traditional British diplomatic limousine for those too junior to rate a Rolls-Royce or a Daimler, and must be included here, even though they effectively expired in 1954. The name lingered into the 1970s on the Chrysler-built Sceptre, but the luxury, long-wheelbase Pullman with 4.0 litre engine and limousine division between chauffeur and charges had gone.

This had an ancient, side-valve engine except in its last year as the Mark IV. The Snipe and the Super Snipe were large cars, but the Pullman was bigger still, with over-

Fins and other wild embellishments seem to have constituted the American idea of a touring car in 1957, when Cadillac produced this Eldorado Brougham. The names were equally elaborate.

all length of 17 ft 8 ins and a weight of two tons. The owner/driver version was the Imperial, another imposing title. Apart from their size and image the cars were undistinguished, but they were members of a vanished breed.

Another vanished marque, this time from Italy, was Iso in its various forms, principally the Rivolta and the Grifo, which was a two-seater coupé. Neither must be confused with the 1954 Isetta from the same company, which was a miniscule bubble-car like a hard-boiled egg with a 200 cc motor-cycle engine. As different as chalk from cheese, one might say, as the big Isos were supposed to do 162 mph. The various Isos were most Italian in appearance, with American overtones and Chevrolet vee eight engines of up to 7.0 litres producing nearly 400 bhp (a later model, the Iso Lele, used a vee eight Ford engine). There were never many of them, even in the production years of 1962 to 1974. The original inspiration was from Renzo Rivolta, who in the end sold out to an American. Bertone provided the first bodies on a chassis not unlike that which they supplied to Gordon-Keeble; Giotto Bizzarini was the mechanical designer. Renzo Rivolta died in the late 1960s, and the new company (run by his son), hired Paolo Dallara from Lamborghini, but all this was after the time of their classics, the Grifo or – better still – the Rivolta.

Jaguar hardly need to be introduced; their slogans of 'space,

Below
Citroen's DS, introduced in 1963 as the 'car of the future', had everything hydraulic – including suspension, steering and brakes.

Right
Citroen have lost money most of their life but produced some good cars, like this 130 mph SM with Maserati vee six engine and variable-ratio power steering.

Opposite, lower
Delage appeared after the Second World War with a 3.0 litre version of their six-cylinder D6, shortly before being absorbed by Hotchkiss.

pace and grace' surely lifted them into the luxury bracket and most people give them credit for making fine machines. In terms of ride and silence, they still set the standards although none of their cars is very young and they are no longer sold at the give-away prices featured by the company when they were a new name trying to make their mark.

The best of Jaguar's current line is perhaps the long-wheelbase, 12-cylinder, 5.3 litre XJ 12 almost the ultimate in luxury. This company,

Opposite, top
This Humber Super Snipe of about 1965 was the last of their big limousines.

Opposite, lower
The Iso Rivolta looks handsome, with a 260 bhp vee eight Chevrolet engine powering an A3 Lusso Grifo model of 1964, with chassis design by Bizzarini.

Below
The last-ever Isotta-Fraschini was this rear-engined Monterosa 8C of 1947, with a 3.4 litre vee eight and five forward gears. Only 20 were ever made.

Bottom
'Grace, Pace and Space' was the Jaguar slogan, and this 420G version of the Mark X exemplified it all in 1967.

incidentally have a dual personality, having also made some very fine sports cars. One of their best-ever models was a two-door coupé version of the XJ12, known as the XJC, but, alas, it had a very brief life, although everyone spoke well of it.

All Jaguar and Daimler saloons are now made with what used to be the long wheelbase (112.83 inches) while the 12-cylinder, sohc-per-bank engine has been with us since 1971. One may have power steering, automatic transmission, air conditioning, electric windows and even real, cow-leather upholstery, which is not common now. The XJS is attractive too, but in view of its limited accommodation it is more of a sports car.

In the same sort of idiom is the British Jensen, powered by an American vee eight, this one from Chrysler and running up to 6.3 litres. Jensen were in production from 1936, but only in small numbers; they are best known for their grand tourers of 1963 onwards. There had been earlier models in fibreglass, some with Austin engines, but the seller was the Interceptor (a confusing situation as a 1949 six-cylinder also used this name). The 541 and the C-V8 were good, fast tourers but not as high in the luxury stakes as the models from 1965 onwards, which had everything plus room for four. There was even a four-wheel-drive model called FF, which was expensive and sold in small numbers, but which might well be the one to choose now for its rarity value. Like so many other good triers Jensen eventually went out of business in the 1970s, after an American, Kjell Qvale had taken over in a bid to save the company.

Naturally there must be a Lincoln Continental, but the question is, which model? The name was first used by Lincoln in 1941 after forming part of Ford's Zephyr line-up. It was then used, war years apart, until 1948 and re-appeared in 1956. American auto writers say the Continental Mark II of 1956 was the 'most beautiful Lincoln' of the year. Well, it was very big, slab-sided with an egg-box, chromium grille and distinctly ponderous

lines, but it did win the Industrial Designers Institute Award for excellence in automotive design. It weighed 5,190 lbs and only 3,012 were made, with a vee eight of 6.0 litres. After 1961, all Lincolns were known as Continentals, which upset the fans tremendously.

We have talked a lot about Mercedes in previous chapters, but they did make the limousine to end all limousines – the 600, introduced in 1963 with a 250 bhp, 6.3 litre vee eight engine, three doors either side, and seats for seven or eight people. Four of the rear-seat passengers could sit facing each other and play cards, hold a conference, or even a séance if they felt so inclined. There never has been anything like it: the Super or *Grösser* Mercedes, 20 ft 6 ins long with a 12 ft 10 ins wheelbase. People have put gussetts in

Above
The line was always right in Jaguars, and this very rare 1949 Mark V drophead is still lovely.

Opposite, top
Jaguar's magnificent XJ12, with 5.3 litres and single ohc per bank. At the price, it must be the best saloon car in the world.

Right
The first Jensen Interceptor of 1950 used a 4.0 litre, six-cylinder Austin engine with steel body, unlike the glassfibre 541 which followed.

the middle of Ford Granadas or big American cars to achieve the same effect, but who wants to know?

Mercury came from the Lincoln Division of Ford Motor Company in 1938 (as well as being the messenger of the Gods) and grew up to be 7.0 litres large with nearly 400 bhp from their vee eight by

1969. It was seen as a scaled-down Lincoln in the medium-price range, and the one to look for was the 1964 Mercury Park Lane, the 25th anniversary model with acres of metal covering boot and bonnet. Few of their other models would have won any prizes for beauty with their toothy chrome grins and busty bonnets. The Park Lane had a 10 ft 8 ins wheelbase, which, if not quite up to Mercedes 600 standards, was no minicar. The engine was a vee eight of 7.2 litres and 345 bhp. The car had clean lines with not too many embellishments, but a rather unappealing, inward-sloping back window as seen on the British Ford Anglia of 1960. It was BIG and not ugly and sufficiently fast and comfortable to qualify as the God's messenger.

No collection would be complete

A lazy, Chrysler vee eight combined with Jensen standards of comfort and handling made the Interceptor a tremendous long-distance cruiser in the 1970s. This is a Series III model from 1972.

without an NSU Ro80 saloon, the only non-piston-engined car of its kind, sadly mourned by many fans of the Wankel engine. The German NSU company came into being in 1905, but did nothing startling until they produced the Ro80 in 1968. They had earlier sold the Spider, a Wankel-engined version of the tiny, 600 cc Prinz, but this does not concern us here, except that it was the forerunner of the Ro80, a handsome machine which made many friends with its silence and untraumatic travel. The semi-automatic transmission with a gear-lever but no clutch was a mistake (it used a torque converter), but the engine was smooth and would rev to the skies, so needing something other than a normal transmission set-up. This Wankel had twin-rotors and there were always sealing and other problems which gave the engines, if not the cars, a bad name, and eventually killed them off. Production ceased in 1972.

Packard started as a great name and finished as warmed-up Stude-bakers, so it is essential to pick the right period for an enduring model. The company had been around for 59 years when it died in 1958. A model called the Patrician sounded promising, but even bigger was the eight-seat Executive Limousine of 1953, with a 10 ft 7 ins wheelbase and a 180 bhp,

5.3 litre engine, a straight-eight when everyone else had gone Vee. The year after it was made came the merger with Studebaker and the end of Packard as a leader.

Pontiac was an Indian chief before becoming a famous name in US motoring, credited in 1926 with being the first to use oil and fuel filters, an air cleaner, crankcase ventilation, automatic advance, main bearing shells, full-pressure engine lubrication, and the Silentbloc type of spring shackle bushing. No doubt some of these claims could be contested. Pontiac started out as a sidekick to the Oakland, another long-lost make. They shared a common engine in the early days, but the later Pontiacs, which used Chevrolet, Oldsmobile or Buick parts, were more desirable. Their biggest car before 1954 was the Star Chief, with a 10 ft 4 ins wheelbase – nearly as big as Lincoln or Cadillac – but it, too, had to manage with a straight-eight engine when all the others were vees, although a vee was eventually installed, even in the

For those who prefer Teutonic efficiency to the more traditional forms of luxury transport, Mercedes still make cars like this 350 SLC of 1972.

Star Chief. The vintage year was 1959, with new, wide-track styling and suspension and some marvellous model names like Bonneville, Parisienne and Catalina Vista and a choice of engines like the Strato Flash with 5.7 litres and lots of horse power.

The original sporting estate car was the Reliant GTE (Grand

Touring Estate) designed by Tom Karen of Ogle Design and produced by the Reliant Motor Company, who achieved fame by selling one to Britain's Princess Anne (who then had trouble with the speed limits). It was a pretty shape in glassfibre, clothing standard Ford mechanical parts, with either manual or automatic transmission, allied to the 3.0 litre British Ford vee six engine. The body design deserves a lasting place in history, if only because it led to the concept of the hatch-back–a now ubiquitous feature on ordinary production cars. The original coupé had been the Scimitar and the new one, introduced in 1969, was the Scimitar GTE. The car grew up with a longer and wider body so that the later versions perhaps qualify best for our grand touring class, although the original smaller and slimmer one handled better and was less soggy. In this chapter, however, perhaps ride matters more than handling.

Top
Reliant's glassfibre GTE is unique, with a Ford vee six engine in a station wagon, a cramped rear but good performance. This car deserves to be preserved as the first of the successful hatchbacks.

Above
It must have been one of the world's largest-ever front-wheel drive automobiles. The 1973 Oldsmobile Toronado came with no less than $7\frac{1}{2}$ litres of vee eight with which to haul its considerable bulk around the highways.

Rover are traditional makers of comfortable touring cars, but their latest offerings are the best, as they have the comforts of earlier models allied to much improved handling and roadholding. We refer, of course, to the 2300, 2600 and 3500 SD1. This is the biggest British hatchback, and sets high standards of road-holding, handling and passenger comfort. It has many little novelties, such as the direction of warm air into the doors to prevent rust and, although not a complicated design owing to the need to keep cost down (its producers, British Leyland, have some problems), it is well conceived and executed. The vee eight 3500 with automatic transmission is the ideal, as gear-noise in the smaller-engined, manual models is very noticeable. In addition to its other merits, it has those splendid, Dunlop Denovo tyres, which enable one to keep going for 50 miles or so after a puncture.

Someone will ask why there is no

Rolls-Royce in the luxury car section, and the answer is that we have had a Bentley, which is, nowadays, exactly the same thing except for the shape of the dummy radiator shell. A Rolls will no doubt creep in somewhere under another chapter heading, particularly when we deal with specialist cars in the different engine categories. Suffice to say, Rolls cannot make enough machines to satisfy the customers, so it is perhaps a bit superfluous to go into their merits, unless one is prepared to wait a couple of years for one's transport.

If Rolls-Royce are a company who prefer to wait until others have tried and tested new ideas, the same could most certainly not be said of the Tucker Corporation of Chicago, USA. Immediately after the Second World War, they hired Alex Tremulis, former designer of Auburn, Cord and Duesenberg cars, and he came up with the Torpedo, which was absolutely crammed full of new ideas.

The bodywork was relatively conventional, except that it sported three headlamps at the front, the middle one being steered along with the front wheels to provide illumination round the curves; inside, there was crash padding, a collapsible steering column, safety belts, a pop-out windscreen, recessed door handles and other safety features, virtually all of which have subsequently become legally compulsory on American automobiles.

Under the skin, almost nothing was conventional. The engine was a flat-six unit developed from a light alloy, ohv helicopter engine built for Bell helicopters by a firm that used to be Franklin, about who we have written elsewhere. This air-cooled unit was modified and given a sealed-liquid cooling system and its 5,500 cc gave up to 166 bhp. It was mounted at the rear of the car,

Opposite, top
Renault's 30TS uses a vee six engine shared with the big Peugeots and Volvos, but some think it the best of the three.

Opposite, lower
Beloved of conservative executives and politicians, the Rover 3.5 litre coupé was sufficiently reliable still to be common on British roads ten years after its 1968 introduction. With a Buick-based vee eight and 160 bhp, it could top 115 mph and had power steering and automatic transmission as standard.

Below
Rover stuck with the Buick-based vee eight engine when they introduced the five-door 3500 in 1977. It was an instant hit with both public and press, who voted it Car of the Year.

with the radiator behind it.

The suspension was revolutionary, too, with self-damping rubber cartridges providing independent springing for each wheel some 12 years before Alec Issigonis' Mini, while aircraft-specification disc brakes were fitted to all four wheels. With a wheelbase of almost 11 ft and a height of over five feet, this $1\frac{1}{2}$ ton car was capable of almost 120 mph.

Only 49 Tucker Torpedos were ever made, all of them prototypes of one sort or another, as a result of which no two were ever quite alike. Tucker was never happy with the specification as described, having plans to build his own engine – a 9.6 litre monster, still a horizontally-opposed six – and to include other revolutionary features. The transmission, for example, was to have been automatic, including a torque converter and direct drive to the rear wheels. The cars he did build had to make do with four-speed manual boxes fitted with pre-selector electric operation, although some were fitted with another of the company's innovations: a Tuckermatic transmission with only 30 basic parts.

The company's owner, an engineer named Preston T. Tucker, was sued for fraud and other things and, although cleared in 1950, the time and money spent caused him to abandon further production plans and the name vanished.

10

1939–79: The Legacy of Le Mans

Alfa Romeo is an honoured name, but in terms of recent sports-cars there is only one model to consider: the Montreal, made from 1970 onwards and powered by a smaller version of the four-overhead-camshaft vee eight engine used in the Type 33 sports-racing car. In the Montreal, the engine was only 2.5 litres (against the racer's 3.0 litres)

The demarcation between saloon cars and sports cars has become rather blurred in recent years, thanks to the exploits of companies like Alfa Romeo, who won sports car events (this is the Nürburgring 6-hour race in 1967) in what were obviously saloon cars (like this GTA driven by Bianchi and Rolland).

but it had a useful 200 bhp, which was quite sufficient for road use, giving it a top speed of 137 mph and a standing-start quarter-mile time of 16 seconds. It had a five-speed gearbox, rear-wheel drive, and a fierce-looking, three-door body with tailgate and two-plus-two seating. Bertone designed the body after a long association with Alfa, and it had his mark about it: rear-seat passengers could not be too large or have any legs. It was a dream-car, but one you could afford. Most Alfa models nowadays are normal saloons or coupés, and this was about the only model with sufficient performance to call a real sports car.

Opposite, top
Renault-Alpine's entry into the 'super-car' stakes, the A310, with mid-mounted engine. Initial examples could be had with an 1800 cc, four-cylinder engine, but the model to have will be the vee six one, so far used only in competition.

Opposite, lower
With a 210 bhp, 2.9 litre, twin-ohc, inline-six engine originally designed by W. O. Bentley for Lagonda, the Aston Martin DB3S had the sort of historical background which guaranteed classic status. The DB3S added to this by racing successfully all over the world (twice second at Le Mans) and, as with this 1955 example, proving an excellent road car.

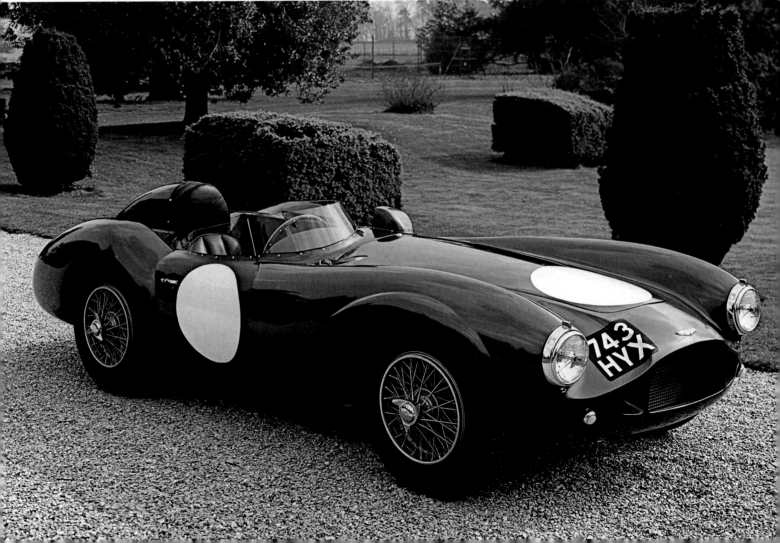

Sydney Allard built some very different cars, with powerful American vee eight engines in crudely-cobbled-up frames designed only to go quickly without much emphasis on creature comfort. They grew out of the cross-country trials specials which Allard made for himself in London from about 1934 onwards, but they did not go on the market commercially until after the Second World War. Each was a kind of four-wheeled motorcycle (except for the rather terrible-looking saloons) with enormous power and straight-line acceleration, and they were gone by 1958. There was no other vehicle quite like an Allard, with its De Dion rear end and burbling Cadillac vee eight, but it was hardly what one could call refined.

Alpine comes from Dieppe, used to be Renault Alpine, and have won many rallies in convincing manner. Since 1955, they have made sports cars to use, rather than promenade machines. They began with small engines, like the 845 cc Dauphine unit, but it is a different story now and the 1.8 litre A310 is very purposeful indeed, offered for sale with 140 bhp, five-speed gearbox and servo-assisted discs all round. The alternative is the fibreglass Berlinetta 1300 which the works used for rally victories; the one you can buy is a little tamer, but still not exactly slow and was quite capable of

Above
Aston Martin survived by the skin of their teeth and are now successful. This is their fastest current model, the 5.3 litre vee eight Vantage.

Opposite, top
It won't bite you, it just looks as if it might. A horrid-looking Alvis-Healey of 1952; fortunately, very few were ever made.

Right
BMW's new wonder, the M1, in this case the Group 4 racing version with 470 bhp at 9,500 rpm and a top speed of 190 mph. The one you can buy isn't much slower.

winning the Index of Performance in the Le Mans 24-hour race. It is a very small, handy machine with the engine at the rear, calling for some skill from the driver for best results.

Is an Aston-Martin a sports car? Well, it was very much so in the past, even if the modern, vee eight ones are more like luxury saloons or businessman expresses. It comes down to the old question of definition, and one might have to take a model of a year or two back to qualify as a true sports car. The Zagato-bodied lightweight of 1959 was the machine to find but there were very few of those. Certainly, one must go back to the days of the six-cylinder engine (before the cars became bigger and heavier). The engine began as a 2.6 litre unit from W. O. Bentley's pen, but the 3.7 litre of 1959 was new, although still a six-cylinder dohc. It all began

with the DB2, which was a bit uncivilized in some ways and became fatter, more bulbous and heavier. Best of all were the last sixes, including the DB6, which had gone up to 4.0 litres; even if this was not a real sports car, it would carry four people reasonably fast, with good handling and road-holding.

The British big-banger, the Austin Healey was a mechanical crudity which tended to grill its crew with engine heat and drag its bottom on the ground to the detriment of the exhaust system, but it

grew a reputation for being rugged and fun to drive, so finding favour with sporting young men. There were three versions, starting with the original four-cylinder, two-seater with the 2.7 litre engine from the A90 saloon made by Austin and known as the Healey 100 or BN1. Later (1956) came the first six-cylinder 2,639 cc known as the 100/6 or BN4. Finally, with the 2,912 cc unit from the Austin and Wolseley 99, it was the BN7 or 3000. There is now a cult following for the fours, but the 3000 was the lusty one which won rallies and, in

works-tuned form, was a real eye-opener. The Big Healey died in 1968, and the one to have was a late model with wind-up windows and a good hood, so that it was not too Spartan. Maximum speed was around 120 mph for a good one, and there was no pretence at silence, nor any masking of the machinery performing rather close to one's legs.

Is the Corvette a sports car? Most Americans – probably all Americans – would say yes; certainly it has made its mark in competition since appearing on the scene in 1953. It sold 300 that year

214

Opposite
When the Chevrolet Corvette Sting Ray appeared in 1954, it was the first real American sports car and one of the first production cars to use glassfibre bodywork. As with this example from the initial year, the cars all came in blue.

Above
By 1971, the Corvette had matured to this more familiar shape, but still retaining glassfibre bodywork. The engine had grown some, however, with over 7.0 litres available in some versions, providing real straight-line performance, even by the best European standards.

and nearly 10,000 by 1969. The one sold today, of course, bears little relation to the original, 1953 model. The code name of the original project was Opel, just to confuse people, and there were quite a few things wrong with it. The original designers were given only 12 months to get it into production, and the 'Vette was initially a disaster, prodded into continued life only by Ford's introduction of the Mustang. It was too slow and didn't handle, but a vee eight in place of the ageing six gave it performance, and Zora Arkus-Duntov came from Belgium to mastermind the overall transformation. He ran one at 150 mph, which helped sales, then put in a four-speed manual gearbox, fuel injection, and steering which worked. But, as has happened so many times, the weight also went up, although the glass-fibre body helped restrain it.

Which was the vintage year for Corvettes? The 1963 Sting Ray was a good one but had drum brakes, while some of the later, big-bodied versions (1968 on) could be had with nearly 400 bhp. Fastest of all were those fitted with the 7.5 litre vee eight, before they were strangled by the addition of all that clean-exhaust equipment. The Corvette remains America's only production sports car and has been offered in many varieties during its 25-year life. Everything has been available at one time or another, from a 'promenade' car to a full-house racer.

Cisistalia of Turin really did start a trend when, in 1946, they set about creating a sports/racing car out of the standard production parts then obtainable from other manufacturers – very much the way in which so many small sports car builders operate to this day. The Cisistalia 202 was largely based on Fiat components, with one of that company's 1,089 cc ohv engines forming the power unit, albeit in revised form with balanced crankshaft, special connecting rods and pistons, larger valves, modified porting and manifolds and a 7.5:1 compression ratio, all of which resulted in 50 bhp at 5,500 rpm. The cylinder block was cast iron, with a light alloy head and, while the basic car came with one vertical carburettor, one could buy multi-carburettor options.

The suspension was by wishbones and a transverse leaf spring at the front; coil springs and a solid axle at the rear, with hydraulic damping all round and drum brakes.

Around this was wrapped a low, flowing body by Pininfarina, with aerodynamic lines and light alloy construction, noted for its simple and tasteful design, with wings integrated into the main body and a general look which was well ahead of its time. The standard car weighed well under a ton and could

This 1968 styling exercise by Bertone was called the Carabo. It proved to have certain practical problems for people.

travel at 110 mph, but the factory also produced ultra-lightweight, spider versions for competition and one of these was driven into second place on the 1947 Mille Miglia with the great Tazio Nuvolari at the wheel. Around four dozen of the various models were sold in the first year of production.

Cunningham from California hardly made production sports cars, but they could be bought in 1952 and 1953 as the C4R, when Briggs Cunningham needed to sell enough cars to satisfy homologation for racing purposes. There were roadsters and coupés, designed by Michelotti and built by Vignale in Italy, for which 135 mph was claimed from a 210 bhp, vee eight Chrysler engine, but only ten of each were built out of the scheduled 75 and the company closed in 1955.

From sunny California to the land of the rising sun for a Datsun 240Z, a rugged sports car and one of the few to emerge from Japan. The car came on the market in 1969 with

Opposite, top
An elegant little Hotchkiss Ten of 1939, when the fashion was for popular cars to be streamlined. This was one of the last cars made in France before the Second World War.

Opposite, lower
Cunningham of California made a few cars for sale as well as racing at Le Mans and elsewhere. This open two-seater version appeared in 1952.

a 2.4 litre, sohc unit pushing out 160 bhp and was aimed at the US market. It was then developed for rallying and took two wins in the East African Safari. It was powered by a six-cylinder version of the four-cylinder Bluebird saloon-car engine, and a total of 153,000 were exported in 1970–73, of which no less than 130,000 went to the US.

The 240Z was a good-looking, clean-cut coupé with two seats, very much in the hairy, 'man's car' image of the defunct Austin-Healey – plenty of noise and not so much comfort. It was also regarded as a

Jaguar E-type competitor, although not really similar except that both had six-cylinder engines. The 240Z had a five-speed gearbox, and sold well until superseded by the 260Z, which looked much the same, but came with 2.6 litres, a hatchback and had a four-seat version as an option. Since then, the engine has grown still further – to 2.8 litres in the USA, but the basic concept has changed hardly at all.

The Mangusta is an animal which eats cobras. Alessandro de Tomaso comes from the Argentine but lives in Italy with his wealthy American wife. He dabbled in Formula One racing, produced a Vallelunga sports car, which did not do much, and then produced a car called the Mangusta which –

with a 4.7 litre, Ford vee eight – produced up to 506 bhp when fitted with fuel injection and a five-speed gearbox.

The Mangusta had handling faults and was developed into the Pantera, which was much better and was really the one to have. Later, De Tomaso (who now owns Maserati and all sorts of other companies) sold the Pantera and the company bearing his name to Ford, along with Ghia. The Pantera itself was a two-seater, with 5.75 litres of mid-engine, about 160 mph and exceptional handling. It was very much a car of its time (now) and had few equals.

Just down the road in Modena, of course, is Ferrari and all his wonderful creations. Choosing a Ferrari is more painful than choosing a hat for a woman; there are so many mouth-watering choices that it is hard to know where to begin, or end. Although the company make the best-known and most highly-regarded road-going sports cars in the world, they have only been going since the Second World War. Their first model was a 2.0 litre V12 around 1947, but a real Ferrari must have a larger engine of 3.0 or 4.0

Above
The car that really upset the sports-car market, especially in the USA, Datsun's immortal 240Z sold unbelievably well. This is a later, 260Z, but the shape has remained basically the same through all subsequent developments.

Right
Perhaps the best-known and best-loved Ferraris of them all were the 250 Series, with 12 cylinders mounted in the 'right' place (in front). This is a 1962 GTO.

litres to represent the house style. The 250 was well-regarded but it was more of a racer in its quicker forms, lacking creature comforts. (Every schoolboy knows, by the way, that in the 12-cylinder models, which means most of them, the type number-like 250 – is also the capacity of one cylinder, so you multiply by 12 for the engine size).

The later 330 did not find much favour among afficionados, who preferred a Daytona, a Super America, Tipo 500 Superfast or a Tipo 365 California. Some of these go back a bit, the Super America hailing from 1956–7, but they all went like the proverbial scalded cat and were wonderful to look at. Different coachbuilders supplied

bodies, so there was an enormous choice of styles. The Super America finally had a 4.9 litre engine, which was nice, but the California was slightly later (1959) and could be had in a Spider or open version. They were all super-cars and the choice of type was entirely a matter of bank balance and personal prejudice. There are no bad Ferraris, but – like beer – some are better than others. The Daytona, for example featured a transaxle with its 4.4 litre engine and offered about 180 mph. The more modern cars are bigger and

more 'road-going' than the early ones, more supple in suspension, but still in the top class for handling. One would really need a separate Ferrari book to do them all justice. We can even have a mid-mounted, flat 12 engine in the Berlinetta Boxer, but this does not seem to be a true Ferrari, even if it does offer 188 mph. It does not,

after all, have the right, V12 configuration. A keen man really needs more than one Ferrari to do himself justice. And one for his wife or mistress or both.

We have delved a little into Jaguar saloons, but the sports cars are another matter. The E-Type (or XKE in the US) was a marvel in its day, but to be really superior one

Above
This is a Jaguar, believe it or not, although scarcely recognisable as such after Michelotti had finished his styling exercise. It started out as an E-Type, but was called a Jaguar Le Mans.

Below
The Jensen-Healey was a 1972 combination effort by Donald Healey and Jensen, with a Vauxhall engine made by Lotus. It did not save Jensen.

needed a C or D Type, which were basically racers. Various people are now making imitation ones, but the originals are the only ones the worth pursuing, even if the fakes look and perhaps even go as well.

The family began in 1948 with the XK120, which startled the motoring World with its combination of performance and comfort. Maybe it didn't stop too well, but neither did Bugattis and no-one seemed to mind. The original XK did 130mph on its first press demonstration run, which was good even if it did have the help of an undertray and a high-ratio back axle. The C-Type (or 120C) was built to win Le Mans. It had bigger valves with different springs, bigger carburettors, and 204 bhp. Brakes were improved, and the aluminium body was different, having a one-piece front end with lifting bonnet and wings like a Triumph Herald. The back end was the same, with access to suspension and so on. There was a 40-gallon fuel tank in the back, and the rear suspension used special torsion bars.

The D-Type, also made for Le

Mans, was entirely different, identifiable by the fin on its rear. It won three times. Where the C-Type had a space frame chassis, the D had a monocoque like a modern F1 car. It was a much better car; it went faster and stopped more easily. It had alloy wheels which were lighter than the wire wheels of the C. It also had a dry-sump oil system on the engine, which meant that this could sit lower in the car. It was only 12 ft 10 ins long and weighed 18 cwt, 150 lb lighter than the C. Most people found the D so much better than the C, that one had to select a D if the choice were available. Sixty-seven of them were sold, 18 to the US. Top speed was around 180 mph and, running gently on the road, it could average 30 mpg. What more could one ask?

Somewhere for the luggage, perhaps, which is why the E-Type was a much better bet for the road, with enough performance and better brakes after the first year or two.

Back to Italy for the second of their famous trio of supercar makers, Lamborghini, which is facing a very doubtful future. It began in 1963 when Cavaliere Ferrucio

Lamborghini had trouble getting his Ferraris serviced and vowed he would build a better car himself. His first featured a 3.5 litre, 4 ohc V12 with six Weber carburetters, which was not bad for a beginner. He stuck with the V12 like his neighbour Ferrari, and went up to 4.0 litres for his most exciting car, the P400 Miura of 1965, with its engine across the tail

and 180 mph on tap for the brave. There have been many other Lamborghini models: the Espada, the Jarama, the little Urraco and the Countach, but it is for the Miura that he will be remembered. The Miura looked like a hungry shark sliding along the road and was about as defiant as a car could be. It was very noisy and very frightening and will never be repeated.

Lancia is a classic name in motoring, and their best postwar sporting car was the Stratos, which came to us in 1973 after Fiat had taken the company over. It was very much a sport-biased machine with the Ferrari-designed, 2.4 litre, vee six Dino engine. The full title was the Stratos HF Coupé, it was mid-engined, and it carried all before it in European rallying, taking cham-

Opposite, top
Jowett's Jupiter was based on their Javeline saloon, with flat-four, horizontally-opposed engine. It ran at Le Mans and in the Monte Carlo Rally and acquitted itself well in both.

Opposite, lower
Lamborghini have always favoured individual shapes, as seen on this Espada 400 GT Mk III, which must be the fastest, true four-seat car in the world.

Above
Lancia's Stratos has always been a racer but one you can buy – if they trust you not to kill yourself.

Left
This Lancia Aurelia, with a lovely, wind-cheating shape, did well in competition in the 1950s, including the Mille Miglia.

223

Opposite, top
Also experimental, this Rover/BRM ran at Le Mans in 1965, with a gas-turbine engine. It represents something which shows no signs of happening yet.

Left
Maserati tend to name their cars after hot winds, and this Khamsin is no exception. It has a 5.0 litre vee eight under the bonnet.

Opposite, lower
You can't buy this one, but it's offspring will probably hit the roads in the 1980s. It is the record-breaking Mercedes C111 experimental coupé, with four-rotor Wankel engine. A more recent example has also shattered world speed records with a turbocharged diesel motor.

Below
Oh dear. The World's Ugliest Car title goes without any contest to this Lancia with a Pininfarina body. Fortunately they have stopped this kind of thing.

pionships in 1974, 75, 76, 77 and 78. But in 1973 there was a run of around 400 production cars for homologation purposes. It was a very short machine with a busy look, and a rear section which detached to reveal all the works in the tail. The engine sat across the car behind the driver's head, which was therefore very close to the half-a-dozen carburettors on the other side of the bulkhead. Not a motor car for a middle-aged woman, but a rare and exciting classic for those who love driving and have more than enough skill.

As everyone knows, a Lola is a racing car, but some of the sports cars have been converted for road use, notable by a Mr Sbarro in Switzerland. It made a rather way-out road machine, but no more so than a Ford GT 40, a car which has been treated in the same way by some millionaires, but you probably needed to be both odd and rich to get away with it. This was no reason not to covet one, however, knowing that the neighbours were not likely to turn up with one too. Eric Broadley made the Lola for racing, and there were many types and models, but the conversion required a sports car with two seats, like the GT Coupé of 1963. Engines were to taste, usually a big vee eight from Ford, but a Cosworth DFV would have been a bit wild for road use – or would it?

The modern Lotus is not really a sports car at all, although it may perform and handle like one; it is a full, four or five-seater, and so does not fit the picture. For a true sports car, we would need to go back to a model they do not make any longer but which is still produced under licence by Caterham Cars, – the old Lotus 7. This is a four-wheeled motorcycle with virtually no weather protection, practically dragging the driver and his unfortunate passenger along the ground on their bottoms, accompanied by the sound of a rasping exhaust and wrapped in the most exiguous of bodywork. There is a hood, difficult to erect and which makes it impossible for anyone to get in or out when it is up. Better to get wet and smile. It was originally sold as a kit-car, when British taxes on completed cars made this a cheap way of

Opposite
Exotica from the tradition source of Modena in Italy. This is a 1972 Maserati Bora, with mid-mounted, four-cam vee eight engine and enough performance for any right-minded customer.

Above
Truly desirable property – a 1955 Mercedes-Benz 300 SL 'gull-wing' coupé with six-cylinder engine.

doing things. The trick was to attempt to put it together, then ship it along to your friendly Lotus dealer who would 'check' (and rebuild) it for you. Happily, that is all over and you just buy your Seven, with a variety of wild engines, enormous acceleration, a good thirst for fuel, and the need for a supple and athletic driver who can climb in and out over the sides. It even makes a Morgan look like a limousine and we cannot think of anything else like it.

Next to Lotus comes Marcos, which used to be called the Wooden Wonder. This was a British sporting car with a wooden chassis. Ignoring all the jokes about woodworm and death-watch beetle, Jem Marsh and Frank Costin plodded on from 1961 with various types, culminating in the GT coupé with a choice of Volvo or Ford engines. The driver was almost lying on his back and visibility in the wet was a problem, but that was the price one paid for being different. The wood got lost somewhere along the line and the car ended up fairly orthodox, although it never looked ordinary with its low, sleek profile. It was a brave and different car, even if the mechanical layout was mundane with a front-engine. Marcos died about 1972 as carmakers, although the Mini-Marcos, which cleverly used plastic panels to turn a Mini into a tiny sports car, soldiered on.

The third of the trio of Italian giants is Maserati who have the most honoured name in some circles for their racing activities, which we have investigated before. Originally, they made only racing cars, and a very few, two-seater sports cars, but after the Second World War, they went properly

Left
Last of the desirable MG's? The MGA coupé of 1962 came with a 1.6 litre, 72 bhp, pushrod, ohv, B-Series engine with disc brakes, good handling and reliability. There were some made with twin ohc engines and these, despite being temperamental, are now in great demand.

Opposite, lower
Over 100 mph was claimed for the diminutive Panhard 24 CT sports coupé in 1964, despite only 848 cc and 60 bhp. The model disappeared when Citroen took over the factory in 1967.

into the business of producing road cars.

Some people decry the 3500 and such models, preferring something like the Zagato-bodied 450S Le Mans coupé or the open Mille Miglia version of 1957. These were real racers; for those with a tamer spirit, how about the 5000 GT with Monterosa body, the Bertone version, or even the Frua of 1963? From more recent times the Ghibli,

Indy, Bora, Merak and Mexico, were not to be sneezed at. Perhaps the later family of hot winds, from which were derived all the type names, were more civilized and urbane than the early cars, but it depended on what one wanted. The vee eight Khamsin, for example, reached 168 mph, which is enough.

Next to this, purely for alphabetical reasons, we arrive at MGB, although anything less like a Maserati would be hard to imagine. The MG is a tame little beast after 17 years production with not much modification, and one would have to choose the closed coupé GT version, which is much prettier than the open tourer and more useful. There is nothing exciting

Modern-day fresh-air fans can enjoy wind in their hair and part with lots of money, with cars like the 1978 Panther Lima, based entirely on Vauxhall running gear, but with a performance which belies such mundane mechanicals. This one even has a turbocharger.

Opposite, top
Only the hardy need apply: wind-un-the-hair motoring with vee eight power in the Morgan +8. This goes very well in a straight line, but is not the most stable device round corners. Motoring as it used to be.

Opposite, lower
A General Motors product to satisfy the sporting tastes of European customers, the Opel Manta was an instant success, despite being little more than a tastefully re-styled Ascona saloon. This is a 1972 1.9 litre SR.

Above
The first classic Porsche, still much in demand among enthusiasts despite its curious handling, was the 356 Coupé. This immaculate example was built in 1951.

about it, with an ancient, iron, pushrod 1.8 litre engine, only four cylinders and big thumpy wheels, but it has served many people well and remains one of the best-looking cars of all time. There was a six-cylinder version called the MGC, but this had too much weight on the front and tended to go straight on through hedges.

We have been into the Morgan saga before, and the postwar ones were not that different from those made before the Second World War, except that they had more power and brakes and could shake your liver even harder at the higher speeds. Inevitably, one would like a Plus 8, which has been around since 1968 with a vee eight Rover 3.5 litre pushing out 160 bhp, enabling one to have one's head blown off in the wind at 125 mph. A Rover manual gearbox comes with the engine unit and while an automatic would be much nicer, it would not suit the Morgan image of brutality and defiant anachronism. There is not much more to write about the Morgan; the engine sits at the front and drives the wheels at the back, there is a minimum shelf for two people to sit on and a minimum cover keeps some of the rain off their heads. But people want to keep it the way it has been since 1910, and Morgan can't make enough cars to satisfy demand, which means they must surely be classics?

Being a pure racing car and a one-off as well, the Nardi of 1955 probably shouldn't be here at all, but it deserves a mention for some of its technical novelties. Built by Enrico Nardi for two Frenchman to tackle the 1955 Le Mans 24-hour race, this car was built like a catamaran, with one pontoon containing the driver and the other one containing a 64 bhp, twin overhead camshaft, 750 cc engine. The platform in the middle contained a surface cooling radiator and a tiny hole which masqueraded as a passenger compartment to meet the contemporary regulations (which demanded two-seaters). Nardi's opinion of the regulations could best be judged by the fact that he even made good use of the passenger compartment – the lid was also an air brake! The whole machine was streamlined, with enclosed wheels, looked fabulous but didn't really work.

Opel come from Germany and their only sports car to date was the pretty little GT Coupé of 1969, made from Kadett saloon bits with

Car Of The Year in 1978, this is one Porsche that doesn't have a rear-mounted, air-cooled engine. It is, of course, the 928, with 4.5 litres of front-mounted, water-cooled vee eight and magnificent roadholding, performance and comfort.

a 1.9 litre, ohc engine, disc brakes and retractable headlamps. With the right motor (there were options) it would do 115 mph and handled well. For some reason, not many were made, although it was well liked.

Matters are a little easier now that we have disposed of the Big Three from Italy (Ferrari, Lamborghini, Maserati) as well as most of the lesser and smaller beasts, but we must include Spain's only sports car since the Hispano Suiza left Barcelona, the late-lamented Pegaso. This was made between 1951 and 1958 (in the old Hispano works, curiously enough) by a truck company, Empresa Nacional de Autocamiones SA. It was a jeweller's joy, with four overhead camshafts in a dry-sump, 2.5 litre vee eight putting power to the rear wheels through a transaxle with five speeds. Nothing about it was simple, with a De Dion rear end and torsion bar suspension, but it was Spain's pride and joy. They called the first one Tipo Z102, and there were later and lesser models with smaller engines and less complications. But a full house car came with anything up to eight Weber carburettors or a Roots supercharger. Only 125 of all the various types were ever made, so each was a collector's item.

To go with the big machines, we might have a little German device – preferably an air-cooled Porsche. The two latest models, the 924 and 928 are water-cooled and front-engined, which somehow seems a sacrilege after 30 years of rear-engined, air-cooled classics. The 924 is actually a reversion to the basis from which Porsche started, cobbling up sports cars out of production VW or Audi saloon parts, which does not make a collectable classic car.

No, there is only one model to

Right
Another sporting saloon, the Saab Turbo; not as innocent as it looks, being the first really workable, road-going turbo-car.

choose, and that is the 911S in any of its many forms, which did so much for so many on the road, on the track and in rallies. There was, of course, a Carrera version as well, but that is going a bit far for road use and makes one rather conspicuous. A standard, 2.7 litre version of the 911, with its flat-six engine at the rear, was very satisfactory despite all its vices. For normal people, 150 mph or so without effort is quite adequate! One doesn't want to get involved with turbos or flat 12s or complex racing machinery, and should be happy with a relatively cooking machine that is a pleasure to drive.

11

4 Cylinders or Fewer: Workhorses of the World

If anyone took the time and trouble to do his sums, there is little doubt that he would discover that more people drive four-cylinder cars than those of any other configuration, and that this has probably been so almost since the motor-car was invented. Most of the really big-selling, mass-production cars have had four or fewer cylinders: Ford Model T, Chevrolet before 1928, Citroen 2CV, Austin, Morris, Fiat, Jeep and so on. Taxation has played its part, particularly in France (where it killed off the big engine) and in Italy. In Britain, long-stroke engines were encouraged under the old RAC formula, which took no account of stroke.

Most people started with singles, although Daimler had a twin by 1899. Cylinders were cast singly, then in pairs on a common crankcase, before the monobloc came along. There have been cars with one, two, three, four, five, six, eight, 12 and 16 cylinders and by diligent searching it might even be possible to fill in the odd numbers, as there were radial or rotary aircraft engines with seven and nine cylinders. Some makes use the number of cylinders almost as a trademark: Ford had four until he took to eight; Chevrolet started with six, went to four and then reverted to six; Bugatti liked eight and Ferrari 12. Lanchester tried two, four, six and eight, while Jaguar always liked six until they discovered 12. Rolls-Royce tried a three and an eight, but their cars were usually sixes until recent times.

What we want to look at in this chapter are the best, most successful or most intriguing fours, the ones worth keeping for some outstanding virtue or maybe just a quirk which made them likeable.

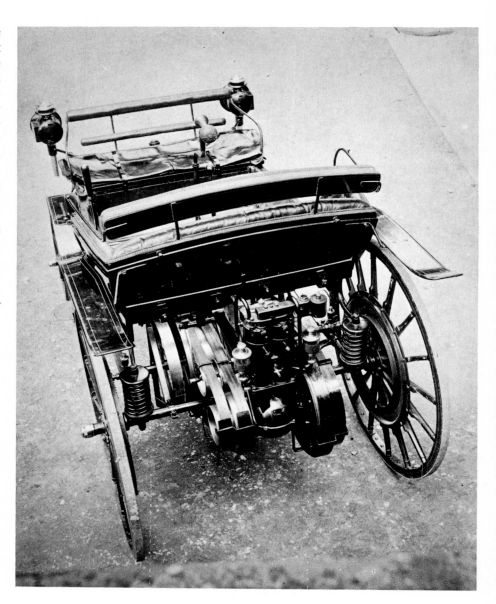

First coil-spring suspension? First belt-drive transmission? An early Daimler from Bad Connstatt, probably made in 1895.

Spyker are usually credited with making the first six, but who made the first four? Panhard, before they disappeared, used to advertise themselves as the world's oldest car-makers, and they had a four in their catalogue by 1905/6. Like

most people, they used Daimler or Benz engines in the beginning, as these were the only ones made. The first British car was supposed to be made by Lanchester, (although some credit John Henry Knight with one in 1896) and Lanchester had a four by 1904, his Model 20 with water-cooled 2,472 cc, ohv engine.

All of them, however, were anticipated by the first Mercedes of

Beans are not the most popular choice among discerning collectors, many of whom hold that they only sold in the late 1920s because there weren't enough cars around to satisfy the market. This 1925 14 hp tourer, with a four of 2,750 cc, is more modern than its predecessors.

1901, which we have heard all about, but which did have four cylinders of 116 mm × 140 mm, 5.93 litres, 35 bhp at 1,000 rpm and 45 mph. De Dion, another early bird, ran a team of four-cylinder *voiturettes* in the ill-fated Paris–Madrid race of 1903, but this was their first four and so was later than Mercedes. Alternatively, there was Peugeot, who claimed to have sold the first petrol-driven car in France, but by 1902 they were offering only 'four-cylinder cars on Mercedes lines' according to contemporary lore.

Léon Bollée was another pioneer, but his four was in 1903. There were few other makers at that time, two being Alexandre Darracq, who raced (but didn't sell) a four in 1902, and de Dietrich, who also had a 1902 four. The early Americans were all singles, so it looks as if Mors made the first four in 1899 and Mercedes made the best one, as fitted to the Mercedes Sixty which, as already discussed, was the original prototype of the modern car.

We have been into the merits of the Model T, the Austin Seven, the Morris Cowley (or Oxford) and the Fiat Mouse, which were some of the best examples of fours in terms of practicality, long life, design merit and market impact. But many others have left their mark on the history of the motor car and these are worth seeking out.

We have considered some of the bigger and later Alvis cars, but their 12/50 of 1923 onwards carved out its own niche for rugged simplicity. It had a simple, pushrod ohv four of 1,500 cc producing only 50 bhp and with no design quirks, but it made many friends for its reliability. The bodywork was not as impressive as the later Speed Twenties but there were some good-looking sports two-seaters with pointed tails, even if the tourers and saloons were a bit

mundane. The 12/50, which lasted until 1932, deserves its place for becoming such a pillar of the Vintage movement and a stepping-stone for so many drivers.

Austin may have been famous for their Seven, but another model which endeared itself to many British families in the 1920s was the Heavy Twelve-Four. This must

Opposite, top
The archetypal vintage car, W. O. Bentley's first 3.0 litre, with long stroke, single-ohc, 70 bhp engine. It appeared at the London Motor Show in 1919 and this car, the first, is seen with Bentley himself at the wheel.

Opposite, lower
The first real Bugatti production car, a Type 13 of 1910 with 1,327 cc, four-cylinder, ohc and two valves per cylinder.

not be confused with the Light Twelve, a six-cylinder machine which did nothing right and did not help the company name. But the Heavy Twelve of 1,661 cc, a worthy side valve which could just about drag itself along by modern performance standards, was indestructible and ran until 1936, rivalling the long life of models like the Model T and the Silver Ghost. It usually had solid and heavy, closed coachwork, although there were tourers, sometimes with railway-carriage-hoop-like handles, an external luggage grid, and a stern upright mien. It would carry great weights at up to 45 mph, more or less for ever.

Bean made a four in 1919–26 and again in 1928–29. It varied in size from 1,794 cc up to 2,297 cc, was side-valved and no racer, but it was

Front-wheel-drive was the chief innovation on this BSA Scout of 1937–39, with a 1,204 cc side-valve engine, 32 bhp and a top speed of 65 mph.

cheap to buy and many survived. Before becoming Bean, it was Perry, and after it was Bean it became Hadfield Bean. People were rude about it, but the 2.3 litre Fourteen was not a bad-looking car, with sporting rear-quarters and a rear-sloping screen plus rakish wings.

Among famous four-cylinder engines, the two Bentley units – the 3 and the $4\frac{1}{2}$ – can hardly be left out. We have touched on Bentley in general terms, including their sixes, but should look more closely at the fours. Only 2,472 four-cylinder Bentleys were ever made, 1,639 of

The first electric starter to be fitted in mass production was American, as you might expect. It went on Cadillac's 5.5 litre, 30 hp tourer in 1912, this particular car being made the following year.

3.0 litres and 733 of the 4.5 litre, but they have probably made as much noise in motoring history as the millions of Model Ts and Jeeps. The first, four-cylinder 3.0 litre Bentley was sold in 1921 to a rich, young man called Noel Van Raalte, and the marque lasted less than ten years before going broke. The 3.0 litre was 80 mm × 149 mm with four valves per cylinder operated by a single ohc. It was unremarkable, producing only 70–85 bhp, yet it became a legend.

The 4.5 litre, which came in 1927, was a bigger 3 or a cut-down, six-cylinder 6.5 litre, according to which historian you read. It still had four valves per cylinder and a non-detachable head, which did not make life easy for mechanics. The cars were built like battle cruisers, which is maybe why they lasted so well.

BMW have escaped the net, except for their luxury cars, while their most famous model – the 328 sports car of 1937 – was a six-cylinder. Probably their most successful and reliable four-cylinder model was a postwar saloon called the 1602 which sold in great numbers and was developed into a more sporting device, with 2.0 litres and fuel injection: the 2002ti, with 120 bhp and 110 mph top speed. This was a straight-forward, two-door saloon, front-engined, rear-drive and with a single-overhead-camshaft engine, but it had reliability plus reasonable performance allied to economy and put the company back on its feet after a difficult period when the 'bubble-car' boom ended, and motorcycle production declined.

There was even a four-cylinder Cadillac once, of which 75,000 were sold between 1906 and 1914. It was called the 30 Horse Power and had separately-cast cylinders, together with the luxury of copper water-jackets. It had the usual planetary

gearbox with which most US cars started, but later models offered an orthodox, manual gearbox with three ratios, and the complication of a two-speed axle as well.

The Chrysler-Matra-Simca Bagheera wins a place as the only car designed with three seats in the front and none in the back, which can lead to all kinds of witticisms. It looked like a world-beater but had only a four-cylinder, 1,294cc Simca engine in its tail and just topped 100mph. In some senses, it was a phoney (like the Rancho from the same stable, which pretends to be a super-safari car but is really for the promenade), but the Bagheera was a nice enough

Left
Modern Citroen 2CV, still much the same car as was envisaged by its designer in 1939, although now with proper lights, seats and bodywork.

Opposite, lower
Citroen's Light Fifteen (or Traction Avant) was sufficiently lively in its day to succeed in rallies – this one is finishing the 1950 Tulip in Holland.

Below
1920s' rivals on the open road: a 'Bullnose' Morris Cowley is about to be passed by a 'Royal' Clyno.

little pseudo-sports car and had novelty value, even if it was no Ferrari-beater.

Then there was the car with which every French student had his first love affair, the Citroen C. Nicknamed the Citron (lemon) in France, because most of them were painted yellow, it was called the Clover leaf Citroen in Britain because of its open, torpedo bodywork with upturned tail. Thousands were made and it was one of the first designs which took account of the actual needs of the public, with a host of useful and/or economy features.

It was the first Citroen with coil ignition and the first car anywhere on which exchange parts were offered at fixed prices and with standard repair charges. Each buyer was given a workshop manual. It only had one door, on the passenger side, with a spare wheel firmly bolted across what would have been the driver's access.

The engine was a four-cylinder, 856cc monobloc with an aluminium block, detachable iron head, 55mm × 90mm bore and stroke, electric starting and a conventional three-speed transmission. It was

Although designed in Britain, the GN Tourer found a manufacturer and a market in France, where it sold in 1921 with an air-cooled, 1,087 cc twin.

rated at 5 hp in France and at 7 hp in Britain, but either way there wasn't much actual power, the unit giving perhaps 11 bhp. The car was tiny, however, measuring only 10 ft 8 ins × 4 ft 5 ins overall, and it only weighed half a ton, so that speeds of almost 40 mph were possible.

Touring and coupé bodies were available, and later versions, with two inches extra length, included a van. Cheap, economical to run, charming to look at and apparently indestructable, it was supposed to be a woman's car until everybody decided to have one. They are still eagerly sought after to this day.

We included Citroen's 2CV elsewhere, but have not admitted the car which brought front-wheel drive to millions, the Light Fifteen or Traction Avant. This was a real innovation when it was introduced in 1935, with torsion bar suspension, monocoque body/chassis construction, wet cylinder liners *and* fwd. It had 1.6 litres, a funny gear-lever sticking out of the dash, and later came a long wheel-base model with a 1.9 litre engine; known as the Big Six, this needed a very wide street in which to turn round. But a standard, black Traction Avant had a musical exhaust conjuring up images of Inspector Maigret. It was as French as the Metro and Gaulloise.

There have been so many fours that we are bound to leave out some good ones, but the idea is to distill the essence of the best. So what is missing? What about the Clyno, which was not terribly good but was the great thing in its day, until the company went bust? It competed with the Morris Cowley and the 10.8 was the one to have, with a Coventry-Climax, 1,368 cc side-valve. They were Britain's third-biggest at one time, but faded away by 1928, shortly after introducing their own engines.

A little-known British sports car

Opposite, top
You needed a fur coat to travel on one of these in such conditions. This Fiat 60 of 1904 had 10.0 litres spread between its four cylinders, plus chain drive and detachable wheel rims.

Opposite, lower
A chapter on four cylinder cars without a Ford Model T is unthinkable, so here is one. They eventually made 16½ million of them, so it must have been good.

with handling way ahead of its competitors was the Cooper, made by the racing car firm which dominated the 500 cc Formula 3 class after the Second World War. Their attractive little two-seater with a no-nonsense look could be had in 1949–54 with various engines; although some of these were sixes (Bristol and Jaguar) the earlier fours had either Vauxhall or MG power plants. It was a most handy little fun car, inexpensive to repair, and it was a pity that it remained in such small production. The engine was 1,203 cc or 1,250 cc depending on make, and it used two SU carburettors; with cycle wings, it was much nicer to drive than the big makers' cars.

The Ford empire was built on the four-cylinder car, and – ignoring the Model T – there were, of course, the A and the B, and a whole family of British Fords, including the first £100 saloon car, the two door model 8 hp of 1935. The Model Y was another of the first, mass-motoring products (like the Austin Seven) but it was not a lovely thing, with transverse leaf springs (which let it roll about) and a side-valve engine. The Eight was joined by the Ten, an egg-shaped thing, also not lovely. They fore-shadowed a whole gamut of Anglias and Prefects which switched names and engines in bewildering fashion, and the only remarkable thing about them was that a lot were sold. They lacked character either in appearance or performance, and the first of the Ford fours which might be considered a classic was the later Escort, which proved a wolf in sheep's clothing in rallying and racing and has been made in millions since 1968. The first Escort was in 1955, with a 100E sidevalve 1,172 cc engine, but the modern versions have always had overhead valves in various engines from 1,098 cc up to 2.0 litres. The

Even mighty Mercedes made do with fours in their top cars of early times. This 1910 device boasted 35 bhp and a top speed of 80 km/h.

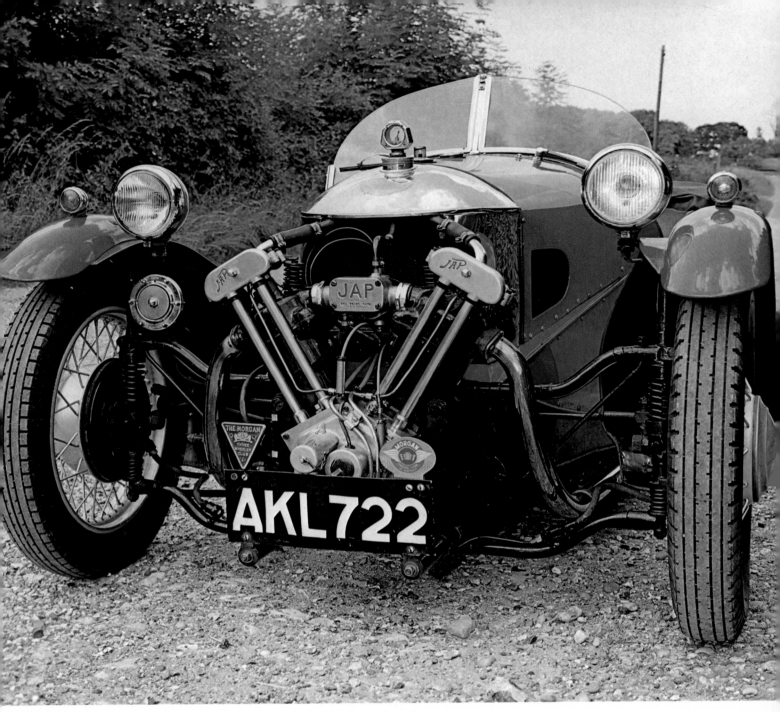

hot ones are the Mexico or RS models, quite different from the normal cars. The most remarkable thing about the Escort is that it is entirely unremarkable, with a front engine driving the rear wheels and no frills at all. A good work-horse.

Two small-production, British sports cars deserved a better fate. The first was by Gilbern, makers of the only motor-car ever built in Wales. It was sold originally as a kit-car and came with a spaceframe chassis and a glassfibre body of pleasing lines. Various engines could be had, but the four-cylinder, MGB unit of 1,800 cc gave this light car a reasonable performance.

The other one was from Ginetta, who are still with us but now only make a six. Their four was a kit car with a glassfibre body in open two-seat form (later came a coupé) and the best were the early ones with Ford or MGB units, as in the Gilbern. There have also been vee six and vee eight versions.

One might also include the H. E., a British car made by Herbert Engineering from 1919 to 1931. It was a quality product, and the fours ran until 1929, with side-valves and around 2.0 litres. Most were tourers.

After such worthy vehicles, we must have something a bit more far-

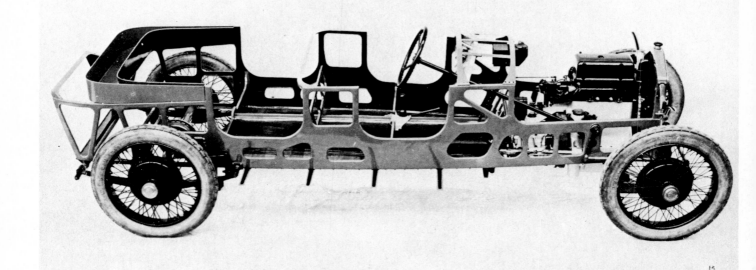

Opposite, top
The first car with unit construction was the Lancia Lambda of 1922, with independent front suspension and a typical, narrow-angle vee four.

Left
The world's fastest-accelerating four-cylinder motor car, the Lotus 7. Now made by Caterham Cars of England, it can be had with big-valve Ford 1,600 cc twin cam power and the ability to beat everything but a Ferrari or a Lamborghini from 0 to 60 mph, after which the aerodynamics take over and slow things down.

Above
The Mk1 Lotus Cortina in appropriate pose, driven by the late, great Jim Clark to victory in the 1964 British Saloon Car Championship. This Ford twin-cam powered saloon led to the 1960s and '70s profusion of sports saloons.

fetched, so how about a 1912 Pic Pic from Switzerland. This was never made in millions but was successful in racing and was different. There were a number of four-cylinder models, ranging from 12 hp up to 23/40, and this larger one had a rather Mercedes look about it, being a sporting two-seater with spare tyres strapped on the back – and not just for show on the dirt roads that predominated at the time. They were noted for their silent running and elegant coachwork, quite apart from their competition successes, and seem to have been a paragon of every motoring virtue. By 1914, they had front-wheel brakes and hydraulic shock-absorbers, years ahead of anyone else, thanks partly to the Hispano – Suiza designer, Mark Birkigt, who was Swiss.

Renault are very much four-cylinder people and have been for a long time, so that one is hard put to choose a single model worthy of preservation. They started with singles and twins and have had some sixes and eights, but the Régie was really built on successful fours, like the current range from 4 up to 20, with only the vee six 30 on top.

Before the Second World War, they made a very large four-cylinder of 2.4 litres with side-valves, sold under the slogan 'There's more room in a Renault' but, by and large, their cars were undistinguished and did not catch the imagination, except perhaps the Juvaquaine of 1937 with a 1,003 cc engine in a good-looking two-door saloon. The big sellers were the

postwar cars, the already discussed 4CV of 1945–61, the Dauphine (so disliked by insurance companies), the R4 (that strange carry-all with unequal wheelbase) and the rear-engined R8. The company did a complete switch from rear-engine to front-engine with fwd, beginning with the R4, and this one was perhaps the most classic of them all, even with its funny steering and gear-change.

The R5 is much more civilized and modern, more of a motor-car and less of a load-carrier; the R16 is also a worthy machine, spoilt by its looks. Come to that, the R12 has its merits too, with performance allied to economy, although again it is not beautiful.

Warming to the theme of good old fours, one should consider the Riley, a British sporting machine of the 1920s and 1930s. We say 'sporting' as, although many of them were saloons, they somehow had a name for being just the thing for bright young men. Perhaps the lightweight fabric bodies on some Nines gave them this image, as well

Above
A latter-day addition to the ranks of four-cylinder classics, this is no ordinary Porsche 924, but a 1978 turbo.

Opposite, top
Pre-dating the Volvo-Renault-Peugeot engine-sharing scheme by 20 years, the 2.0 litre Standard Vanguard engine was used by Morgan, Swallow Doretti, Peerless, Warwick, some tractors and this, the Triumph TR3, which sold and raced successfully between 1954 and 1961.

Right
Cheap and adequate, the 9 hp Riley Imp of 1935 was almost the A-H Sprite of it's day.

as their use in trials, rallies and races. We went into Riley before, and it is true that they were not all fours, but the major models were. The Nine from the Vintage period (pre-1930) with 1,087 cc and short pushrods from high twin camshafts was the classic, but this basic engine went into the 1.5 litre saloon after Riley had become part of the Nuffield empire. If one wanted an early fun car, one could go for a Nine in one of its many variations –

even a Brooklands real racer. The
later 1.5, which went on to 1955,
was more sedate and refined but
was rather heavy and needed to be
helped by the addition of twin
carburettors. It had leather and
wood and all the attributes then
considered desirable, but was quite
orthodox apart from its use of

torsion bars and the high-cam
engine. It also started the fashion
for black imitation leather stuck all
over the roof. It was undeniably a
nice-looking vehicle in its day and
motored well.

The 2.5 had much more power
and speed, but its poor steering lock
and a great long bonnet combined
to make it a bit of an embarrassment
when emerging from side roads or
in tight corners. There were a few
drophead coupé versions of both
1.5 and 2.5 litres which were
desirable.

Also in the big league among
fours is Rover's most famous and
best-selling model, the Land
Rover. This company were long
noted for comfortable, leather-
bound cars for doctors and vicars,
although they did experiment with
air-cooled twins, ohc fours and the

famous Light Six of 1930, which
beat the Blue Train from St
Raphael (on the French Riviera) to
Calais. Few people except Dudley
Noble, who planned it, knew that
the train averaged only 40 mph.

But such antics have nothing to
do with the sober Land Rover,
which began life in 1948 as a sort of
grown-up Jeep with the four-
cylinder, 1,600 cc engine from the
Rover 60. It went from strength
to strength with bigger engines,
longer wheelbase and all kinds of
special equipment to be a world-
wide best seller for 30 years. It must
figure in our story as a workhorse if
not as a glamour machine and as a
forerunner to the Range Rover, a
very different sort of vehicle which
began a trend that tempted all sorts
of manufacturers into the cross-
country car market.

The Jeep itself should also be included of course, although not in its modern vee eight form but in the original (Second World War) rugged, open four-seater design, as made by the Willys Corporation and used by the Allied Armies in Europe. It was pulled by a 2.2 litre four which used petrol at a prodigious rate when driven fast, but it had four-wheel drive and could go anywhere. Millions of Jeeps ran all over Europe and many still do and, although the Land Rover has usurped the Jeep as a farm vehicle in some countries, the Jeep is probably a permanent institution.

From the Continent we should also look at one of the most successful French cars of its day, the Salmson of around 1927 with a twin ohc, 1,100 cc motor in a smart two-seater which did well in racing. The earlier versions were fascinating, as they had a single pushrod operating each pair of overhead valves, pushing one and pulling the other. They were attractive-looking little cars and went well for their size. For the

Another manufacturer with a distinguished sporting record was Salmson of France, who produced this Grand Sport with an 1,100 cc twin cam engine in 1925. The company were among the many who later suffered at the hands of MG.

ohc models, the suffixes were GS and SS. There were saloon bodies, but the open two-seater was much more the right style. The Salmson had lots of peculiarities but was a good goer and somehow captured the spirit of the open French roads of the late 1920s. It was a desirable acquisition, although a friendly French mechanic to go with it would have been useful too.

One cannot overlook the Beetle from Volkswagen, which beat the Model T in numbers produced and lasted even more years; it really began before the Second World War, although not produced for civilians until later. It was laughable, if not tragic, that the British experts, who could have had the factory for nothing after the war, said that the car would never sell and that they did not want it. Many millions are now roaming the

The original 'people's car' came from Germany, of course, in the immortal shape of the Volkswagen Beetle. This car, still recognisably the same basic design in 1977 as it was in 1947, demonstrates the benefits of persevering with a model range by making continual, detail improvements.

world! The 1303 Cabriolet has become a snob car for the young of Europe, while the sedan Bettle is still made in South America. It began as a robust, 1,131cc runabout with a backbone chassis and rear-mounted, flat-four, air-cooled engine, which grew eventually to 1,584cc, and the body stayed static apart from cosmetic changes. Initially, there were no luxuries – not even a fuel gauge – and a piece of bent pipe by the driver's left foot turned the fuel on or off or selected the reserve; if kicked by mistake when overtaking it was bad news. Handling was eccentric and there were all sorts of crudities, but it sold millions all over the world and must be included in any definitive list of immortal cars.

VW produced another worldbeater in more recent times. This was the little Golf Diesel: the smallest, most successful, dieselengined car so far, which offers wonderful benefits to people living in those countries where diesel fuel is half the price of petrol. If the use of such cars spreads, governments will, of course, put the tax up to spoil the diesel's advantage, but this does not detract from the technical merit of the VW. All previous diesels needed some special starting technique (with heater plugs or other means of introducing heat to the cylinder head) to fire the fuel, which was then kept ignited by a compression ratio of 20:1 or so. But in the Golf, the driver can – in moderately warm weather – just switch on and start up, as in a petrol car; there are heater plugs but they need only be used for a few seconds, if at all. Admittedly, the Golf sounds like a London bus when ticking over, but on the move it is just like a petrol car, with adequate performance and 50 or 60 mpg. The company commissioned the car during the 1973 petrol crisis and it was ready for test in three months. It uses the 1,500 cc engine from the petrol car, suitably strengthened and modified, while the overhead camshaft belt drive

Opposite, top
One that got away: this Triumph Roadster was shown at the Paris Motor Show in 1945, but never went into production.

Opposite, lower
The Volvo liked by enthusiastic drivers, the PV444 had only 1.4 litres and 40 bhp, but it won lots of rallies, sold outside Scandinavia and was made from 1944 to 1961. Volvo's have only got bigger since then.

Below
Based on the 2.3 litre Sunbeam-Talbot 90, the two-seater Alpine was a sports car for the masses, its appeal greatly enhanced by competition successes like Stirling Moss' Alpine Rally Gold Cup win in 1954.

also turns the injection pump, which is clever. Top speed is 87 mph and power output is the same as the 1100 cc petrol car – 50 bhp. It is 50 per cent slower to 60 mph (18 secs against 12) but this does not show up in normal driving.

12

5 or 6 Cylinders: Is more always better?

Whether the world ever *needed* a six-cylinder car is a good question, but someone sold the idea that six meant smoothness and superiority. When? Well, the long-defunct British firm of Napier claimed to have the first production six in 1905, but most people now accept that Spyker of Holland beat them to it, with an innovative, four-wheel-drive device of 50 hp in 1903.

The most famous six of all time, however, was probably the Silver Ghost. Despite being on the market for nearly 20 years (from 1906 to 1925), very few were made, so that its fame must be a tribute to the publicity powers of someone, perhaps Claud Johnson, who was known as 'the hyphen in Rolls-Royce'. Napier sixes also enjoyed a tremendous reputation, but they were dead by 1924 and made little mark on the industry.

There must have been thousands of six-cylinder models, but how many had a real effect on motoring history? Most Britons think of the US as the land of the vee eight, and this is so today, but there were many famous American sixes in the past (notably from Chevrolet). After Napier and Rolls-Royce (who was only one year behind Napier with his first six), the only English maker that springs to mind is Talbot, whose cars were designed by the Swiss, Georges Roesch. They were notably good, ranging from a rather slow 65 model to the distinctly rapid, 3.5 litre 110, and all were ahead of their time, silent-running and trouble-free. Other names worthy of mention are Wolseley, Hotchkiss, Lagonda, Mercedes, Bentley and Hispano, ignoring the other side of the Atlantic Ocean for a moment. Of these, Wolseley was nearly ruined by a dreadful machine called 'The Silent Six' until rescued by Bill Morris (Lord Nuffield). Morris himself, or rather his company, made an appalling, ohc six-cylinder just after the Second World War called the Morris Six, later to become the ohv Isis. As if history were repeating itself, there were

Opposite, top
One of the world's first six-cylinder production cars, the Napier 30/35 of 1913, this one with a Cunard body.

Left
By 1917, America was already a six-cylinder country, with cars like this Winston seven-passenger touring model.

Wolseley versions in a series of badge-engineered cars called the 6/80. These models ran from 1948–58 as Morrises, from 1948–54 as the Wolseley 6/80 and from 1956–59 as the Series I and II 6/90, which was fitted with the 2,639 cc ohv unit. Both the ohc Morris Six and the 6/80 were villains and did not last long or sell well.

Audi have confounded us all by producing a five-cylinder engine, a rare configuration for a petrol engine, although Mercedes produce a five-cylinder diesel and there were three-cylinder-Rolls-Royces once upon a time.

Audi may set a trend with their five-cylinder 100, which offers 136 bhp from 2,144 cc (against 115 bhp from 1,984 cc in their four-cylinder engine). One therefore gains more than one-fifth in power from a one-twelfth increase in size.

Although Bentley made sixes, there were only three models: the $6\frac{1}{2}$-Litre, the Speed Six (which was almost the same thing) and the 8-Litre. Only 100 of the 8.0 litre models were made and 544 of the other two combined, so it was very much a minority product; it was another public relations triumph, however, because we now think of Bentley in the context of the six, when he really did much better with fours.

In Europe, BMW have recently espoused six-cylinder engines for their smaller cars (they have long used them in big ones) and the response of most critics has been, why? The old 1500/1602 series were well liked and well behaved and the succeeding '3' series cars carry on the tradition, as do the '5' series. But the 520, 525, 528 and 530 have all gone six, and the 520 offers an extra 13 mph (from 99 to 112) at a point where it can be little

Opposite, top
A famous six-cylinder: the 1937 Mille Miglia Alfa Romeo, with 2,300 cc engine and coupé body.

Opposite, lower
Fangio and Sala in their 3.0 litre, six-cylinder Alfa Romeo on their way to second place in the 1953 Mille Miglia.

Above
A rare car, the convertible DB5 Aston Martin of 1965, with the classic straight-six engine built at Newport Pagnell.

used and at a cost of 27.4 mpg instead of 28.8 mpg. One wonders why BMW, whose fours have done so well, have made this move, unless they think that the six has more prestige and will sell better. In practical terms, the 520 offers 122 bhp against the 90 bhp of the 518, but then it is a bigger unit at 1,990 cc against 1,766 cc. In arithmetical terms, an increase of one-eighth in size has yielded an increase of one-third in power, although the reasons may be quite unrelated to the number of cylinders.

Since this company have an enviable reputation and sound engineers they must consider the six a worthwhile concept.

Chevrolet was another story and, in 1929, introduced their Ford-knocking advert; 'A six for the price of a four', which referred to the famous Stovebolt Six. It had 50 bhp from a 3.2 litre ohv and lasted right through the 'Blue Flame' series until 1955, when they produced a lightweight vee eight. Before that, the six went through the Second World War in trucks. Chevvies had straight sixes and Fords had vee eights in basically similar vehicles supplied to the Allied forces. After the war, even the Corvette started with a six.

La Salle, another General Motors make, agreed with Ford, ignored the six and ran on vee eights. But Oldsmobiles from the same stable were six-cylinder vehicles from 1930, although they had used vee eights from as early as 1915 and had the first American, L-head vee eight cast en bloc. They brought the eight back in 1932, but

the six ran alongside, as the F-31, and sixes accounted for three-quarters of Oldsmobile production in the 1930s. Their F-34 six had only six horse power less than the 84 bhp, L-34 eight-cylinder.

Another GM division, Pontiac, also abandoned the vee eight for an L-head, 3.3 litre six in 1932 and stayed with sixes up to 1954. The six then lived on for the Canadian market.

The Americans realised the benefits of the multi-cylinders early on, with straight and vee eights, but they made some fine sixes too. The Chrysler Red Head of 1924 was one, with a 3.3 litre block, and it went on until 1933, when most models became slaves to the eight, which had arrived in 1931. The De Soto was another Chrysler model which surrendered to the eight in 1930, but before that it had used the Chrysler Six and sold 100,000 in a year. They stretched the wheelbase of the De Soto by five inches to take the eight, and offered the six in stylish models like the Victoria Cabriolet. In fact the eight never

sold as well as the six, and was dropped in 1931. The 1932 De Soto had a freewheel, a vacuum-operated clutch, and was offered in eight body styles with the bored-out six-cylinder. It also had Chrysler's Floating Power, which was a rubber engine mounting, front and rear. The L-head six went up to 3.5 litres in 1933 and the compression ratio up from 5.2:1 to 6.0:1, which sounds low today.

In 1934, De Soto's only model was the Airflow, a Chrysler design which has been called the ugliest car ever. As the total output of cars in the US slumped from 4,794,898 in 1929, to 1,860,185 in 1932, this was not really the time to bring in a radical new model, even if it did, as the advertisement claimed 'bore a hole in the wind'. De Soto had their worst year in 1934, managing only about half the previous year's sales – just 11,447 cars. They kept on with sixes after the Second World War, until 1954, when vee eights were everywhere.

Dodge was another Chrysler division to push the six, which they took to in 1929 after favouring fours. The old Dodge Brothers Victory Six used a unit of 3.4 litres and in 1932, like De Soto, it acquired the Floating Power gimmick. Dodge dropped the eight in 1933 as well, and stayed with the six, the 3.6 litre L-head giving 87 bhp at 3,600 rpm. They ran with straight sixes right up to 1959, and then switched to what they called a slant six.

Plymouth, yet another Chrysler line, ran a six up to 1955, when the vee eight came in, so superseding a power plant in use since 1933. Plymouth had Floating Power, too, sold with 'the smoothness of an eight, the economy of a four'.

Henry Ford, who jumped from a four to a vee eight when he brought in the successor to his Model A in 1932, ignored the six until 1941, although the old vee eight went on until around 1949. Perhaps the most notable six-cylinder Ford was the cheaper version of the Mustang from 1964 on, but it was the vee eight model which really mattered and Ford of America doesn't figure much in the six-cylinder saga.

In Germany, however, Ford take a very different view. Many of their cars for the world markets are made there. The Capri must be one of their best sellers ever, as not many modern designs run for ten years, and the styling has only been changed to include a hatchback door. The 60-degree vee six engine comes in various sizes from 2.0 litres up, and powers what they call the Taunus in Germany and the bigger Cortinas and Granadas in Britain. Another example of rationalisation. Ford have no straight six, and, with the vee four confined to trucks these days, make cars only with straight fours or vee sixes which must be a unique situation for a big manufacturer.

The Hispano-Suiza was virtually a one-model car after 1919 and certainly was always a six, apart from an abortive V12. The model

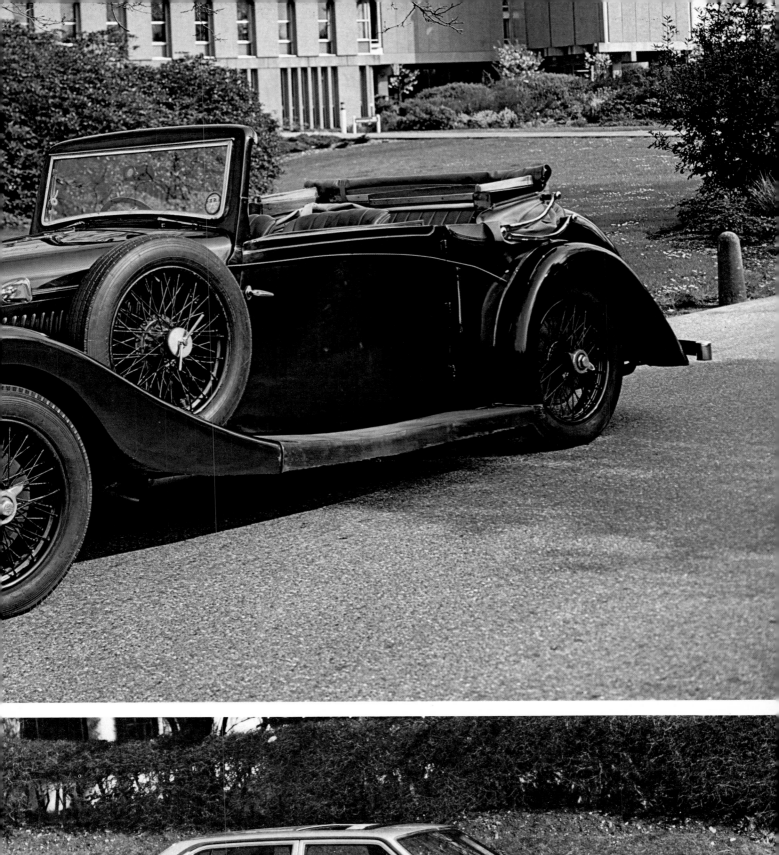

was the H6B, and the H6C or Boulogne was its more sporting derivative. The B had 6.6 litres and 135 bhp delivered at 3,000 rpm from six cylinders of over 1.0 litre apiece. There was a single, overhead camshaft and one advanced practice was the use of steel liners in an aluminium block, derived from their experience in the manufacture of aero engines, some of which were used in British machines in the First World War. The sporting C went up to 8.0 litres using 110 mm × 140 mm and used a seven-bearing, pressure-fed crank, also ahead of its time. The famous brake servo (adopted later by Rolls-Royce) was driven off the gearbox and imposed a slight delay while the works wound themselves up, but the car was capable of 85 mph when

this was a considerable speed, and it had comfortable suspension as well. The Hispano, made in both France and Spain was, of course, designed by Mark Birkigt.

The independent firm of Hudson relied on their Super-Six right through the 1920s, when they called themselves 'the world's largest manufacturer of six-cylinder cars'. Later Hudson moved on to an eight, but the Essex Terraplane – which also sold in England – used the Super Six Hudson engine, a 3.15 litre unit producing 70 bhp at 3,200 rpm. They continued to build sixes right up to their purchase by Nash in 1954, including a revamped one called the H-Power with 145 hp from a 5.0 litre side-valve.

The Hupmobile company tended to go for fours and eights until they

Above, top
This special-bodied Bentley belonged to Woolf Barnato, who financed the company until he changed his mind and let them go broke in 1931.

Above
When BMW finally resumed car production in 1952, their first product was the 501 saloon, with a 1,971 cc six based on pre-Second World War designs. It was solid and well-made.

Opposite, top
This was the comfortable BMW, but not the fast one. It is the 320 cabriolet, with 2.0 litre engine, a contemporary of the 328.

Opposite, lower
This really is a fast BMW – a modern saloon developed for racing – but the skills of German tuning firms are such that one can run almost as potent a car on public roads, money being the only limiting factor.

produced the 70 bhp, Century Six in 1930. The sixes then went on until Hupmobile merged with Graham-Paige in 1940. Up to 1934, the sixes and eights were quite different cars but, with the so-called Aerodynamic model, they offered either engine in the same body, with headlights faired into the wings.

Jaguar's XK engine made a much bigger mark and went on for longer, starting in 1948 and still going strong 30 years later. It was a 3,442 cc (83 mm × 106 mm) twin ohc unit, producing various amounts of power from 160 bhp upwards according to tune, and it first saw life in the XK 120 sports car. There

should also have been a four-cylinder 2.0 litre, but this was never made because the big one took up all the production facilities. The six is a lovely looking unit which has been modified in various ways and produced in many sizes from 2.4 to 4.2 litres with very few problems. True, early 2.8 versions did tend to consume their pistons, but the answer was found. Jaguar saloon and sports cars still offer a high standard after all this time, and the shapes wear well, even if the late-lamented E-Type did eventually lose its charm.

Another independent, Kaiser-Frazer used an L-head 3.7 litre six from Continental when they came

onto the market in 1947. This 'Red Seal' engine produced 100 bhp in the K100 Special, and the K101 Custom four-door sedans. They featured 'Cradle Ride' which put the passengers between the axles. They ran sixes, ultimately with 118 bhp, until the end came in 1955.

In the Vintage years and into the thirties, Lagonda were certainly in the six-cylinder market more than anything else. True, their famous 2.0 litre was a four, but the 3.0 and the 4.5 litres were all sixes and the later V12 was only made in very small numbers, so we can basically regard them as a six-cylinder firm. The 16/80, which was a six-cylinder version of the 2.0 litre, was

less popular than the equivalent four, but the 3.0 and, more particularly, the 4.5 were well liked both then and now. There were some appealing open tourer bodies on the 4.5 which had 4,453 cc from 88.5 mm × 120.6 mm and gave about 150 bhp. It was an orthodox pushrod machine with a Meadows engine, a mite heavy, but a good slogger at low revs.

Mercedes have been six-cylinder people from 1921, with the 16/50

Road-going version of the newest BMW supercar, the 160 mph, mid-engined M1, which gives the company a Porsche-Ferrari-Lamborghini – beater at last.

Benz limousine (before the Mercedes-Benz link-up) until the present day, although they now use a vee eight in some models. Their biggest production numbers must have been in the 220 series of 1958 onwards.

It is curious that Morris/Wolseley made so many bad sixes as, in addition to those already listed, there were the horrible little Hornets of the 1930s with tiny pistons like egg-cups and a horrendous vertical dynamo doubling as an ohc drive, which filled itself with oil. The original Hornet (1931–33) also had a terrible steering lock and took 169 feet

to stop from 40 mph. Nevertheless it sold with various fancy bodies, wire-mesh lamp-guards, badge-bars and all the trimmings.

The Nash, which came on the market in 1916 and ran up to 1957, ran sixes as well as eights, one famous model being the Ambassador Six. They were much publicised for having seats which converted into a bed. From 1945 to 1954 they made only sixes, mostly under the Rambler label, designed by Pininfarina. One feature was the first, cheap air-conditioning system. Model names eventually included Statesman and Ambassador as well as Rambler, and there was

even a Nash-Healey sports car (of which only 150 were made) using Donald Healey's name, Pininfarina design, and Nash manufacture. In 1953, a hardtop was added to the Nash-Healey and a further 162 were produced.

Opel, a General Motors company with the enormous resources of one of the world's biggest firms behind them, use only four cylinders in-line, except in their 1978 Monza and Senator models, which have a 3.0 litre straight six called the E engine. So we see a conflict of opinion, with Ford on straight fours and vee sixes, and GM on all-straight engines. The Opel, with Bosch L-Jetronic fuel injection, puts out 180 bhp at 5,800 rpm against 138 bhp from Ford's vee six of the same size, which uses a Weber, twin-choke down-draught 38/38 carburettor. The comparison is

Right
The best-looking Bristol of all, the early 401, 2.0 litre, six-cylinder saloon with divided windscreen and wind-cheating shape.

Below
The first of over 50 million Chevrolets, this model came off the line at Detroit in 1912.

interesting but proves nothing unless we go into all the factors involved. Injection alone offers a big power boost, and Opel do not offer a carburettor alternative at all in some markets, so it is difficult to compare like with like.

Packard, sadly no longer with us, were basically eight-cylinder people but also made some sixes, notably in 1937 with the 'junior series'. There was also a Packard

Left, top
Belgium's most magnificent car, the Albert I Excelsior of 1922 onwards was compared by many with the contemporary Hispano-Suiza H6B of France. The Albert came with a 5,350 cc, ohc six, vacuum-servo brakes and 100 mph performance.

Left, centre
The car looks more dated than the aircraft, although there are still plenty of both around. The car is a Mk 1 Ford Zephyr of 1959 with 68 bhp, 2.5 litre six. It came with independent front suspension and ohv. The aircraft is, of course, a de Havilland Comet.

Below
Frazer-Nash Mille Miglia model of 1949, with 2.0 litre, six-cylinder engine offering 125 bhp at 5,500 rpm with open two-seater body.

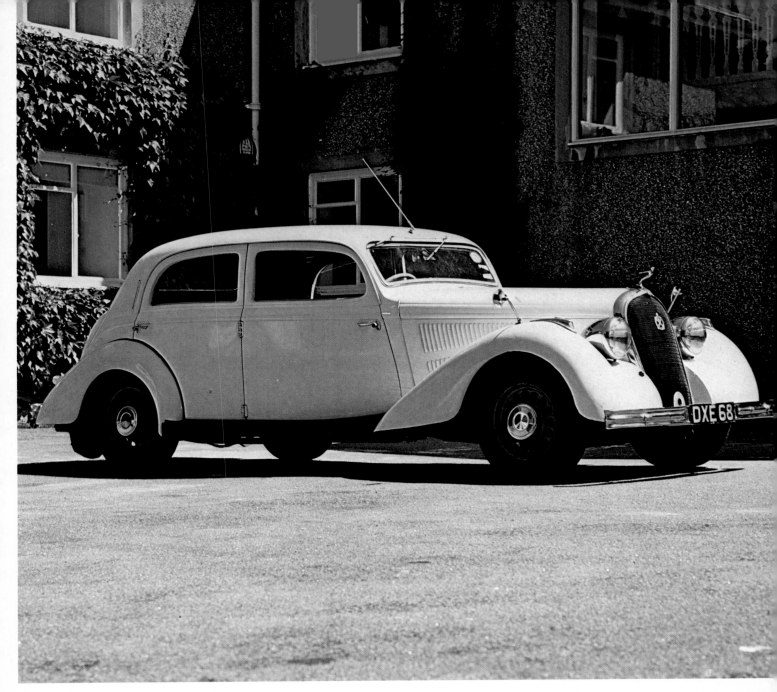

Opposite, top
Fiat's much-underrated 130 coupé which had good looks and, with 3.2 litre vee six power, adequate performance. Sadly, it never seemed to sell and Fiat dropped the model in 1977.

Opposite, lower
Smallest and, for many people, most delectable Ferrari of them all, the Dino 246 with its mid-mounted, transverse, vee six engine. Named after Ferrari's son, it brought Ferrari motoring to a whole new section of the population.

Above
Developed from the car which won the Monte Carlo Rally in 1932, the 20 CV Hotchkiss 686 appeared in 1936 with a 3.5 litre, straight-six. Production of this model was resumed after the Second World War and continued until the mid 1950s.

Six in 1936, the 115 C (which referred to the wheelbase), which used the body of the eight-cylinder 120 in a shorter car. The Six had 100 bhp from 3.8 litres and side valves, with eight different body styles and 65,400 were sold. Their best year was 1937, but in 1938 the Six grew longer by seven inches and was given a V-shaped windscreen. In 1940 the Six became the 110, then the vee eights came and Packard disappeared into Studebaker.

Studebaker were themselves into sixes, having an all-six line-up in 1920, and they did not move to eights until 1928, with the President Eight. Although six or eight cylinders could then be had in the President, Commander and Dictator, by 1931 there was only one six, the Studebaker Six. This was joined in 1932 by the Rockne Six, named after a famous football coach, but it lived only for one year, selling 23,000. The financial troubles which led to the end began at this time, but the famous Studebaker Champion, designed by Raymond Loewy, came in 1939, and was cheaper than a Ford or Plymouth, with a side-valve 2.7 litre six and 78 bhp; they sold 72,791 Champions that year. Postwar sixes included a revamped Champion and the later Flight Hawk of 1953 which had a sporting image.

Not many of these were made: The Lanchester Dauphin 2.5 litre six of 1953, with coupé coachwork and 90 bhp transmitted through a fluid flywheel.

Roesch's Talbots were excellent but had their eccentricities, like a dipstick which pushed down to drain the sump, so that it paid to check the oil oneself and not ask the gas-jockey, who might suddenly find himself standing ankle-deep in dirty oil. Then there was silent starting, without benefit of reduction gear, which even 24 volts could not master. But even with such peculiarities, his six-cylinder engine – particularly in the Talbot 105 of 2,969 cc (75 mm × 112 mm) with 100 bhp – was delightfully sweet-running and free of temperament. It usually had a Wilson preselector gearbox, but there were some, mostly the 2,276 cc Nineties, with a knife-through-butter, right-hand manual change, although this had a rather strange clutch spring which could be troublesome. Roesch's theory was that one should put in fuel, oil and water and just drive, leaving any repairs to the factory; this annoyed the garage trade who could not solve little mysteries, like how to remove the engine. The answer was simple: one started by removing the back axle and worked forward, which one found out only after wrestling with the unnecessary excision of chassis cross-members and other structural items which should never have been touched!

These cars were unusual for their time (the 1930s) in having really effective drum brakes and a one-shot lubrication system to all important points, worked by a plunger next to the famous dipstick. No special tanks needed filling – it was all automatic apart from a pull on the plunger from time to time. Roesch must rank high in the six-cylinder heirachy as he never used anything else after his 10/23 four of 1923. The balance of his engines was marvellous to behold, and they ticked over so slowly that one could count the revolutions of the fan!

Willys, when they ceased to be Willys-Overland in 1930, came out

Opposite, top and bottom
Is it the real thing? No, this is a modern Lynx Replica of the famous D-type Jaguar, which is probably the nearest one can get to a Le Mans winner these days. The engine is genuine enough, however, being a Jaguar dohc six, albeit of non-racing origins.

Above
Lancia's 1913 Theta had six cylinders and five pedals: one for the starter, one for an exhaust cut-out, plus the normal three.

The Talbot man, Georges Roesch, was one of a celebrated band – like Louis Coatalen (the Sunbeam man), Birkigt, Bugatti, Bentley, Royce, Lanchester, Renault and others whose work lives on: today we never know who designs anything apart from those who make racing cars, like Broadley, Chapman, Philippe, Colombo and the rest. Issigonis is one of the few exceptions.

with a six or eight-cylinder alternative in their new car, and soon dropped the four altogether, although it came back for the Jeep. The Great Six was a smart roadster with a vaguely Rolls look about the front. The Model 66, a more sporting roadster, came with a 10 ft wheelbase and 87 bhp. Jeeps kept Willys out of the car market for a while, but they were back in 1952 with a side-valve, 2.6 litre Six called the Hurricane in Aero-Ace and Aero-Wing models. Later, the Lightning Six offered 75 bhp and the Hurricane 90 bhp, but by 1953 Willys had gone with Kaiser.

This review of both independents and big makers shows that the six had a bigger influence in the US market than many people realise. They were late switching from L-head (side-valve) to F head (ohv) but used the six-cylinder configuration from early days until the coming of the vee eight.

Whereas the US six tended to be a poor relation of the eight (or more)

cylinder car, the reverse was the case in Europe, where the six was up-market compared to the four, being fitted to expensive and sporting machines. This remains true today, except that America has become the land of the vee eight while the four still reigns in Europe. It is hard to think of a European eight except Rover (and Morgan) and, formerly, Triumph and MG, while the twelve is confined to Ferrari and Jaguar, now that Lamborghini are tottering. The vee six is a newish concept for mass-production, and is now found in Ford, Peugeot-Renault-Volvo models and in small numbers in Maseratis.

The Peugeot-Renault-Volvo 2.7 litre vee six is one of the most interesting engine developments for a long time as it is powering cars from three different makers in two countries. In the Renault 30, it produces 131 bhp at 5,500 rpm for a top speed of 115 mph, while the other two give similar results differing only in detail: Peugeot claim only 114 bhp from the same engine at the same revs, but 117 mph top speed, using two Solex carburettors while Renault fit a Weber. Volvo use an SU HIF 6 and claim 125 bhp at 5,250 rpm and 117 mph in their 264DL model. The engine uses a light-alloy block and head with four main bearings and wet liners. Weights are: Peugeot 3,065 lbs, Renault 2,911 lbs and Volvo 2,948 lbs. One would expect the massive Volvo to be heavier, and its blunt shape to have more effect on performance, which may be the case, as Peugeot quote 21.7 mpg,

Renault 16.3 and Volvo give no figure at all. Peugeot also offer a 604 TI with Bosch K-Jetronic fuel injection and a claimed figure of 25.9 mpg.

There are parallel cases of Fords for the British market being built in Germany and/or Spain, British Leyland vehicles in other Continental centres, and some Chrysler cars in France, but it is hard to recall a petrol engine which is shared between several makers. This will, of course, be the pattern for the future, particularly with Fiat/Lancia, Peugeot/Chrysler/ Citroen, VW/Audi, Leyland Cars of many colours, and all the other combinations of the future. There has been consultation between Leyland Cars and Datsun, and between Peugeot and Renault, while General Motors have branches everywhere. One of the latest developments in passenger cars, for example – anti-lock braking – has been developed by a German company (Bosch), and appeared first on both Mercedes and BMW. This may have little bearing on six-cylinder cars, but it is quoted to show the way things will go, with more international collaboration, a smaller number of makers in each country, and major components like engines shared, so that assembly plants can become just that.

Opposite, top
A Mercedes 300S Roadster, shown for the first time at Paris in 1952.

Opposite, lower
This toothy grin came from Pininfarina, who 'styled' the 1953 Nash Airflyte Custom Country Club Hardtop Convertible, with Le Mans Dual Jetfire engine! They must have employed more copywriters than engineers.

Top
The British Standard company made this six-cylinder Roi des Belges tourer in 1907.

Centre
Triumph's 2.0 litre, six-cylinder saloon was used as a rally car with success, as was the subsequent 2.5 with petrol injection. This is Paddy Hopkirk on the 1969 RAC Rally.

Bottom
The Hotchkiss Model 686 of 1949, versions of which won the Monte Carlo Rally in both 1949 and 1950.

277

13

8 Cylinders: Safety in Numbers

It would be a long job to make a list of all the world's cars which have used eight-cylinder engines, and nearly as difficult to decide which were the most famous. The United States has always had an affinity for eight cylinders, and although they are today used in vee form in most American shopping cars, the US straight-eight was once something to be proud of.

Bugatti, too, was a major protagonist of the eight although there were four-cylinder Bugattis before 1922. His cars have appeared in earlier chapters, but the classic one was the Type 35 (there was a four-cylinder version of this, known as the Type 37, but this is almost the exception which proves the rule). The other covetable model was the 57SC with a supercharged straight-eight of 3.3 litres. Bugatti was originally opposed to the super-charger and was reluctantly forced into it after the Fiat racing victories of the early twenties.

Every major US maker has had a V8, most of them for a long time. Chevrolet were traditionally six-cylinder cars and stayed that way until 1955, when their 4.3 litre, ohv vee eight appeared with 162 bhp to start with, although this was increased as time went on. If one had to pick a classic vee eight Chevvie, it

Opposite, top
The epitomy of modern Bentley cars, the S2 Continental, with lightweight, aluminium bodywork by H. T. Mulliner, a 6.2 litre Rolls-Royce vee eight and automatic transmission.

Opposite, lower
A vee eight convertible of the 1970's, Aston Martin's Volante of 1978 had a 5.3 litre engine, four double-choke Weber carburettors and supercar performance.

Below
Join the queue behind Arabia's richest oil sheiks if you want one of these—Aston Martin's incredible, expensive, vee eight Lagonda, with space-age electronics, performance and comfort to match.

Above
A most handsome Type 57 Torpedo
Bugatti of 1936 with the straight-
eight engine beloved of Ettore, and
the firm's own coachwork.

Right
Eight-cylinder power, 1966 style. A
Buick Wildcat convertible, with 6.5
litre engine.

Above
The *concours d'elegance* setting for this Lancia Dilambda is redolent of the
early 1930s. Unlike the Lambda, the Dilambda had a separate chassis, along
with a narrow-angle overhead camshaft vee eight engine of four litres. Almost
1,700 of them were made between 1929 and 1932.

would be the Corvette, after Arkus-Duntov had put the vee in place of the six.

Chrysler made fours and sixes until 1931, when they slotted in a couple of straight-eights called the CD and the 6.3 litre CG which could be had with Le Baron bodies. The dreadful Airflow of 1934 was also an eight and lasted three years, losing money, until it gave way to the Airstream. The eights went on in various guises up to 1951, when the first vee eight – the 5.4 litre ohv unit – appeared; at the time, it produced more horse power than any other engine in the US.

Sidelines to the Chrysler eight story are provided by Cunningham (who used a 180 bhp Chrysler unit in his C1, which finished 18th at Le Mans and won at Watkins Glen in 1951); Sydney Allard in England (who used some Chrysler units in his rather special trials and road cars); Facel-Vega in France (who used the 4.5 litre Chrysler 'hemi'); and Jensen in England (who used the same unit, changing the work-aday cam covers for smart, expensive-looking ones but otherwise leaving it alone).

The alphabet naturally brings one to Auburn and Cord, which were of the same empire. Errett Lobban Cord first produced the L-

29 Cord with a 4,934 cc Lycoming engine which simply had to be an eight. This model came in 1929, which could not have been a worse year, as it coincided with the Depression, and only 4,400 had been sold when it faded in 1932. But Cord came back in 1935, with a strange-looking, space-age affair designed by Gordon Buehrig with front-wheel drive, but with a vee eight of 4,730 cc, still from Lycoming. This was the 810 and two years later came the 812 with supercharger and 195 bhp. There were two-seater, tourer and sedan versions of the 810, and a saloon in the later series, with chrome outside exhausts and a very futuristic air.

Supercharging was retained on the 851 Speedster, on which the centrifugal blower turned at six times engine speed, running at up to 24,000 rpm in order to produce 150 bhp from 4,590 cc. Although only a two-seater, this car had a wheelbase of 10 ft 7 ins and weighed

Below
The one with the egg-box front is a Chevrolet Caprice Classic Sport Saloon of 1976 with pillarless construction and, of course, a big vee eight engine. Perhaps a Classic only in name.

Bottom
The car on the left is a racing special produced as a private venture by General Motors styling chief, Bill Mitchell. It's shape led directly to the 1963 Stingray – one of which is on the right – which replaced the more bulbous early Corvette.

When it was introduced in 1956, the Chrysler 300B was billed as the world's fastest production saloon. With a 6.25 litre vee eight, it certainly had more horsepower than anything else, including the rival Ford Thunderbird. Only 2,023 of this GT model were ever built, with all-leather upholstery and 'Powerflite' transmission.

well over 1½ tons, making the presence of 12-inch, hydraulically-operated drum brakes on each wheel most welcome, especially as three-figure speeds were quite possible

Looking at famous straight-eights, Delage and Duesenberg are two of the names which come up at once. Delage made his name with sixes, but the D8 from 1929 onwards was the one to remember. It was a straight-eight of enormous proportions, in a chassis with a wheelbase of either 10 ft 10 ins or 11 ft 11 ins and reminded one more of a locomotive than a motor-car. It used a four-speed gearbox, forced cooling with both pump and fan, and coil ignition, which was then a bit new. The D8 had a relatively small-capacity engine (for its external size) of only 4,050 cc, with pushrod ohv, 77 mm × 109 mm. There was an in-between chassis of 11 ft 8 ins, but they all tended to be big cars, with an 85 mph maximum. This was improved to 100 mph by the Grand Sport of 1932, which started at a wheelbase of 10 ft 3 ins but went up to 10 ft 10 ins like the D8. In 1934 came a smaller D8 with 2,668 cc and independent front suspension with a transverse leaf and wishbones. When Delahaye took over Delage they made the eights even bigger, with 4,300 cc, then 4,743 cc but these later ones did not please the marque's fans as much. There were not many D8s made, but their name has lingered on, like those of other small producers such as Bentley.

The same might be said of Duesenberg, regarded as the ultimate American car, yet they ran only from 1920–1937. To those outside the US, it is always a surprise to discover that the Duesenberg had only eight cylinders; it somehow seemed to deserve

Above
One of the rare Cunningham C3 coupés, built by Vignale to a Michelotti design in 1953 with a 220 bhp Chrysler vee eight engine.

Left
The chassis of Sydney Allard's first special in 1937. With a 1934 Ford vee eight and divided-axle independent front suspension, it was later clothed in a Bugatti GP body.

more, especially as it was credited with 129 mph in SJ form and zero-to-100 mph in 17 seconds. But an eight it was, right from the Model 8 of 4.2 litres, which lasted to 1926. But the ones enthusiasts speak of with bated breath are the J and SJ, which had a 6.9 litre motor made by Lycoming (who, with Duesenberg, belonged to E.L. Cord). The SJ was supercharged, but both had twin, chain-driven, overhead camshafts and four valves per cylinder. This was new to America and came from the racing cars, which had three valves per cylinder and were said to owe something to Bugatti, who used a similar layout.

The Duesenberg had the most of everything: bigger, faster, costlier, heavier and more desirable. It was one of the greatest eights and was supposed to develop 265 bhp at 4,250 rpm.

One of the earliest eights must have been that installed by the Swiss brothers Charles and Frédéric Dufaux in their 1905 racing car. This had four pairs of 125 mm × 130 mm cylinders to give a total capacity of no less than 12,760 cc, which produced an impressive 120 bhp at 1,300 rpm and carried the one ton machine along at 93 mph. The engine needed over 14 gallons of water to keep it cool, while fuel was gobbled up at such a rate that 22 gallons of it had to be carried.

The United States is the real home of the vee eight however, apart from straight-eight men like Miller, Stutz and Duesenberg. The first popular, mass-produced vee eight must have been from Ford, who introduced a 3.6 litre, 70 bhp one in 1932 and sold a million a year by 1935. This car won the Monte Carlo Rally in 1936 and 1938, assisted by some peculiar 'fiddle brakes' which allowed one rear wheel to be locked at a time to help in the driving tests which determined the results. There was also a small Ford vee eight of 2.2 litres, called the Model 60, introduced in 1936, but this was one of many units with very limited performance. It was sold in England too, but had a short life in more senses than one.

A very different eight came from the British firm of Hillman in 1928, described as the cheapest eight-cylinder car on the market, although there cannot have been many competitors. A straight-eight, it was called a 20 Horse Power, had ohv, and there was a two-door model known as the 'Segrave Model' after the famous racing driver. At the 1930 London Motor Show, a new version called the Vortic appeared, but it did not make a great impression.

The Horch company of Germany also favoured straight-eights for their giant cabriolets, which looked brutal and aggressive. The Horch 300, designed by Paul Daimler (son of the famous pioneer), appeared in 1925 with 3,230 cc and twin ohc. The cars got steadily bigger until 1930, when the company switched to new, sohc eights of 4.0, 4.5 and 5.0 litres, this engine running until 1939.

The Isotta-Fraschini company used four-cylinder engines until their designer, Giustino Cattaneo, went for a one-model programme after the Second World War with a 5,880 cc straight-eight with alloy block, three-speed gearbox, and 80 bhp at a pleasantly low 2,200 rpm. This was the Tipo 8 and many were sold in the US. Later came the 7.4 litre 8A, the 100 mph 8A SS, and the 8B, the end of a glorious era.

In England, a famous name to favour the straight-eight was that of Frederick Lanchester, who introduced his Thirty in 1929 with an ohc engine of 4.5 litres (78.7 mm × 114 mm) with a four-speed gearbox. This one ran from 1928 to 1933, offering 82 bhp at 2,800 rpm, and his only other eight was the Special S-8 of 1936–39 with 4,625 cc (80 mm × 110 mm) which was quite different, although it had the same chassis dimensions (wheelbase 11 ft 10 ins and track 4 ft 8 ins). It used half-elliptics all round whereas the Thirty had cantilever rears, like all Lanchesters from 1919 to 1931. The Thirty weighed over two tons, could achieve 85 mph and was free from vibration; it could also be had with a French Weymann flexible body which aided its silence and smooth running.

In Italy, one of the most inventive and ingenious designers, Vincenzo Lancia, used a vee eight as early as 1922 in his Trikappa, with 4.6 litres giving 98 bhp. This was parallel with the four-cylinder Kappa and the Dikappa sports model. Lancia was always a vee man, and even his fours were in this configuration with a narrow angle. Later on, he produced the vee eight, ohc Dilambda as companion to the four-cylinder Lambda, using two Lambda engines joined as a unit. The included angle was only 24 degrees, but Lancia was not con-

sistent in the angle of his cylinders and over the years had used 14 different ones, including three variations in the different Lambdas. The Dilambda was the last model to use a letter of the Greek alphabet until 1972, when the modern Beta came along, the Greek letters meanwhile being used rather oddly for trucks. For cars, he switched to the names of Roman roads (which had been named after the daughters of emperors and magistrates) like Artena, Astura, Appia, Augusta and Aurelia. The Dilambda was a big, heavy machine in the tradition

Opposite
A fast car from a small firm, the British AC Cobra, with a 330 bhp, 4.7 litre Ford vee eight. Inspired by an American, Carroll Shelby, cars like this finished fourth at Le Mans in 1964 and 1966. The interior was not noted for its creature comforts.

Below
Ferrari is better known for his V12 engines, but this car proved him capable of creating superb vee eight units, too: a 1977 Dino 308 GT4 2+2.

of Hispano/Isotta/Rolls, but some had attractive cabriolet and sedanca coachwork. It was very flexible, a popular virtue at the time as it avoided gear-changing.

La Salle, the cheaper Cadillac line, also ran a vee eight in the late 1920s but moved to a straight-eight from Oldsmobile in 1935. They went back to a vee eight before dying in 1940.

Locomobile, whose policy was to make everything themselves and use no ready-made units, gave in and used a Lycoming 4.9 litre straight-eight near the end in 1929. Their own engines had been fours, and the new one failed to save the company.

Leyland made a 40 hp Eight designed by the 'Welsh Wizard', Parry Thomas, the most costly British car of 1920; only 18 were ever made, but at least one still exists. In Europe where eight cylinders has been the preserve of the favoured few and not the popular makes, Leyland found themselves with two competing vee eights (the

Rover and the Triumph), both in mass-produced cars and neither a big money-spinner. This unusual situation was a by-product of the fact that Triumph were already part of Leyland when Rover came along in 1967, and each set of engineers and directors was too pig-headed to give up their own vee eight. Perhaps if there had been some more rational decisions in those early days the company would be in better shape now. Certainly they did not need two vee eights, whose production was minimal even before the Triumph one disappeared with the death of the under-rated Stag. The Triumph unit was a 2,997 cc vee eight, with overhead camshafts, putting out 145 bhp at 5,500 rpm with an iron bloc, and alloy cylinder heads; the Rover unit (née Oldsmobile or Buick) was a 3,528 cc, 90 degree vee eight with light alloy block and head producing 143 bhp at 5,000 rpm. There was obviously no need for both in one company.

The Stag, a convertible with

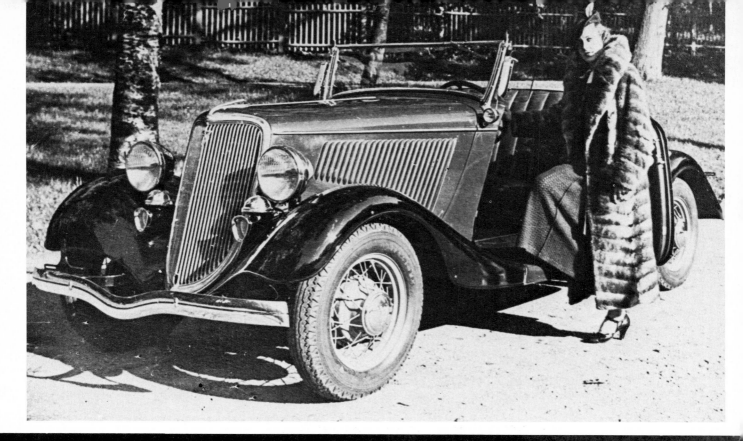

removable hard-top, came on the scene in 1970 and was dropped in 1977. The engine was said to be a delicate unit with inadequate main bearing area and was subject to overheating and stretching of the camshaft drive chains with ghastly results when valves met pistons in an unscheduled manner. Nevertheless, many gave good service, but the few tainted the many in the eyes of trade and public, and some insurance warranties refused to include Stags. A pity, as

Opposite
Miss Finland of 1934 shows off a Ford Model 40 drophead coupé with vee eight engine and a rumble seat.

Below
The Lancia Astura Streamline of 1938 had bodywork by Pininfarina and 2.6 litres of vee eight power.

it was a handsome and unusual car with all-independent suspension and was one of the few fresh-air cars left. It was heavy and solid, with a built-in, removable roll-bar over the top. With power steering, electric windows, tinted glass, and other good points, it was a very complete motor-car for the money, available with either automatic transmission or overdrive.

The Rover unit was introduced in 1968, when Rover bought the drawings from Buick and reworked the engine. It appeared in the Rover 3500, Range Rover, MGB (and Morgan, which is not a Leyland car). It has now been dropped from the MG, which rests on its ageing 1,800 cc four-cylinder. As luck would have it, Rover and Triumph are now in the same Leyland division and could well be using the same engine, which might have kept the Stag in production. Rover's car was the old 2000 saloon with the vee eight engine dropped in. It was a good design for 1964, using a De Dion rear-end, four-wheel discs and bolt-on body panels for easy repair.

Lincoln are thought of as 12-cylinder people, but they made a vee eight back in 1921, with 5.8 litres putting out 81 bhp. Then Ford took over and the twelves came in until 1948, but a vee eight returned in 1949.

Maserati in Italy were eight-cylinder people too, but only made racing cars until after the Second World War. Alfieri Maserati, one of six brothers, began racing with a vee eight, actually half an Isotta-Fraschini aero engine, and then moved on to straight-eight, twin ohc, Diatto GP cars built by Maserati. The brothers took over the Diatto cars when the latter firm gave up racing, so Maserati started racing with straight-eights after reducing the capacity from 2.0 litres to 1.5 to suit the then-current formula. Later came the straight-eight 8CTF which won the Indianapolis 500 in 1939 and 1940, and the 4.5 litre vee eights of 1957. In road cars, they began using vee eights with the four-door saloon Quatroporte, which was never a

great success, and then used a 4.7 litre vee eight in the Mexico, Ghibli, Indy, Bora, and Khamsin. The biggest vee eight, the 4.9 litre, gives 320 bhp and a top speed of 168 mph. All the modern Maseratis are magnificent.

A machine made for racing was the Mercedes-Benz 300 SLR of 1955. This was quite different from the one you could buy, which had six cylinders, produced 215 bhp from 3.0 litres and was said to be a pig to handle. The SLR had a straight-eight of 2.98 litres offering 310 bhp, more power from less than half the size and a top speed of about 160 mph. This is hardly a fair comparison as one was a racing car pure and simple, the other a tourer, but the SLR was one of the great eight-cylinder cars of all time. It ran up to 7,500 rpm to give its power from a square engine of 78 mm × 78 mm and was, of course, the machine in which Stirling Moss and Dennis Jenkinson won the Mille Miglia at just under 100 mph in 1955. It was the year in which Levegh crashed into the Le Mans crowd in a W196 (using the same engine), the company pulled out of racing and no more development was done. Otherwise . . .

In this racing context, one must mention the American Miller, who set records which stood for generations. Harry Miller, from California, was involved in the Bugatti-Duesenberg aero engine scheme and then worked with Duesenberg to produce a 3.0 litre, dohc straight-eight for Indianapolis in 1921, where it did not in fact run as it was not completed in time. But Miller went on to build track-racing machines in the US and his speciality was the front-wheel-drive eight with eight carburettors, which appeared in 1924. The Miller 91, as it was called after its 1,500 cc power plant, had a centrifugal supercharger (which Duesenberg also used) running at five times engine speed. It produced 154 bhp at 7,000 rpm and in 1926 filled nine of the first 10 places in the Indianapolis 500-mile race. There were two Miller road cars, but not with the straight-eight

Looking like something out of a gangster movie, the La Salle was a poor-man's Cadillac in 1931, with a 5.8 litre, side-valve vee eight, high standard of finish and a relatively low price.

engine used exclusively for racing. One, in 1928, used a 325 bhp vee eight, the other, which appeared in the year of his shut-down, 1932, was a V16, but Miller went bust before it was finished and the buyer had the rest of the work done elsewhere.

Another great eight was the Minerva, by a company which made do with fours and sixes until 1930, when they produced two big, straight-eights, a 6.6 litre AK model and a 4.0 litre 22CV AP model. This was hardly the time for big luxury cars, and the Belgian firm started on the slippery slope to extinction. They did produce another vee eight at the 1937 Brussels motor show, with a Ford unit mounted transversely and driving the front wheels through a torque converter. It also featured all-independent torsion bar suspension, but only three prototypes were made.

Packard were another firm with eights, the first being a 5.9 litre straight of 1923, which displaced the famous 12-cylinder Twin Six and offered 84 bhp. The eights ruled as Senior Packards, which were joined by the 3.7 litre, Light Eight 120, and continued until 1939. They came back after the war until they merged with Studebaker. The body dies for the Clipper model were sold to the Soviet Union on President Roosevelt's request and became the Zis and Zil Russian limousines.

Pierce-Arrow, a great American name, used a straight-eight from 1939 to replace their previous six. It came in two sizes and by the following year there was a choice of three. They then went for 12s, but retained the eight until they closed in 1938. They were majestic cars with some splendid coachwork.

The French firm of Renault, now government-owned, were mostly famous for economy cars and rather ugly shapes, but they did once venture to an eight. This was the 7.1

290

litre Reinastella of 1929, a giant machine with the radiator in front of the engine, rather than under a coal-scuttle bonnet behind the motor as on all other early Renaults. The Reinastella had the look of a Chicago gangster car, running boards and all, and was one of a range of various sizes, including the Primastella (13.9 hp) and the Vivastella (27 hp).

Stutz were another American make devoted to the straight-eight and involved in racing, although with sports-car events like Le Mans

rather than GP events. Stutz began with four cylinders in 1911 or so, but switched to eights with the 4.7 litre known as the Vertical Eight in 1926. It was designed by a Belgian, Paul Bastien, who worked for Métallurgique, who mostly made big fours. His overhead camshaft Stutz put out 92 bhp at 3,200 rpm and used a worm-drive rear axle like Rover, Peugeot and others. This permitted a low-built design and it was sold as The Safety Stutz. It had hydraulic brakes, only two years after Chrysler claimed them

Above
It is a tribute to the Range Rover that it can be included in a book about cars. With the vee eight engine used in the Rover 3500, this is the only vehicle truly to combine cross-country capability with comfort and adequate performance for the open road.

Opposite
A potential classic of the future – Leyland's TR7 fitted with the Rover vee eight engine, providing effortless performance. This is an early rally version, with over 300 bhp from an engine that had been only slightly modified.

EXN 767

as a 'first', but these used water with added alcohol.

The racing version which ran at Le Mans and elsewhere was known as the Black Hawk and had a slightly bigger (4,883 cc) engine. The touring car had a 75 mph top speed, but the racer did 106.52 mph at Daytona to set a record. Frank Lockhart died trying to set a new World Land Speed Record, but his was not a true Stutz as its 16-cylinder, 3.1 litre engine came from Miller – he achieved 225 mph before it crashed.

There is a footnote to the six-versus-eight controversy, as Stutz ran against Hispano-Suiza at Indianapolis for a $25,000 wager in 1928, but broke down after 19 of the 24 hours. The French coachbuilder Charles Weymann, father of the flexible Weyman body (fabric on a wooden frame) put up the money and Frederic E. Moscovics, president of Stutz took the bet.

Three Stutz Black Hawks ran at Le Mans that same year, one finishing second in the hands of Bloch and Brisson. They ran again with superchargers in 1929, when one finished fifth, but in 1930 and 1932 they failed to make the finish.

Some of the roadgoing Black Hawks were fitted with striking bodies, like the AA tourer of 1927 and the Convertible sedan of 1928. These included such innovations as a device behind the gearbox which stopped the cars running backwards down hills; and a 'Variable Booster Brake' which adjusted the amount of servo assistance. The model name was rather spoiled by a cheaper, six-cylinder Black Hawk in 1931, but that car need not concern us here. Stutz went out of business in 1935, although someone produced a modern car called a Stutz Bearcat in the 1970s and people like the late Elvis Presley bought them.

Sunbeam were later allied with Hillman and the designer, Coatalen,

Opposite, top
Spain's only recent makers of luxury cars, Empresa Nacional de Autocamiones produced Pegasos in the old Hispano-Suiza factory from 1951 to 1957. Only 125 of the cars were ever made, including this pair of Z-102 Berlinettas, each with a 210 bhp, 2.8 litre, four-ohc vee eight, dry sump lubrication and a five-speed transaxle.

Opposite, lower
Last of the US muscle cars, the Pontiac Firebird Trans-Am of 1975 provided incredible acceleration and interesting corners in the days before US emission regulations made such vehicles illegal.

Below
From a more spacious age comes this Renault Reinastella, with special *sedanca de ville* coachwork by Binder of Paris. It was Renault's first-ever straight eight, appearing in 1929 with 7.1 litres, coil ignition, unit gearbox and transverse leaf rear suspension.

had been with Hillman in 1909 before he joined Sunbeam. There was an eight-cylinder, 3.0 litre Sunbeam racer of 65 mm × 112 mm, but no road car. There would have been a 4.5 litre, straight-eight Sunbeam in 1936, designed not by Coatalen but by Georges Roesch, but it was never put into production. This engine had the 3.5 litre Talbot dimensions of 80 mm × 112 mm, with ten main bearings, and, as in all Roesch designs, the valve gear was very light. The car in which it was to have gone was very Humber-like with independent front suspension by transverse leaf.

The Sunbeam which won the French Grand Prix in 1923, giving Britain her first such win for 21 years, was a straight-eight, as were all the major contestants in the 2.0 litre formula of 1923. Fiat used superchargers. The Sunbeams were said to be copies of the Fiats, – 'Fiats in green paint' as one critic said – but the Bugatti and Rolland-Pillain conformed to the same layout. All these were works racers, although some of the Sunbeams still exist and examples of the others are in museums; they are all relevant to the straight-eight story.

The Czechoslovakian company, Tatra, made some vee eight models from 1934 onwards with aerodynamic bodies and air-cooled engines. Their 3,400 cc unit offered 95 mph and it is said that several senior Nazis came to a bad end during the occupation thanks to the handling faults of this machine with its engine behind the rear axle à la Volkswagen. This Type 77 was designed by Hans Ledwinka, a famous name, and his later (1937) Type 87 was good for 100 mph, which decimated the Party cadre even more, especially in winter. In 1957, the Tatra 603 came along, still with an air-cooled vee eight at the back, this time of 2,472 cc. Some people never learn. It had three headlamps in a row inside the grille and a rather bulbous look.

14

12 Cylinders or more: Too much of a good Thing?

Off-the-cuff most of us would think that the 12 or 16-cylinder car was a fairly rare sort of beast, yet there have been almost 20 makers of 12s and ten of 16s through the years. This is by no means a complete listing, but they are the ones known to most people, without digging up rare prototypes made (or catalogued – not always the same thing).

Sixteens should surely rank as classic cars on the grounds of rarity, although most of them were racing

Opposite
Marmon's magnificent swansong, the 9.1 litre V16 of 1931. With an all-alloy engine producing 200 bhp, it was the last car made before the Indianapolis firm went bust.

When Packard made this V12 Cabriolet in 1938, half their labour force were involved in making such cars, which accounted for only eight percent of sales; this 7.0 litre Cabriolet was therefore one of the last 'Senior' Packards, more mundane stuff being issued after 1939.

cars or prototypes. As there have been so few, we might dispose of them first.

Not many people remember that Alfa Romeo made three different 16s and that one model, the Tipo 316 of 1938, finished second and fourth in the Italian Grand Prix of that year, while two cars also ran in the 1939 Belgian GP. Most people call the famous Tipo 158 eight-cylinder car half of a Tipo 316, but Alfa put it the other way round and say that the Tipo 316 was two 158s. Either way, the Tipo 316 engine had a 60-degree vee of 2,958 cc, with one supercharger for each bank of cylinders and 440 bhp at 7,500 rpm. It was, of course, a single-seat racer, first seen at the Tripoli GP in 1938.

The other two Alfa 16s were prototypes, the Tipo 162 and 163, and used an entirely different vee of 135 degrees and 2,995 cc. The Tipo 162 of 1939 was a front-engined single-seater producing 490 bhp at 7,800 rpm, with four superchargers, but the Second World War put an end to it. The Tipo 163 was a rear-engined, two-seater racing coupé with closed coachwork of almost wedge shape, wider at the front than at the rear and sloping down from the driver's head to the tail. These two prototypes appeared to share the same engine – all the dimensions agreed – plus other details like four valves per cylinder and twin magnetos. Six 162s were made but only one 163.

The British company, BRM, who have not had a lucky history, made two 16-cylinder racing cars in its time, both failures, but worth recording on account of their complexity and cost. Best known was the 1.5 litre, V16 with egg-cup pistons and two-stage supercharging, supposed to give 600 bhp at 12,000 rpm but which never kept its promises, and was best remembered for breaking its driveshaft on the start-line at its first appearance in 1950 – after three years development. The V16 staggered on until 1955 without any real success, at which point the designers abandoned all this complexity for a straight four-cylinder.

In 1966, their chief engineer, Tony Rudd, produced two flat-eights joined together to make an H-16, but this was just as bad as the old V16. It was too heavy and blew up often. Jackie Stewart finished second at Spa in an H-16 and the great Jim Clark actually won the US GP of 1966, but this was cheating from our point of view as he had the engine in a Lotus. BRM went back to another V12.

Probably as little known as the V16 Alfa was the V16 Bugatti, but in view of Ettore's standing no reviewer could possibly leave it out. It was not really a car engine, but must have its place among the might-have-beens. Bugatti had to leave his Alsace home during the First World War as fighting was going on there, and in Paris he produced for the French Government a 500 bhp 16-cylinder aero engine consisting of two eight-cylinder units side by side with their cranks joined by gears, rather as in BRM's H-16, except that the latter's were one above the other. The French Government did not fancy the machine much, however, and sold it

GP 4831

to the Americans, who asked Mr Duesenberg to look it over. Bugatti's favourite mechanic, Mr Friderich, was sent over to the US to help, and from this arose the Bugatti–Duesenberg collaboration. They went on playing with the machine until the war ended, but Bugatti engines were always criticised for poor cooling of valve guides and seats, and this was probably a fault in his aero engine, which apparently never flew.

From all these rather tentative

Left
A big car in every way, the V16 Cadillac broadcasts its superiority to anyone who cares to look. With 7.4 litres, 185 bhp and a wheelbase of 12 ft 4 ins, it sold 500 a year between 1930 and 1938.

Below
The Daimler Double-Six engine, a 40/50 hp unit of 5.6 litres.

Opposite, lower
The original Daimler Double-Six (the name is now used for Jaguar derivatives) appeared in 1931. This is a specially-lowered sports model.

efforts, we come to one of the most successful 16-cylinder production engines of all time, the Cadillac. They began with a single-cylinder, went to a four, then vee eight, and finally V16 with a beautiful-looking, 7.4 litre unit producing 165 bhp at 3,400 rpm. The designer was Ernest Seaholm, with Cadillac from 1923 to 1943. In 1930 it was the world's first production 16, with a 45-degree included angle and mounted on a 12 ft 4 in wheelbase. This V16 went on for seven years before a cheaper one arrived, with a much wider, 135-degree angle and side instead of overhead valves. Only 511 of them were ever made, and the 16 then disappeared from the Cadillac line-up. During its reign there were some wonderful-looking cars, like the 452B Sedanca of 1932, the 452A Roadster with pram-irons in 1931, and of course, the Fleetwood Sedans. Film Star Walter Pidgeon was one of many customers for the convertible, with its 7.4 litre V16. Cadillac sold 2,500 of their V16 in 1930 (although it was

Depression time) but sunk to a total sale of 3,173 cars of all models in 1933. The narrow-angle 16 is an American immortal; the wide-angle V16 is not talked about.

A contemporary of the Cadillac was the Marmon V16 of 1931, but this brought the company to ruin. It was, nevertheless, a motoring milestone in the United States, coming from a company based in the sporting centre of Indianapolis, and it

A pair of 12-cylinder Ferraris – a traditional classic from 1962 in the shape of a Berlinetta Lusso 250 GT, with front-mounted, 3.0 litre V12; and (below) the company's latest offering, their far-from-traditional Berlinetta Boxer, with 4.4 litre mid-mounted flat-12 producing 360 bhp, an output which would have been respectable in a Formula One car only a very few years ago.

was one of the most massive engines ever made. A 9.1 litre motor in light alloy, it was said to produce 200 bhp. Equipped with a three-speed gearbox, the mighty Marmon had enormous flexibility and torque.

The V16 Maserati Tipo V4 of 1929, known as the 'Sedici Cilindri', was made up from two, Tipo 26B engines mounted on a common crankcase. It was a pig to drive, and only Alfieri Maserati and Baconin Borzacchini managed it. Borzacchini put up the fastest speed for a racing car on a road-circuit up to 1929 when he averaged 152.9 mph over 10 kilometres of the 25-mile Gemama track in Italy. Alfieri did a 124.2 mph lap in the 1929 Monza GP and this stood until 1954, while Borzacchini won the 1930 Tripoli GP with the only V4

car ever made.

Later came the V5, which was similar but bored out to 5.0 litres (4,905 cc) and with 360 bhp at 5,500 rpm. This was still a single-seat racing car and, although only one was made, two more 16-cylinder engines were put into speed-boats. The V5 won the 1932 Rome Grand Prix and was second in the Monza GP, but when Rugieri tried some records at Montlhéry he lost control and was killed. It raced again in the Tripoli GP in 1934, and crashed. Taruffi survived, but the V5 didn't.

Harry Miller, who was involved in the Bugatti-Duesenberg V16 aero engine, made mostly eights, but was involved in two 16-cylinder projects. One was an abortive World Land Speed Record machine which was to have been driven by Barney Oldfield, with a 5.1 litre engine, dohc and four-wheel drive. The other was the four-wheel-drive, road-going sports car, presumably related to the record-breaker and with a V16 engine. This one came in 1932 and was his last fling.

So we come again to Stutz, who made fours, then eights, and – when rivals like Cadillac, Packard and Lincoln were making 12s and 16s – called their eight-cylinder 1931 Bearcat the SV16, although it did not have 16 cylinders. They went one better with the DV32, which still had only eight cylinders, but which did have four valves per cylinder and double overhead camshafts. Stutz thus never made a 16, but (by using numbers which referred to the quantity of valves) fooled many people into thinking that they did.

With all these many-cylindered things out of the way, we can turn to the relative simplicity of the 12s. The first such engine to be put into series production was made by Packard, who introduced their Twin Six in 1915 with aluminium pistons, detachable cylinder heads, left-hand drive and a left-hand gear change. With a relatively modest price, it was actually their only model until 1920 and a racing version did 149.9 mph at Daytona

(the missing 0.1 mph must have been rather frustrating).

Keeping matters in their logical, alphabetical order, however, first (as usual) comes the Italian Alfa Romeo concern, who have made fours, sixes, eights, 12s and 16s. Their hall-mark for many years was the double overhead camshaft. In modern times they have made 12s for sports and grand prix racing in Brabham-Alfas, but these do not count as we cannot use them on the road in the way we might have used a racer from the past with two seats, wings, lamps and so on. Alfa's first 12 was the Tipo A of 1931 which had two of the famous 1,750 cc engines side by side. Four of these cars were made, with two of everything right back to the differential. Total capacity was 3,504 cc and output was 230 bhp at 5,200 rpm. The driver changed gear on both boxes at once with a lever linked to both. They won the Coppa Acerbo and Susa-Moncenisio races.

Then there was the famous

Bimotore, but this had two engines of eight cylinders each, front and rear, so was not truly a 16, or was it? There was also the Tipo 12 C of 1936, but this was a single-seater racer, of which six were made. Tazio Nuvolari won the Vanderbilt Cup race in the US with this 4.0 litre car.

Yet another 12-cylinder racer came in 1939, this time with a 4.5

Opposite, top
The man who has done more than anyone else to popularize the mystique of the V12 – Enzo Ferrari himself.

Opposite, lower
The giant Fiat 520 of 1921 used a 6,805 cc V12 divided into two groups of six and rated at 60 hp.

Below
Leyland's big cat – the 500 bhp Jaguar XJ 5.3 Coupé raced in the 1977 European Touring Car Championship. Although very fast, it was soundly beaten by the BMW team and did nothing to help Leyland's ailing image.

litre, 60 degree vee putting out 430 bhp at 5,800 rpm. Four of these were made. The following year saw a V12 of 3.0 litres, and this time three were made, so it is all very confusing. There was even a saloon-car prototype with a 60 degree V12, the Tipo S10 and S10SS, of which two were designed for the 1941 Mille Miglia, which never happened, of course. They were a normal four-door saloon and a shorter coupé respectively, both front-engined. The engine was different again, this time a 3.5 litre producing 140 bhp at 4,700 rpm.

The Tipo 412 arrived in 1939 with yet another 60 degree V12 this time of 4.5 litres with 220 bhp at 5,500 rpm and an open, two-seat body. It had three carburettors and no supercharger. Another was the rear-engined, Tipo 512 of 1940–41, which had what we would now call a 'boxer' engine with two sixes in opposition. It was again a racer, of only 1,490 cc, but offering 335 bhp at 8,600 rpm. Parts were made for three cars, but again the war stop-

ped construction.

Long after the Second World War, there was another V12 Alfa, this time a sports-racing prototype called the Tipo 33 of 1971–72, which won the Targa Florio, Brands Hatch 1000 Kms and Watkins Glen Six Hours in 1971 and which subsequently took the World Sports Car Championship by winning almost every round. This one had 440 bhp at 9,800 rpm. One way and another, Alfa must have produced more different V12s than anyone, even if they did not make many of each.

The American Auburn company (1900–1937) made singles, twins, fours, sixes, eights and, eventually, a V12 of 6.4 litres in 1932 with the famous Columbia two-speed axle. It did not sell in spite of a low price. Its V12 was a 6.4 litre job with a 45 degree angle and a bore and stroke of 79 m × 108 m. A Speedster model captured many records and Auburn were involved with Cord and Duesenberg as recorded earlier.

Cadillac's V16 has been men-

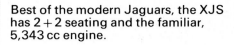

Best of the modern Jaguars, the XJS has 2 + 2 seating and the familiar, 5,343 cc engine.

tioned, but they had a 12, too. This came in 1931 with 6.0 litres and ohv and it ran until 1927. The 12 shared a lot of bits with the 16, which made for economy, and both were 45 degree vees. The V12 had a bore of 79 mm and the V16 only 76 mm, and in fact the four engines in the range (there were V8s as well) were really variations on only two.

The British Daimler company produced a V12 in 1937 called the Double Six, a monster thing of 6,511 cc with ohv and 142 bhp. The most interesting one was the drop-head coupé which was quite different from the royal saloons and performed more like a sports car. There were not many of them, but they were distinguished by being extremely low on the ground. In modern times (1972 onwards) the name was revived on a Jaguar with a fluted Daimler grille superimposed on the front of the bonnet, and this was, in fact, a very good car. The one to have was the two-door coupé from 1974 onwards, which was not in production for long. It had the 5.3 litre, dohc engine producing 265 bhp, usually with automatic transmission, power steering and all such driver conveniences; for swift silent travel it could not be bettered.

Delage and Delahaye also made V12s. There was the racing Delage of 2.0 litres which won the French and Spanish GPs in 1926 with 190 bhp from its four-ohc V12; and an earlier, 10.7 litre V12 of 1923, with which Réné Thomas took the World Land Speed Record at 143 mph. Then there was the imposing, 1937, 4.5 litre V12 Delahaye (the same firm by now) with 238 bhp and 165 mph from a sporting two-seater, with a Cotal electric, pre-selector gearbox. With a De Dion rear axle, this was raced with success in GPs, and some simpler versions were sold to the public.

Ferrari is *the* name in twelves, and to list all his models would be impossible. There are so many

Opposite, top
Designed by W. O. Bentley, the last of
the 4.5 litre Lagondas was the LG6 of
1938. With a four-carburettor V12
producing 180 bhp the car could be
driven from seven to 103 mph in top
gear without jerking. Rated as
Bentley's finest design, Rapide
versions finished third and fourth at
Le Mans, but production ceased soon
afterwards.

Opposite, lower
Much loved by both gangsters and
the FBI in the late 1920s, Lincolns
were noted for their superior
performance. This 1928 model came
with 6.3 litres of V12.

Above
Early efforts by Ferruccio
Lamborghini included this 400 GT
coupé of 1966, with 4.0 litre, four-
ohc V12 and around 400 bhp.

desirable Ferraris – in fact *all*
Ferraris are desirable – that choice
is purely a matter of taste. Not so
long ago, the 330 GT, which was
the least popular one, could be
bought very cheaply but times have
changed now. They are all beautiful, they all go extremely fast and all
give a driver much pleasure. Ferrari
are fortunately in a healthy state,
unlike the other two Italian 'supercar' companies, and they are making so many more cars than used to
be the case, that the earlier and less
common models may become more
sought-after. Certainly the four-
cam GTBs were (like the 275) a race
apart and much less bulky than the
modern cars.

What every young man fancied in
the 1920s was a Hispano-Suiza,

who were rather like the Ferrari of
their times. The company name
was a combination of the Spanish
words for Spanish and Swiss, de-
noting the fact that their cars were
made in Spain and designed by a
Swiss, Marc Birkigt. The fact that
they were better known as a French
firm, with production from Paris,
merely serves to confuse us.

In 1931, they produced their
most exotic car, the T12, with a 60
degree V12 engine arranged as two
rows of six cylinders, each with its
own range of accessories. There
were thus two water pumps, two
magnetos and just about two of
everything else, except for camshafts, of which there was only one,
located in the centre of the vee and
driving the overhead valves by

means of pushrods and rockers. The cylinder heads and blocks were in cast aluminium, with steel liners, while the crankshaft ran in seven bearings operating alloy pistons via tubular connecting rods. With square dimensions of 100 mm × 100 mm, this masterpiece of engineering produced an easy 220 bhp from 9,425 cc, and was the largest engine in production any-where at the time. Not satisfied even with that, the company in-troduced an 11.3 litre version in 1935, which really was something.

Such was the power and flexi-bility of this engine that the lowest ratio in the three-speed box was 5.4:1 – about the same as top gear on most other cars – while top gear was an amazing 2.75:1, giving well over 100 mph. And all this in a car that tipped the scales at 2½ tons and boasted a wheelbase of up to 13 ft 2 ins! This was one car which could never be accused of being ordinary.

The young Briton of today, of course, hankers after a Jaguar. This company share their mechanical components with Daimler, and we have already included a Daimler saloon. The Jaguar to have, how-ever, was an open two-seater E-Type sports car. Now unfor-tunately out of production, this grew a bit middle-aged after the early models, with longer wheel-base and more width, but it had ample power and no need of auto-matic transmission, as it could do most things in top gear. There was a splendid burble, breath-taking per-formance, and not enough noise to upset those that might otherwise be upset.

Lagonda had a V12 just before the Second World War, designed by none other than W. O. Bentley. This came in 1937, produced 180 bhp, and could go from walking speed to more than 100 mph smoo-thly. They made some particularly beautiful cars with this engine, and the Rapide drophead was a joy indeed. It was a 4.5 litre with single, chain-driven ohc per bank, and was very heavy – the short-chassis, sporting Rapide was the one to have. Low-speed steering was hard on the wrists and it was none too quiet at speed, but it was lovely to look at.

Lincoln have been mentioned in earlier chapters, but their V12 was a famous one used by many US presidents. Their V12 arrived in 1932 with the famous KA and KB series, the latter offering 150 bhp from 7.2 litres. They also had vacuum brake boost. The KA ser-ies, with its 6.2 litre motor, did not last long and was dropped in 1934 and the KB with the bigger engine went on alone. By 1936, Lincoln had 18 body styles. President Franklin Roosevelt had a 'Sunshine Special' V12 Lincoln convertible in 1942 which, with bullet-proofing, weighed 9,300 lbs. Lincoln stayed with the V12 until 1948, when the real classic – the Continental – was dropped. It did not re-appear until

Opposite
One of Lamborghini's fabulous V12 engines, capped by four, triple choke Weber carburettors.

Below
Wilhelm Maybach graduated from making airships (with Count Zeppelin) to making cars under his own name. This is his 1938 Cabriolet, with a 200 bhp, 8.0 litre V12.

1956 and then not as a 12. The pre-1948 version had a majesty of size although not always a pretty car.

From the United States back to Italy for a famous V12 from Lamborghini. This came on the scene rather sensationally in 1963 as a four-cam, 3.5 litre V12 with six Weber carburetters. All his subsequent cars were V12s until more recent times, when sixes and eights crept in, but the company is in

Left
The 5,990 cc, V12-powered Horch could be bought in a variety of wheelbases and body styles in the Germany of 1933.

decline. The most famous model was the Miura, named after a fighting bull, with a V12 placed across its tail. Like Ferraris, they were all fast, dramatic, incredibly noisy (especially inside) and quite unlike any other motor cars.

Another Italian V12 was by Lancia, and appeared in 1919 as a 7.8 litre ohc with a 22 degree angle (Lancia liked odd angles for his vees). This one produced 150 bhp but few were made or sold. A pity it did not survive, as there were no bad Lancias.

In Italy, too, Maserati favoured sixes and eights, but first tried a

V12 in the Tipo 250F/T2 of 1957, a 2.5 litre machine, of which only two were made; a different version, a 3.5 litre Tipo 57 (350S) remained a one-off. The unit used in the Tipo 250F came back in the Tipo 63 (Birdcage) racer of 1961 and ran fourth at Le Mans. Three were made. A fourth V12 appeared in 1961, this time of 3.0 litres in the

One of the last Pierce-Arrows to roll off the production line at Buffalo, New York, the 1934 convertible could be had with either a 5.5 litre or a 7.0 litre V12, but very few were sold and the company finally folded in 1938.

The engine of the Pierce-Arrow sat noticeably low in the car and was located well behind the classic radiator.

Scuderia Serenissima car at the Pescara GP. A 60 degree unit, it put out 320 bhp and was capable of 187 mph in the Tipo 64 sports car, which was rather squat and ugly. This appeared to be the same engine as in the Tipo 63 Birdcage, although both were enlarged from the 2.5 version. Most confusing.

Maserati had still another V12 in 1964 in the Tipo 8/F1, a 1,500 cc, dohc, transverse unit with Lucas fuel injection, but it was never used. The Tipo 9/F1 went into the 3.0 litre Formula One Cooper-Maserati of 1966, with 360 bhp at 9,000 rpm. It used an incredible 24 ignition coils, mounted over the gearbox, while a later Tipo 10 used three valves per cylinder. There have been no V12 road cars.

The fecundity of Alfa and Maserati in producing V12s to the tune of about half-a-dozen each, puts companies who had only one such model rather in the shade. But the German Horch company, which from 1932 was a member of the Auto Union Group (with Audi, DKW and Wanderer), produced an outsized motor-car with a V12 of 5,990 cc. This machine, capable of 90 mph, came in Models 600 and 670 and often carried majestic, cabriolet coachwork. It was sold at a much lower price than similar cars. However, the V12 did not sell well – it was introduced in 1931 during the depths of the economic depression – and gave way to a vee eight by 1933.

Two British vehicles now claim attention – one of them perhaps the most prestigious of all, the Rolls-Royce Phantom III, introduced in 1935. This was a 7.3 litre V12, which stayed in the catalogue up to 1939. It was the first Rolls with independent, front-wheel suspension (which was of doubtful value) and the power-plant quite obviously stemmed from the aircraft engine made by the same company for the Schneider Trophy air races of 1929 onwards. The R-type-engined Supermarine seaplane won

315

This late Bugatti of 1939 has elegant lines which look forward to the post-war period. The T57 was Bugatti's last true production model – 800 were made between 1934 and 1939.

the 1929 and 1931 races with 2,350 bhp from 36.7 litres. This engine was developed from the Buzzard, itself a development of the Kestrel with a bigger bore and stroke. It originally produced 925 bhp, but was put to one side as a failure for use in big flying boats. It is hard to resist the story of the Phoenix rising from the ashes, but it is so apt. The Merlin, which powered the Supermarine Spitfire, Beaufighter, Defiant, Halifax, Hurricane, Lancaster and Mustang and which can be called the engine which won the Second World War, was developed from 'failure' of the Buzzard. But the aero link is tenuous, as the V12 in the Phantom car was also the same size as two 20/25 car engines on a common crankcase, giving 7,340 cc and a power output of 165 bhp at 3,000 rpm. This increased from

1938 to 180 bhp with the adoption of four-port cylinder heads. The PIII dispensed with magnetos in favour of two coils, and had a single overhead camshaft per bank in the vee. It used American-style, hydraulic tappets, which made it quiet, but discarded these in later years as owners found them troublesome. The independent suspension also had a GM look about it. The V12 engine was shorter, but the radiator was thrust further forward, making some of the bodies look awkward, although there were some beauties, too. It could reach 100 mph if not overbodied and could do zero-to-60 in 16 seconds, but it was flexible in the extreme – a silent, top-gear car, which is what luxury is all about. It had an easy to-use gearbox with right-hand change, and a huge, 48 ft turning circle, while finding which of the plugs was missing was a chauffeur's nightmare.

A lesser-known British V12 came from the fine old firm of Sunbeam (since lost within Rootes, Chrysler, and now Peugeot). Their immortal Sunbeam Tiger (not the 1960s road

car) of 4.0 litres was made up of two blocks of six in a V12 and produced 306 bhp at 5,300 rpm from 3,976 supercharged cc. The car weighed only 18 cwt, used a 75 degree vee and took the World Land Speed Record at Southport Sands, England in 1926, driven by Sir Henry Segrave at 152.33 mph. Before being named the Tiger, the Sunbeam was called Ladybird. The engine consisted of two blocks of the type used in the 2.0 litre Sunbeam with which Segrave had won the 1923 French Grand Prix.

There was also a 1,000 horse power Sunbeam, with two V12 engines in four blocks of three giving 44,888 cc, and which Segrave took to the Land Speed Record in 1927, at 203.78 mph, but these were Matabele aero engines. Finally there was a 12-cylinder Sunbeam racer in 1913 called Toodles V and with 9,048 cc.

Tatra have the last word, with their 6.0 litre V12 Type 80, producing 100 bhp in a swing-axle design dating from 1930, which was said to be particularly lethal. Unusual though.

Acknowledgements

The publishers are grateful to the following individuals and organisations for the illustrations in this book:
AC Cars Ltd.; Alfa Romeo; Audi NSU; *Autocar*; George Bishop; BMW; Griffith Borgeson; Bristol Cars; Neill Bruce; David Burgess Wise; Chrysler; Citroen; *Classic Car*; Coys of Kensington; Detroit Public Library; L'Editrice dell'Automobile; Hans Edwards; Fiat; Ford Motor Company; The Henry Ford Museum; The Free Library of Philadelphia; General Motors; The Hamyln Group Library; David Hodges; Ray Hutton; Lamborghini; Lancia; Leyland Cars; Lucien Loreille; Ozzie Lyons; Maranello Concessionaires Ltd.; Mercedes-Benz; *Motor*; The National Motor Museum; Peugeot; Charles Pocklington; Porsche; Cyril Posthumus; The Royal Automobile Club; Renault; Rolls-Royce Motors Ltd.; Maurice Rowe; Saab; The Science Museum; Shell; Nigel Snowdon; Jasper Spencer-Smith; Vauxhall Motors Ltd.; H. Roger Viollet; Volvo; David Winter; Nicky Wright

The publishers would also like to thank the following owners for making their cars available for photographs:
The Auburn-Cord-Duesenberg Museum; The Briggs Cunningham Automotive Museum; Wirt Fairman; Homer Fitterling; Bill Goodwin; John Hare; Phil Hill; The Hillcrest Motor Company; Jim Lepke; Dennis Mitchell; Bud Oser; Charles Schetelage; Ralph A. Scott; David Spegal; G. W. Walker; "Yesterdays Wheels"

Index